American Protestantism in the Age of Psychology

Many have worried that psychology has corrupted American faith, eroded citizens' virtue, and weakened community life. But the social history of three major psychospiritual movements since World War II – Alcoholics Anonymous, The Salvation Army's outreach to homeless men, and the "clinical pastoral education" movement – finds the opposite. These groups innovated a practical religious psychology that nurtured participants' faith, fellowship, and responsibility. They achieved this by expanding the definition of what constituted therapy to include religious traditions and spiritual activities. They turned to clergy and lay believers to deliver therapy. These efforts enhanced the three movements' success in reaching out to people who were socially alienated and religiously disenchanted. By fostering community and responsibility among some of America's most disaffected citizens, psychologically infused religious programming helped foster the kind of society our liberal democracy requires.

Dr. Stephanie Muravchik is an Associate Fellow at the Institute for Advanced Studies in Culture at the University of Virginia. She holds a PhD in American History from the University of Virginia and was previously a Fellow at the Miller Center of Public Affairs at the University of Virginia.

American Protestantism in the Age of Psychology

STEPHANIE MURAVCHIK

*Institute for Advanced Studies in Culture
University of Virginia*

CAMBRIDGE UNIVERSITY PRESS
Cambridge, New York, Melbourne, Madrid, Cape Town,
Singapore, São Paulo, Delhi, Tokyo, Mexico City

Cambridge University Press
32 Avenue of the Americas, New York, NY 10013-2473, USA

www.cambridge.org
Information on this title: www.cambridge.org/9781107010673

© Stephanie Muravchik 2011

This publication is in copyright. Subject to statutory exception
and to the provisions of relevant collective licensing agreements,
no reproduction of any part may take place without the written
permission of Cambridge University Press.

First published 2011

Printed in the United States of America

A catalog record for this publication is available from the British Library.

Library of Congress Cataloging in Publication data
Muravchik, Stephanie, 1970–
American Protestantism in the age of psychology / Stephanie Muravchik.
p. cm.
Includes bibliographical references and index.
ISBN 978-1-107-01067-3 (hardback)
1. Pastoral psychology – United States – History. 2. Protestant churches –
United States – History. 3. Clinical pastoral education (Movement) – History.
4. Alcoholics Anonymous – History. 5. Church work with men – Salvation
Army – History. I. Title.
BV4012.M785 2011
253.5′2097309045 – dc22 2011002211

ISBN 978-1-107-01067-3 Hardback

Cambridge University Press has no responsibility for the persistence or accuracy of URLs
for external or third-party Internet Web sites referred to in this publication and does not
guarantee that any content on such Web sites is, or will remain, accurate or appropriate.

For my parents

Contents

Acknowledgments		*page* ix
Abbreviations		xi
1	The Fall and Rise of Psychoreligious Cooperation	1

PART ONE. THERAPY AS MINISTRY IN CLINICAL PASTORAL EDUCATION

2	The Priest Must Drink at the Scientific Well	28
3	Being the Love of God	60

PART TWO. THERAPY AS FELLOWSHIP IN ALCOHOLICS ANONYMOUS

4	Democracy Is a Therapy	83
5	Came to Believe	112

PART THREE. THERAPY AS EVANGELISM IN THE SALVATION ARMY

6	Freud Is Not a Suitable Psychologist	161
7	New Creatures in Christ	205
8	Conclusion: American Psychology in an Age of Faiths	215
Bibliography		223
Index		239

vii

Acknowledgments

Many people made it possible for me to complete this book. My biggest intellectual and professional debts are to Brian Balogh, who offered an excellent education in how to study and teach American history. But, as all Brian's students know, his most important lesson is the example he sets of truly extraordinary generosity, honesty, and creativity as a scholar and a citizen. I also want to thank Grace Elizabeth Hale, who made time repeatedly over the years to assist me professionally and to clarify my ideas about this study. James Davidson Hunter supported this project and created the perfect setting for interdisciplinary research in religious history at the Institute for Advanced Studies in Culture. Gary Laderman graciously agreed to help mentor me on this project, and he even traveled from Atlanta to do so! Edward H. McKinley and Rodney J. Hunter both offered guidance on sources and interpretation. I am grateful to Cita Cook, Joseph Davis, Ellen Herman, Sarah Igo, Robert Kugelmann, Christopher Loss, Catherine Gavin Loss, Heather Anne Warren, and my two anonymous manuscript reviewers. I deeply appreciate the patience and support of my editor at Cambridge University Press, Eric Crahan. It was a pleasure to work with James Dunn, Senior Production and Design Controller at Cambridge University Press, and Shana Meyer, Senior Project Manager at Aptara, Inc.

I was very fortunate to have been a graduate fellow at the Miller Center of Public Affairs at the University of Virginia. Its unique American Political Development fellowship program provided me financial support and invaluable academic opportunities. My research also benefited from fellowships from the Corcoran Department of History and the Graduate School of Arts and Sciences at the University of Virginia.

Acknowledgments

Like every historian, I depended on the assistance of knowledgeable archivists and librarians throughout this project. The Salvation Army was not only very hospitable to researchers, but it even fed me lunch every day I worked in its archives! Its head archivist Susan Mitchem and assistant archivist Scott Day were friendly and helpful. At Emory University's Pitts Theology Library, I relied on Joan Clemons and her assistant archivist Anne Graham. The library's director M. Patrick Graham offered me coffee and useful suggestions. At the General Service Office of Alcoholics Anonymous, I was ably assisted by Judit Santon and Erin Lange.

Writing this book, especially while having primary responsibility for three small boys, made me heavily dependent on family. My parents supported this project in every way possible from the very beginning to the very end. This book would simply not exist without the help they provided, and I dedicate it to them. My husband has been not only an exhilarating interlocutor on the themes of this study during the ten years I worked on it, but he also made its completion possible in the roles of patron, cheerleader, and babysitter. My mother-in-law has supported and encouraged this work in ways both moral and practical, including countless hours of loving childcare. I also want to thank my sister Madeline, aunt extraordinaire, and Garrett Brown for their critical and gracious assistance at key moments.

Abbreviations

Clinical Pastoral Education

ACPE   Association for Clinical Pastoral Education
CCT   Council for Clinical Training
CCTTS Council for the Clinical Training of Theology Students
CPE   clinical pastoral education
DPCC   *Dictionary of Pastoral Care and Counseling*
JPC   *Journal of Pastoral Care*

Alcoholics Anonymous

AA   Alcoholics Anonymous
AV   Alcoholics Victorious
GSO   General Service Office
GSOA   General Service Office Archives, New York City
JSA   *Journal of Studies on Alcohol*
12 & 12   *Twelve Steps and Twelve Traditions* (1952)

The Salvation Army

ARC   Adult Rehabilitation Center
CO   commanding officer
MSSC   men's social service center
MSSD   men's social service department
SFOT   School for Officer Training
SAA   Salvation Army Archives, Alexandria, Virginia

I

The Fall and Rise of Psychoreligious Cooperation

Has America traded its soul for its psyche? Has the quest for our inner selves replaced the quest for God? Would we rather feel good than be good? Has therapy replaced religion in our lives? These questions have been posed, and for the most part answered in the affirmative and with alarm, in what is now a long string of popular exposés and scholarly works dating back to Philip Rieff's 1966 classic, *The Triumph of the Therapeutic*.[1] Early in the twentieth century, psychotherapy had been the preserve of the elite few who were cosmopolitan enough to want it and wealthy enough to pay for it. After World War II,[2] however, it spread

---

[1] This literature, which spans academic and social critical modes of writing, is quite extensive. Some of the most important are: Bellah et al., *Habits of the Heart*; Caplan, *Mind Games*; Cushman, *Constructing the Self*; Fuller, *Americans and the Unconscious*; Furedi, *Therapy Culture*; Gross, *The Psychological Society*; Heinze, *Jews and the American Soul*; Herman, *Romance of American Psychology*; Holifield, *History of Pastoral Care*; Imber, ed., *Therapeutic Culture*; Kaminer, *I'm Dysfunctional, You're Dysfunctional*; Kovel, "The American Mental Health Industry"; Lasch, *Culture of Narcissism*; Lears, "From Salvation to Self-Realization"; Levine, ed., *Constructions of the Self*; Matthews, "The Americanization of Sigmund Freud"; Meador, "Psychology's Secularizing of American Protestantism"; Moore, *In Search of White Crows*; Moskowitz, *In Therapy We Trust*; Nolan, *Therapeutic State*; Pfister and Schnog, *Inventing the Psychological*; Rieff, *Triumph of the Therapeutic*; Rose, *Governing the Soul*; Rose, *Inventing Our Selves*; Scott, *Contempt and Pity*; Taves, *Fits, Trances, and Visions*; Vitz, *Psychology as Religion*; and Warren, "Shift from Character to Personality."

[2] Although the general tendency has been to deplore primarily the popular expansion of therapeutic modes beginning around the time of World War II, a few authors specify slightly different moments as the source of the problem. For example, Pfister locates it in the rise of the American middle class in the antebellum period; Rieff traces the trouble to Freud's epigoni, who could not resist harnessing his ideas to totalizing systems of salvation; and Rice finds it in the rise of what he calls a "liberation psychology" around

American Protestantism in the Age of Psychology

rapidly to the middle class, as popular media extolled its insights and thousands of new counselors made it affordable for many. As a result, by the end of the century we had become, according to one critique, "one nation under therapy."[3] Thoughtful observers have feared that the pervasiveness of this therapeutic outlook has had three intertwined and pernicious effects: It has corroded or corrupted religious faith, fostered ethical laxity, and weakened social bonds. If this is true, it threatens the vitality of our civil society; the cultural bedrock of our liberal democracy. But is it true?

I believe that these critics have not recognized the degree to which psychotherapeutic ideas and techniques changed as they were popularized. As psychology moved into the mainstream, the mainstream – with its considerable religiosity – moved into psychology. Believers harnessed therapy to their own purposes. They innovated psychospiritual programs that *nurtured* faith, virtue, and community rather than supplanting them.[4] Such programs were particularly successful among the socially isolated and spiritually alienated, who often rebuffed traditional forms of ministry, evangelism, and fellowship. I base this conclusion on my study of three psychospiritual programs: the training of seminarians and ministers in psychology, Alcoholics Anonymous, and The Salvation Army's outreach to homeless men.

Some of the earliest efforts to forge convergences between the behavioral sciences and religion in America began among modernist Protestant clergy in the 1910s and 1920s.[5] Their sporadic efforts caught on broadly

---

1960. See Pfister, "Glamorizing the Psychological"; Rice, *Disease of One's Own*; Rieff, *Triumph of the Therapeutic*.

[3] Sommers and Satel, *One Nation Under Therapy*.

[4] I define "religion" as a community-based system of belief and practices based on an apprehension of supernatural phenomena that give the world its ultimate meaning and structure. In the context of this study, "religion" refers generally to American Christianity with an emphasis on Protestants. "Spirituality" refers to the experiential aspects of individuals' attempts to relate their lives to the supernatural phenomena that endow the cosmos with significance, whether or not this effort is aligned with Christian traditions. Similarly, I mean by "faith" an emotionally meaningful belief in any extrahuman, significance-conferring being or phenomena. I settled on these definitions after consulting Albanese, *America: Religions and Religion*; Fitzgerald, *Ideology of Religious Studies*; Fuller, *Spiritual, but Not Religious*; Hamilton, *Sociology of Religion*; James, *Varieties of Religious Experience*; Taylor, *Varieties of Religion Today*; Wuthnow, *After Heaven*.

[5] Catholics pioneered efforts to link psychology and theology almost from the inception of academic psychology. However, the separation of their educational, intellectual, and institutional lives kept Catholic and Protestant pioneers from learning from each other until after World War II. For Catholic pioneers, see Gillespie, *Psychology and American*

after World War II as ministers looked to the burgeoning field of counseling for ways to enhance their pastoral care. Protestant seminaries began offering, and eventually requiring, psychology coursework and hospital chaplaincy internships. During this education, students underwent the same kind of psychotherapeutically informed pastoral counseling they were being taught to provide. Some warned that such an education could pervert Christian doctrine and ministry by "substitut[ing] psychiatry and psychotherapy for the Word and the Sacrament."[6] A minority of seminarians did, in fact, make such a devastating substitution, styling themselves after therapists, whom they admired and emulated. Most found, however, that this new "clinical pastoral education" strengthened their clerical skills and self-confidence, especially by sharpening their self-honesty, enhancing their interpersonal interactions, and helping them mature in their faith.

Gradually, the idea that faith could foster mental well-being and that emotional growth could pave the way to greater faith reached the laity, too. This realization helped a couple of self-described boozehounds trying to stay sober together in the 1930s. They immediately began to pass the word to fellow sufferers, who responded by gathering in small, mutually supportive spiritual groups. The smattering of such groups around the nation soon came to think of themselves as united in a fellowship they dubbed Alcoholics Anonymous (AA). At war's end, thousands upon thousands of inebriates joined the movement and formed new groups. They did not share ministers' admiration for psychologists and psychiatrists. Instead they argued that they themselves provided the best treatment for compulsive drinking. Doctors soon came to agree. As both a type of lay-led group therapy and a fellowship, AA provided an ethical and spiritual education that nudged members toward greater responsibility to others and to God. Although critics have ridiculed the self-help phenomenon, I found that AA not only strengthened members' spiritual and even religious lives, but it constituted a massive democratic civil social institution in its own right.[7]

Catholicism; Kugelmann, "Neoscholastic Psychology Revisited"; and Kugelmann, *Psychology and Catholicism*. For postwar diffusion of Catholic perspectives, see Heinze, *Jews and the American Soul*.

[6] This concern was posed directly as a question to clinical training graduates in Bruder and Barb, "A Survey of Ten Years of Clinical Pastoral Training."

[7] I mean by "civil society" the private, voluntary associational ties that unite members of the public in liberal democracies. See Seligman, *Idea of Civil Society*; Eberly, ed., *Essential Civil Society Reader*.

4　　*American Protestantism in the Age of Psychology*

Although modernist and mainline clergy pioneered the Protestant effort to connect Americans' understandings of psyche and soul, it was not long before a vanguard of evangelical ministers began their own postwar efforts to claim psychology as a handmaiden to faith. The Salvation Army, a small conservative denomination with an enormous social service ministry, was at the forefront of this development. In the three decades following World War II, it gradually recast its evangelization of homeless men as psychospiritual rehabilitation. Drawing on clinical pastoral education and Alcoholics Anonymous and adding its own innovations, The Salvation Army forged psychospiritual convergences. It fruitfully exploited the overlaps between pastoral guidance and therapeutic counseling, Christian fellowship and group therapy, and the Protestant work ethic and work therapy. This therapeutic transformation of traditional evangelical methods was neither secularizing nor atomizing. Quite the opposite. In fact, the army found it nurtured homeless men's religious lives.

From these findings, I conclude that our understanding of the therapeutic strands in American culture must be revised. In the United States, the achievement of mental well-being did not usually replace spiritual interest, as nearly all the literature alleges. On the contrary, many Americans understood it as confirmation of divine concern. The spiritual groups I have studied convinced millions of spiritually and socially alienated Americans that, in their pursuit of well-being, they needed to turn to God and fellowship, and that to do this they had to become more honest and altruistic. Psychotherapeutic perspectives came to enjoy wide appeal among a citizenry who found them useful in the pursuit of moral self-improvement, fellowship, and a sense of connectedness to God.[8]

The Fall of Psychoreligious Cooperation in the United States

Americans have a long history of blending self-healing and inner exploration with spirituality, although this tradition was temporarily eclipsed

---

[8] This argument was made by Fuller in *Americans and the Unconscious*, but it was neglected by the literature on the therapeutic. A cognate argument has been offered by F. H. Matthews, who says Freud's popularity rested on "the easy and valuable inclusion of psychoanalysis into the ethic of service to the community" (60). It has been widely agreed that psychoanalysis and its offshoots became more optimistic and social in the American context; see Hale, *Rise and Crisis of Psychoanalysis, Rise and Crisis of Psychoanalysis*; Matthews, "The Americanization of Sigmund Freud"; and Sheehy, "Triumph of Group Therapeutics."

The Fall and Rise of Psychoreligious Cooperation

in the first half of the twentieth century by the rise of the behavioral sciences. This amalgamation drew on long-term, broad developments within Western culture. Christianity, Protestantism especially, was experienced increasingly in the mind and heart.[9] The emphasis on feeling one's faith began to intensify in the eighteenth century.[10] Religious claims rested less and less on textual, clerical, and social authority than on individuals' intellect and feelings. Immanuel Kant and his intellectual heirs found evidence for faith on the grounds of universal reason. This did not spare faith, however, from the assault leveled by "cultured despisers." By the eve of the nineteenth century, Protestant theologians, beginning with Friedrich Schleiermacher, had begun moving the burden of proof to the inward experience of believers. Their emotions and intuitions verified the existence of the divine realm.[11] The urgency of this project was articulated by the Anglican Archbishop of Canterbury, Frederick Temple, in 1857 when he wrote, "Our theology has been cast in a scholastic mode, all based on logic. We are in need of, and we are actually being forced into, a theology based on psychology."[12]

This theological and philosophical trend had popular analogues in Protestant pietistic and revival movements. They emphasized the importance of *individual believers* over that of corporate entities and of *faith* over other facets of Christianity (e.g., sacrament).[13] In the face of the increasing challenges mounted against religion – and the growing importance attached to individuals' mental lives – the vitality of faith in the West depended increasingly on believers' ability to link psyche and soul. They would need to find evidence of the divine in their own minds. In the process, many also concluded that they could strengthen their psyches through the salvation of their souls.

These developments helped reshape Protestant denominations and the popular theological imagination in the United States. Disestablishment

---

[9] Many starting points are alleged for this trend, which was at least a half millennium in the making. For example, Bellah roots it in the Reformation, whereas Taylor locates its origins during the High Middle Ages. Phillip Cary pushes the date as back as far as Augustine. See Bellah, "The Protestant Structure of American Culture"; Cary, *Augustine's Invention of the Inner Self*; Taylor, *Varieties of Religion Today*.

[10] Heron argues that both the impulse to articulate a "natural theology" and pietism sprang from the common interest in what faith did and should mean for the individual believer. See Heron, *Century of Protestant Theology*, 10–11.

[11] Ford, "Introduction to Modern Christian Theology"; Heron, *Century of Protestant Theology*, 14–21, 24–9; Jenson, "Karl Barth," 24–5.

[12] Rieff, *Triumph of the Therapeutic*, 41–2.

[13] Ford, "Introduction to Modern Christian Theology"; Heron *Century of Protestant Theology*; Holifield, *History of Pastoral Care*; Taves, *Fits, Trances, and Visions*.

6 *American Protestantism in the Age of Psychology*

and the potent leveling impulses released by the American Revolution created a fertile climate for evangelists. They spread across the land with new understandings of the gospels that were individualistic, optimistic, and democratic.[14] Over the course of the century, Americans new and old flocked to Methodist, Presbyterian, and Baptist churches. These new churches emphasized the idea in the New Testament that "whosoever shall call upon the name of the Lord shall be saved" (Romans 10:13). Faith – understood as what happened in one's heart and head – determined the fate of one's soul.

The new importance of feelings and beliefs in Americans' religious lives reflected and influenced profound changes in social relations and culture. For example, a new emphasis on intimacy infused families. Child-rearing shifted from broad multigenerational clans to bigenerational emotional "hot houses" that fostered tighter relationships and intense feelings between members of the nuclear family.[15] Antebellum literature, like the religion that informed it, reinforced readers' complex and "deeper" sense of selves.[16]

The soul and psyche blurred and merged as nineteenth-century Americans perceived a deeper space inside themselves.[17] This initiated a period of free play in which Americans asserted a bewildering variety of claims about what happened inside them and how this connected to the material and spiritual worlds outside themselves. In the antebellum era, many found an inner portal leading to an extra-individual sacred realm, a space that could be inhabited by holy spirits.[18] Thus possessed, some Americans erupted into fits, fell into trances, spoke in strange voices, or

---

[14] Bednarowski, *New Religions*; Finke and Stark, *Churching of America*; Hatch, *Democratization of American Christianity*; Hutchison, *Modernist Impulse*; Wood, *Radicalism of the American Revolution*.

[15] Demos, "Oedipus and America," 63–78.

[16] Pfister, "Glamorizing the Psychological."

[17] Some historians, inspired in large part by Michel Foucault, have argued that this space was invented or imagined. This line of argument is better supported by theory than by a nuanced social history of the type that, for example, John Demos tells. Either way, all acknowledge that Americans did perceive this space. For one of the best books in the genre of a Foucauldian-inspired history of emotion, see Pfister and Schnog, *Inventing the Psychological*. Other Marxian and Foucauldian-inflected works include: Cushman, *Constructing the Self*; Kovel, "The American Mental Health Industry"; Levine, *Constructions of the Self*; Rose, *Governing the Soul*; Rose, *Inventing Our Selves*.

[18] Cary, in *Augustine's Invention*, argues that such a space hailed back to Augustine and was therefore intrinsic to the Western Christian tradition: "From its inception, inwardness meant seeking a glimpse of the soul's inner relation to its divine origin" (10).

The Fall and Rise of Psychoreligious Cooperation

saw fantastic visions. Americans vigorously debated whether such phenomena were physical or religious, human or divine, sincere or fraudulent. Tens of thousands flocked to the new therapies, churches, and entertainments that coalesced around the idea of an overlapping psyche, mind, and spirit.[19] While some merely sought amusement, many sought healing in an age in which doctors could offer little. For example, hypnotist Phineas Parkhurst Quimby (1802–1866) treated almost 12,000 patients.[20]

Many of those most interested in these new forms of hybrid spirituality were motivated by matters of faith rather than, or in addition to, medical concerns. It appealed especially to people who found more traditional religious forms and ideas implausible or uncompelling. In the decades after the Civil War, many of the traditional grounds for faith, such as revelation and the physical world, were undermined as challengers argued that they were the work of human or natural hands.[21] By the late nineteenth century, Congregationalist minister Lyman Abbott echoed the Archbishop of Canterbury when – dismayed that he found no room for God in the new scientific literature – he said that "if I was to retain any really forceful belief in God and immortality, or even in practical morality, I must believe in the trustworthiness of spiritual experience."[22] In the late nineteenth century, personal experience became the one realm safe from challenge to which educated Protestants could turn for validation and confirmation of their religious longings and intuitions. The pietistic trends that had flourished in the eighteenth and nineteenth centuries attuned believers to feeling their faith, to feeling the divine spirit stirring their souls. The immediacy and intimacy of this experience could not be gainsaid by scholars who insisted, for example, that geology and archeology provided a better natural history of the world than Scripture did.

A new development, however, eventually threw this approach into question. It would curtail the ability of Americans to blend their beliefs easily with their healing: the rise of the academic and professional disciplines of psychology and psychiatry. The first psychology laboratory was established at The Johns Hopkins University in 1883, and a few years later the school awarded its first doctorate in the subject. Over

---

[19] Fuller, *Mesmerism*; Fuller, *Spiritual, but Not Religious*; Meyer, *The Positive Thinkers*; Moore, *In Search of White Crows*; Taves, *Fits, Trances, and Visions*, part II.

[20] Fuller, *Mesmerism*, 118–22.

[21] Ibid; Smith, ed., *The Secular Revolution*; Turner, *Without God, Without Creed*.

[22] Turner, *Without God, Without Creed*, 188.

8 *American Protestantism in the Age of Psychology*

the ensuing fifteen years, dozens of schools set up psychology departments. Williams James, one of the most impressive and famous students of the new discipline, published his magisterial *Principles of Psychology* (1890). And scholars of the burgeoning discipline established the American Psychological Association along with multiple national and regional journals. When Lightner Witmer founded the first psychological clinic for patients in 1896, American behavioral scientists entered the field of mental and psychosomatic healing that theretofore had been dominated by lay practitioners such as Quimby and his students.

As with any new field, psychology's early years were characterized by diversity and disagreements over paradigmatic questions about boundaries, foci, and methods.[23] One contentious issue was the relationship of the new field to theology, spiritual lay healing, and claims of religious experience. Neoscholastic scholars began an ambitious program to bridge the worlds of scientific psychology and Catholic doctrine.[24] Some Protestants also felt that psychology could and should retain a close and collaborative relationship with faith, even if it was a heterodox one. This was advocated and practiced by some of the key figures in the founding of American psychology, most famously by William James, who published his lectures on the *Varieties of Religious Experience* in 1902. It became an instant best-seller despite its massive size and erudition.[25] One small subgroup of liberal Protestant researchers began work on the psychology of religion, by which they hoped to explain such questions as why conversions failed, how to nurture ethical development, and what the nature of religious experiences is.

The relationship of psychology to religion was of interest not only to students and practitioners within the new discipline – a broad array of Americans outside it were emotionally, intellectually, and spiritually invested in the matter as well. Some liberal Protestants hoped to draw on the new disciplines to revitalize theologies that they found implausible and church communities they deemed hidebound. National religious magazines such as the *Christian Century* published many articles on the

[23] Bjork, *William James*; Danzinger, *Constructing the Subject*; Leahey, *History of Modern Psychology*.
[24] Gillespie, *Psychology and American Catholicism*; Kugelmann, "Neoscholastic Psychology Revisited."
[25] Random House, Inc., *Online Catalog* [s.v. William James, *The Varieties of Religious Experience: A Study in Human Nature*], at www.randomhouse.com/acmart/catalog/display.pperl?isbn=9780679640110.

The Fall and Rise of Psychoreligious Cooperation

psychology of religion movement and other developments in the young field.[26] Two Episcopalian priests who had done extensive graduate work in psychology in Germany, Elwood Worcester and Samuel McComb, started a clinic at the Emmanuel Church in Boston in 1906. They had as their goal to "awaken faith" in their patients through contemporary miraculous healing. The "mental health clinic" at the Emmanuel Church consisted of individual counseling with a minister, a religious service, and a social meeting. Ministers used relaxation techniques to put patients in receptive states of mind and then suggested healing messages to them. The project sparked an immediate enthusiastic lay response, with patients gathering together at the church even when no events were planned for them. Widespread national and even international media coverage publicized the work of the clinic to an audience of clergy, doctors, and psychologists.[27]

The openness to psychospiritual experimentation, creativity, and contention that prevailed in the first quarter-century of the development of modern American psychology almost vanished during the subsequent dozen years. The year 1908 marked a turning point. That is when the psychologists and doctors affiliated with the Emmanuel clinic resigned amid controversy, implying that the clinic's procedures were not medically respectable. Other doctors attacked the program as well for trespassing on a bailiwick they believed belonged uniquely to them. In the decades that followed, medical professionals successfully claimed monopoly power to heal American mental and psychosomatic problems.[28] When a trickle of ministers in the 1920s and 1930s began to study psychology and offer therapy, the lessons of the Emmanuel movement prompted them to do so covertly, avoiding any challenges to the authority of doctors. When the lay-led spiritual therapy movement Alcoholics Anonymous emerged in the late 1930s and 1940s, its leadership went out of its way to procure the endorsement of the medical and psychiatric communities.

This constriction of free psychospiritual exploration affected psychological research as well. In 1910 William James died. He had been the most respected and widely read psychologist who found common ground between mental and spiritual phenomena. And this outlook had hurt even

---

[26] Meador, "Psychology's Secularizing of American Protestantism."
[27] Caplan, *Mind Games*, 117–48; Gifford, *Emmanuel Movement*, 63–4, 75; Taves, *Fits, Trances, and Visions*, 309–25.
[28] Caplan, *Mind Games*, 117–48.

10   *American Protestantism in the Age of Psychology*

his standing in the field.[29] After his death, no one promoting research into the psychology of religion matched his intellect or stature. Pushed to the far margins in the 1920s, the subfield fell off the map entirely by 1930.[30] At the same time, the ongoing work of Catholic scholars to bridge psychology with theology was confined to their own institutions.[31] During this period, Sigmund Freud became increasingly familiar to educated Americans. He began publishing work arguing very explicitly that readers should be totally skeptical of religious experiences.[32] "Religion is an illusion," he famously claimed.

This atheism was shared by most academic psychologists who had by this time established behavioralism as their dominant mode of inquiry.[33] Concerned entirely with the description, prediction, and control of behavior, they eschewed any interest in the internal goings-on of the human mind as unworthy of a scientific discipline.[34] Behavioralists not only scorned religious explanations for human experience, but they even disdained the concept of the psyche altogether as a kind of bowdlerized soul in disguise. Although the work of Sigmund Freud had come to dominate psychoanalysis by the 1930s – and although Freud advanced a distinctly atheistic concept of the psyche – behavioralists understood that when Americans thought about what they felt and believed deep inside, most thought about their souls and God.[35]

Modern research psychology and professional psychodynamic psychiatry drove a wedge between emotional healing and spiritual beliefs. It became more difficult, especially among the educated, to connect psyche

---

[29] Bjork, *William James.*

[30] Beit-Hallahmi, "Psychology of Religion 1880–1930."

[31] Kugelmann, "Neoscholastic Psychology Revisited"; Kugelmann, *Psychology and Catholicism.* The Protestants whose documents I examined for this study rarely seemed aware or interested in what other Christians engaged in psychoreligious theorizing or programming were doing. The one exception is Bill Wilson, AA founder. The General Service Office of Alcoholics Anonymous in New York has extensive correspondence between Wilson and Fathers Edward Dowling and John Ford.

[32] Freud, *Future of an Illusion.* Some Americans liked Freud precisely because of his utility in mounting antireligious attacks, see Hale, *Rise and Crisis of Psychoanalysis,* 81, 84–5.

[33] Catholic scholars in Catholic colleges and universities were following a different path, but they walked it unaccompanied by those outside their schools, see Gillespie, *Psychology and American Catholicism*; and Kugelmann, "Neoscholastic Psychology Revisited."

[34] Leahey, *History of Modern Psychology,* part III.

[35] Fuller, *Americans and the Unconscious*; Hale, *Rise and Crisis of Psychoanalysis*; Matthews, "The Americanization of Sigmund Freud." The most influential psychoanalyst who argued for a spiritualized psychic realm was Carl Jung, see Noll, *Aryan Christ*; and Noll, *Jung Cult.*

The Fall and Rise of Psychoreligious Cooperation

and soul.[36] With the ascendance of a strongly atheistic bent in psychiatry and psychology, many clergy worried that faith's former handmaiden had become a siren who would lure it onto the dry rocks of doubt and despair. Although psychology had long been wielded as a weapon in debates over the authenticity of *certain* religious experiences and behaviors, it was now used for the first time to discredit *all* religious experience.[37] Behavioral scientists taught that what believers took to be divine glimpses and encounters were merely projections of the psyche. They mistook a shadow for God. One minister even confessed that he was never able to entirely regain his faith after reading Freud's *Future of an Illusion* (1927) and *Moses and Monotheism* (1939).[38]

Given the extent to which American religion had come to rely on the heart's response to the divine, this was a potentially devastating development. Americans agreed they needed to feel their faith and to have faith in their feelings.[39] As one sober alcoholic said after the war, "Ministers and priests are turning to psychology because faith is an act of the mind.... Faith must be built on our psychological experience."[40] This continuing emphasis on feeling their faith and having faith in those

---

[36] Andrew Heinze finds that "after the death of William James in 1910, the idea of a spiritualized psyche virtually disappeared among academic psychologists." See *Jews and the American Soul*, 165–6.

[37] There was a long history of psychological explanations being invoked to debunk false faith. Believers in the eighteenth century who distrusted the "enthusiasm" of the Great Awakening developed psychological explanations to deny that the outbursts of New Lights were true religious phenomena. Jonathan Edwards, who accepted some of the New Light claims, developed tests to distinguish between outbursts of the spirits, demonic impulses, and mere delusions or wishful thinking. The way people behaved at antebellum revivals of the Second Great Awakening was also dismissed by some outsiders as merely the reaction to the magnetic or mesmeric forces that were believed to pervade the human body and influence the mind. Believers long retained psychological explanations as a way to critique religious ideas and expressions that they found insincere or suspect. Whereas in the eighteenth and nineteenth century, orthodox believers used this weapon against reformers, in the twentieth, the reformers – such as the clinical pastoral education pioneers – turned it against the orthodox. Clebsch, *American Religious Thought*, 14; Taves, *Fits, Trances, and Visions*, part 1, pp. 131–202; Hale, *Rise and Crisis of Psychoanalysis*, 81, 84–5.

[38] Frederick Proelss, "What Makes Clinical Experience Pastoral," presentation at the National Conference of the Council for Clinical Training, Inc., October 30, 1957, Atlantic City, NJ, RG 001, Box 160, folder 2483, Pitts, p. 5.

[39] Even the Catholic Church, which distrusted and denounced such trends, acknowledged the dangers and strove to address it through its own sanctioned psychoreligious blends; see Gillespie, *Psychology and American Catholicism*; and Kugelmann, "Neoscholastic Psychology Revisited."

[40] R. W. in Daytona Beach, FL, "Modern Miracle," *The Grapevine* (April 1947): 9.

American Protestantism in the Age of Psychology

spiritual feelings meant that Americans would begin again mixing their psychology with their religion as soon as opportunities arose.

The Postwar Renewal of Psychoreligious Cooperation

World War II provided just such opportunities. It catalyzed the widespread diffusion of psychological knowledge and techniques. Before the war, the ideas and practices of modern psychotherapy in the United States had been limited primarily to bohemian and elite milieus.[41] There were relatively few psychoanalysts and even fewer clinical psychologists. Only small handfuls of allied professionals, such as social workers and ministers, had made forays into counseling the troubled. Educated readers learned about psychology from the occasional magazine article, such as the 1939 issue of *Time* magazine that announced the death of Sigmund Freud and featured him on the cover.[42]

During and after the war, however, the field of mental health expanded vastly as expertise in general acquired great prestige, and as psychological professionals, in particular, convinced the nation of the utility of their services. Scores of psychoanalysts fleeing Hitler took up residence in the United States and began training others. The rapid growth in the population of analysts, however, was outstripped by the thousands of newly minted psychologists who began to offer psychotherapy. Between 1940 and 1970, membership in the American Psychological Association grew 1,100 percent – from 2,739 to 30,839 – surpassing the growth curves of other medical and academic fields.[43] Most of these new PhDs were headed for clinics or private practices rather than laboratories. By the 1950s, most Americans began first to use the term "psychologist" the way they would continue to use it for the rest of the century – as a synonym for therapist.[44] The demand for psychotherapists was so high, and their status so exalted, however, that many other professionals moved into counseling. More and more nurses and social workers, for example, began to remake their professions as therapeutic ones.[45]

The expansion of psychological perspectives was hardly confined to mental health professionals and elites, as it had been before the war.

---

[41] Douglas, *Terrible Honesty*.
[42] Hale, *Rise and Crisis of Psychoanalysis*, 74–9.
[43] Herman, *Romance of American Psychology*, 2–3.
[44] Leahey, *History of Modern Psychology*, 242.
[45] Morris, *Limits of Voluntarism*; Stevens and Henrie, "A History of Psychiatric Nursing."

The Fall and Rise of Psychoreligious Cooperation 13

Ideas from the behavioral sciences were disseminated in mass media and popular books. Dr. Benjamin Spock, a doctor trained in psychoanalysis as well as pediatrics, published the first edition of his best-selling child-rearing manual in 1946. Millions of Americans soon bought copies of his book, which went through seven editions. Popular women's magazines introduced readers to basic psychological concepts such as ego, inferiority complex, and self-esteem, urging them to think about their own lives in these terms. Movies and other popular media were full of stories of war neuroses miraculously and quickly cured by psychoanalysis.[46]

The broad cultural and social expansion of psychological ideas and therapeutic techniques flooded the old guard psychoanalysts, undermining their monopoly on legitimate mental healing. As the pool of psychoanalysts, psychiatrists, and psychologists expanded, so did the diversity of their religious backgrounds and beliefs. Therapy still attracted new practitioners disproportionately from the small minority of Americans who were atheists and religious skeptics.[47] But the larger the pool of psychological pundits and counselors, the more opportunities emerged to blend spiritual and religious pursuits with healing. Immediately after the war, for instance, Americans, Jewish and gentile, snapped up copies of *Peace of Mind*, written by Rabbi Joshua Loth Liebman. He argued that ancient Jewish wisdom and modern psychotherapy converged in agreeing that self-understanding rather than self-condemnation would lead to inner peace, ethical maturity, and strengthened communities.[48] Millions more Americans soon began tuning into Reverend Norman Vincent Peale, whose psychospiritual sermons reached countless households via radio, television, and magazines.[49]

---

[46] Hale, *Rise and Crisis of Psychoanalysis*, 278–99; Heinze, "*Peace of Mind*"; Moskowitz, *In Therapy We Trust*, 149–77.

[47] Such unusually secular Americans hailed from Protestant and Jewish backgrounds. A disproportionate percentage were Jews, who may have embraced secularity as a strategy for overcoming the prejudice and disadvantages of living in a Christian society. Steinberg found in the early 1970s that over one-third of clinical psychology faculty were Jewish. Unlike their Protestant and Catholic colleagues, the vast majority of them were indifferent or even opposed to religion. Heinze shows how overrepresented Jews were in both the academic and popular fields of psychology in this country. Although his argument does not emphasize it, his evidence makes clear how thoroughly secular these innovators were. See Heinze, *Jews and the American Soul*; Hollinger; Steinberg, *The Academic Melting Pot*, table 17c.

[48] Heinze, "Therapeutic Polemics."

[49] Meyer, *The Positive Thinkers*.

Americans turned in ever greater numbers to their clergy for personal advice. Ministers and priests, in turn, began looking increasingly for guidance on how best to counsel their congregants. In American Catholic circles, despite the controversy surrounding the "new psychology," a few pioneers began advocating the adaptation of modern psychology to spiritual counseling.[50] The journal *Pastoral Psychology* was established in 1950 and was soon being read by thousands of Protestant clergy. Seminaries began offering, and even mandating, some training in psychology in their curricula. Even many unchurched mid-century Americans who were loath to consult a minister found that they could not envision healing their own mental problems without spiritual admixture. The men and women who came together to form Alcoholics Anonymous in the late 1930s and 1940s ensured that self-help would also mingle spirituality with therapy. This movement, which began with a mere hundred members in 1939, exploded over the next twenty-five years, eventually reaching millions of Americans.

American Faith in the Age of Psychology

Although this story of the popularization of psychology has been told many times, a key element of it has been neglected; this has led to misunderstanding. The expansion of a therapeutic ethos was synonymous with its democratization and therefore led to its profound alteration. This allowed psychoreligious programs to foster faith instead of disbelief, community in place of alienation, and ethical striving rather than self-indulgence. The majority of citizens gleaned psychotherapeutic perspectives on their lives from books, magazines, radio programs, and movies. Americans sought therapeutic advice from a variety of sources in addition to clinicians: clergy, medical doctors, social workers, nurses, lay therapists, fellow citizens, and even the occasional outlaw and science fiction writer.[51] Thus, concepts inevitably changed in the translation from their original theoretical sources. The therapeutic advice citizens received encompassed techniques and healing agents that bore faint resemblance to those of professional psychoanalysis or psychotherapy.

---

[50] Gillespie, *Psychology and American Catholicism*, 42–3, 90–3, 121–3.

[51] Bednarowski, *New Religions*; Heinze, *Jews and the American Soul*; Moore, *In Search of White Crows*; Morris, "Charity, Therapy, and Poverty"; Sheehy, "Triumph of Group Therapeutics"; Stevens and Henrie, "A History of Psychiatric Nursing"; Crowley, "L. Ron Hubbard."

Therefore the expansion of the therapeutic did not necessarily entail an expansion of introspection – with its presumed concomitant self-absorption and social isolation. It also often meant citizens turned to prayer, fellowship groups, reading, God, recreation, and work. This resulted from the increasingly broad array of Americans who believed they had the authority to offer therapy and the ever-widening array of activities they prescribed. It arose, too, from the strong religious and associational traditions of the United States, which were not easily cast aside. This meant that the success of the new therapeutic ethos depended on its ability to coexist with and support them.[52] Despite the efforts of psychologists to distinguish their science from religion, Americans adapted psychology to serve their long-standing aspirations for faith and community at least as much as their religious and associational lives were influenced by psychology.

Convergences were aided by the fact that in the years after World War II, American popular culture freely intermingled the values of democracy, civil society, science, and religion. Intellectuals, of course, debated the precise interrelationship of these phenomena. But the majority of Americans clamored for facts and fictions about scientific breakthroughs (in which they included psychological ones), affirmed God and attended church, celebrated their democratic freedoms, and flocked to civil associations.[53] Thus, the American "way of life" during the Cold War seemed to encompass both technological and scientific prowess and religiosity. As mid-century church membership rates rose to historic highs, Americans seemed to cherish their freedoms of worship and association as never before. Science was understood as fundamentally democratic: It was transparent, egalitarian, self-correcting. In distinction to common Gilded Age and Progressive-era narratives of a "war between science and religion," science was portrayed popularly as religious: The grandeur and complexity discovered by scientists revealed God's handiwork.[54] Physicists and astronomers declared publicly that what they had found and seen lifted their eyes heavenward. Many Americans thought it entirely reasonable that the burgeoning sciences of mind and psyche could also uncover sublime new spiritual truths, especially since many would have

---

[52] Fuller, *Americans and the Unconscious*; Matthews, "The Americanization of Sigmund Freud."

[53] Balogh, *Chain Reaction*; Boyer, *By the Bomb's Early Light*; Gilbert, *Redeeming Culture*; Putnam, *Bowling Alone*.

[54] Gilbert, *Redeeming Culture*; Larson, *Summer for the Gods*; White, *History of the Warfare of Science with Theology*.

16   *American Protestantism in the Age of Psychology*

averred that there was something fundamentally spiritual in human nature.

Such beliefs were shared by a broad swath of Americans, both inside and outside of religious institutions. This matrix of crisscrossing beliefs was what allowed the three diverse movements this study examines to agree that fostering Americans' emotional growth would nurture their spiritual growth and vice versa. It was also why the groups believed that citizens' psychoreligious development would enable them to participate more democratically in spiritual communities and free society.

Turning Against the Therapeutic Turn

These linkages between democracy and civil society, religion and science, were brought to their fullest articulation by those who came to advocate what became known as humanistic psychology. Their version, however, pushed these commonly shared connections in directions that were exceptionally individualistic and antireligious (although not always antispiritual).[55] Psychologists Carl Rogers and Abraham Maslow became indefatigable proponents of an optimistic new vision of human nature and the essential role therapy could play in bringing about a society that nurtured virtue. Carl Rogers, a one-time theology student who had abandoned faith for psychology, had begun laying out a nondirective therapy method in the 1940s. This approach relied on the clients, rather than the therapists, to direct their encounters, trusting clients to know what was best for themselves and to articulate their own values and sources of healing. It was rapidly popularized among clergy who struggled to deal with the Americans who were consulting them about a wide variety of problems.[56] They were motivated as much by the fact that a client-centered approach minimized the harm that poorly trained and nervous ministers could do as they were by ideological agreement with the presuppositions of Rogerian therapy.[57] An evangelist for his new gospel, Rogers was thrilled with the political implications of humanistic psychology as he saw them play out in the countercultural and student movements.[58]

[55] For definitions of spiritual and religious, see note #4.
[56] A plurality of people (42%) who sought help for psychological problems sought clerical help. Joint Commission on Mental Illness and Health, *Action for Mental Health*, 103.
[57] Holifield, *History of Pastoral Care*, 259–60, 303; Gillespie, *Psychology and American Catholicism*, 121–3.
[58] Herman, "Being and Doing," 92.

The Fall and Rise of Psychoreligious Cooperation

Abraham Maslow, who disliked the interpretation the young protestors and dissidents put on his work,[59] nevertheless went much further than Rogers in adumbrating the utopian society that therapy would help realize. Maslow argued that current societies were terribly flawed. Even American society, despite its superiority to fascist and communist alternatives, suffered from racism, selfishness, social ills such as drug addiction, and all kinds of "stupidities." The most potent source of reform and revitalization lay within the best people. They shared with the best people of all times and places an uncorrupted innate compass that pointed them toward beauty, truth, and creativity. All of humankind possessed such innate sensitivities, but they had been perverted by culture. Self-insight gained through therapy could rectify the distortions. This would pave the way for a society of "healthy individuals," who would "feel brotherly towards all mankind" while maintaining a deep "respect for individual differences." Such a society might be called "eupsychia."[60]

Maslow's utopian vision was shared by many in the humanistic psychology movement, of which he was such an important leader.[61] Furthermore, its general optimism for the democratic and ethical benefits of psychological approaches was shared by a broad audience. Viewing psychotherapy as a tool to release a fundamentally good human nature from the corruptions of culture was a change from earlier understandings. The older psychoanalytic and mental hygiene traditions took the adjustment of individuals to society as their goal.[62]

That anti-individualistic goal began to seem increasingly sinister to many mid-century Americans, whose historical individualism took on a new salience amidst anxieties about oppressive corporatist ideologies abroad and the personal effects of a corporate economy at home.[63] Humanistic psychologists were not the only ones taking aim at the contemporary practice of psychiatry and clinical psychology. Others began

---

[59] Ibid.

[60] Maslow, "Eupsychia – The Good Society."

[61] This is clear in the early articles of the *Journal for Humanistic Psychology (JHP)*, founded in 1961, which set out grandiose hopes for the new movement. See, for example, Anthony J. Sutich, "Introduction," *JHP* 1(1): vii–ix; Carl Rogers, "Some Questions and Challenges Facing a Humanistic Psychology," *JHP* 5(1): 1–5; J. F. T. Bugental, "The Third Force in Psychology," *JHP* 4(1): 19–26.

[62] Gutmann, "Psychology as Theology"; Holifield, *History of Pastoral Care*; Rice, *A Disease of One's Own*; Rieff, *Freud*.

[63] Riesman et al., *The Lonely Crowd*; McClay, *The Masterless*, 189–268; Mills, *The Power Elite*; Mills, *White Collar*; Whyte, *Organization Man*.

18   *American Protestantism in the Age of Psychology*

to criticize psychotherapy for stigmatizing and even oppressing idiosyncratic individuals. An antipsychiatry movement emerged in the 1960s from the writings of analyst Thomas Szasz, who called "mental illness" a myth whose purpose was to marginalize and imprison difficult people. A growing body of work by American and foreign scholars elaborated this and similar critiques.

Although there were differences in the way these authors formulated their critiques of therapeutic ideas and practices in Western society, they shared a sense that a therapeutic regime was hostile to individualism and individual responsibility. Some emphasized it as a form of social control.[64] Others made a case that it contributed to the mollycoddling and infantilization of Americans. This strand of criticism, which continues today, argued that psychology's portrayal of all humans as ill and subject to unconscious forces weakened Americans by making them less stoic, rational, and self-reliant.[65] However, critics disagreed among themselves. Some, for example, felt that the humanistic reformation of psychology – with its celebration of the irrational and spontaneous – only made the problem worse.

A new note was sounded when sociologist Philip Rieff published *Freud: The Mind of the Moralist* (1959) and the seminal *Triumph of the Therapeutic: Uses of Faith After Freud* (1966). These works were not worried about the way psychology could be used to coerce individuals' compliance with the broader culture but rather the opposite: how psychology exacerbated the sense of alienation modern people felt from the societies in which they lived. Rieff traced this development back to Freud himself. But it was probably no accident that he wrote these works in the same period humanistic psychologists first began loudly making known their agenda, which emphasized above all the use of therapy to cultivate a profound distance between individual Americans and their communities. Rieff charged psychology with eroding public commitments and depoliticizing citizens. Therapeutic introspection "more often produce[d]

---

[64] In addition to the humanistic psychologists such Rogers, Maslow, and the other contributors to the fledgling *Journal of Humanistic Psychology*, who saw it this way, also see libertarian work such as Foucault, *Madness and Civilization*; Foucault, *The Birth of the Clinic*; Szasz, *The Myth of Mental Illness*; and feminist work, such as Chesler, *Women and Madness*.

[65] Classic articulations of this line of criticism are LaPiere, *The Freudian Ethic*; and Meyer, *The Positive Thinkers*. The most recent entry in this vein is Sommers and Satel, *One Nation Under Therapy*.

The Fall and Rise of Psychoreligious Cooperation 19

pedants of the inner life than virtuosi of the outer one."[66] This concern with psychology's threat to communal and public life in all its forms – religious, civic, and political – was an increasingly common refrain for the rest of the twentieth century and beyond. Even critiques and scholarship inspired by Michel Foucault's pioneering analyses, with their strong libertarian and anarchist values, worried less about individual freedom than about community commitments.[67] In the forty years following the publication of Rieff's *Triumph*, a huge literature emerged that detailed the pernicious effects of the spread of therapeutic ideas and practices throughout the culture.

This body of work described a "therapeutic ethos" that, first and foremost, distorted Americans' understanding of human nature and themselves. It promoted solipsism. It caricatured individuals as both psychically wounded and significantly unique.[68] Rieff warned of citizens' "devastating illusions of individuality."[69] It seemed to confer supreme value on feeling good and achieving emotional health, requiring endless self-preoccupation and introspection. Under this new cultural imperative, Rieff continued, "nothing [is] at stake beyond a manipulatable sense of well-being."[70]

This distorted sense of the relationship between self and society isolated individuals politically and socially. Delicate and peerless beings needed protection from demands to conform to the dictates of church, community, and polity.[71] Such corporate entities hardly mattered anyway, since a therapeutic perspective misrepresented many human problems as matters of individual disease susceptible to individual diagnosis

---

[66] Rieff, *Freud*, 329.

[67] Cushman, *Constructing the Self*; Pfister and Schnog, *Inventing the Psychological*; Rose, *Governing the Soul*; Rose, *Inventing Our Selves*.

[68] For a succinct historical–philosophical analysis of authenticity, see Taylor, *Ethics of Authenticity*. For a thorough analysis of the way ideas of the authentic self (i.e., "significantly unique") necessarily entailed ideas of being a victim ("psychically wounded"), see Davis, *Accounts of Innocence*.

[69] Rieff, *Triumph of the Therapeutic*, 10.

[70] Ibid., 13.

[71] Rice confines this development to the "liberation psychology" of the 1960s and afterward, but Rogers – one of the movements' most influential leaders – had been publishing and training therapists since the 1940s. Furthermore, even before the Humanistic school declared itself in the early 1960s, Rieff had argued in *Freud* that the profound social skepticism of psychoanalysis from its founding successfully intended to gain patients' critical distance from their families and communities. Certainly, bohemians and clinical pastoral education pioneers used psychoanalytic theory this way in the 1920s and 1930s.

American Protestantism in the Age of Psychology

and cure. As decried by historian Christopher Lasch – who is surpassed only by Rieff in his eloquent, penetrating critique of the therapeutic – Americans "have convinced themselves that what matters is psychic self-improvement.... [T]hese pursuits, elevated to a program and wrapped in rhetoric of authenticity and awareness, signify a retreat from politics."[72] This excessive individualism vitiated duty and virtue. As sociologist James D. Hunter, invoking philosopher Charles Taylor, has recently argued forcefully, a therapeutic perspective cannot bear the weight of our "far-reaching moral commitments to benevolence and justice."[73]

This distortion of self and weakening of the claims of traditional communities and morality put faith at particular risk. "Therapy constitutes an anti-religion," thundered Lasch. By casting doubt on everything outside the psyche, psychology inhibited the ability of people to apprehend the transcendent. It "inculcates... skepticism about all ideologies except those of the private life," averred Rieff.[74] Although not all critics worried about the potential demise of American religion in and of itself, many were concerned it would undermine a key cultural force necessary for the vitality of liberal democracies.[75]

Over the past few years, however, a handful of new studies have challenged some aspects of this depiction of psychology's social impact. In particular, they deny that it invariably promoted individualism, obviated political action, and enervated spirituality.[76] Despite this, almost all scholars continue to assume that the implications of psychology were negative for religion.[77] A few recent titles quickly make this apparent: *In Therapy We Trust* (2001) and *One Nation Under Therapy* (2005).

---

[72] Lasch, *Culture of Narcissism*, 5.

[73] Hunter, *Death of Character*.

[74] Rieff, *Freud*, 255.

[75] Bellah et al., *Habits of the Heart*; Herman, *Romance of American Psychology*; Lasch; Moskowitz, *In Therapy We Trust*; Nolan, *Therapeutic State*; Rieff, *Triumph of the Therapeutic*; Warren, "Will It Preach?"

[76] Fuller, *Spiritual, but Not Religious*; Herman, "Being and Doing"; Herman, *Romance of American Psychology*, ch. 10; Sheehy, "Triumph of Group Therapeutics." Heinze, in *Jews and the American Soul*, finds a different problem with the literature on the therapeutic. He argues that the trend represents not secularization, but rather the displacement of Protestant perspectives from the center of American culture. Nevertheless, the Jewish psychological pioneers he describes were almost invariably secular. The first author to call for a more empirically based, less normative scholarship on the issue was Battan in "The 'New Narcissism' in 20th-Century America."

[77] One recent book, Alan Petigny, *The Permissive Society* (New York: Oxford University Press, 2009), repeats this argument explicitly. Although the book's larger argument draws on a creative array of social historical data, its claim about religion is based on a cultural history focusing on elite messages.

The Fall and Rise of Psychoreligious Cooperation

Although neither book deals with faith per se, they are typical in that both assume that God has been displaced by psychology.

A Revised Assessment of the Therapeutic Ethos

Most critics' conclusions about the effects of therapeutic ideas and practices on faith, however, are not based on the real data of spiritual and religious groups that have adapted psychology to their own purposes. Rather, they were stitched together from bits of historical evidence and plausible inferences. Yet there are philosophical and methodological reasons to question whether the common portrayal of a therapeutic ethos in American culture is entirely accurate. And some of the reasons lie within the literature itself.

To begin with, despite the diversity of the criticism, the critics all agree that psychological knowledge is socially constructed rather than some "pure" discovery of medical inquiry. In fact, clinical psychology's status as a science – that is as a field whose tenets are subject to validation and refutation on their own ground – is no longer firmly claimed even by its practitioners.[78] It follows, therefore, that the inclusion or exclusion of God and community in this cultural practice is neither philosophically nor logically necessary but rather sociologically and historically determined. Furthermore, while one strand of criticism of the therapeutic indicts it primarily for its socially atomizing effects, an opposite strand has condemned psychotherapy for its role in disciplining the individual to the larger society.[79] Although few critics try to synthesize these critiques,[80]

---

[78] Vitz, "Psychology in Recovery."

[79] Invoking an implicitly libertarian or anarchic conception of society, libertarian- and Foucauldian-inspired literature on psychology sometimes emphasizes the oppressive way individual diversity is cast as deviance. Other times, it assumes a socialist or even organic social conception, in order to argue that psychological perspectives are used (by the powers that be) to train individuals to be selfish. I found far more evidence can be adduced for the former claim than the latter, which seems to take social construction arguments into the realm of Positive Thinking (a la Meyers, *The Positive Thinkers*). Of interest is the argument of Peter Stearns, who with no debt to any of these theoretical frameworks, has found that the emotional geography of the twentieth century, infused as it was with therapeutic attitudes, emphasized the control and transcendence of emotions. Americans in the nineteenth century, before the advent and popularization of modern psychology, gave their feelings much freer reign, Stearns, *American Cool*.

[80] Rice (*A Disease of One's Own*) suggests that the latter critique was accurate until about 1960, prior to which psychology had a disciplining function. He alleges that the former critique has been on target ever since, given the change in psychotherapy's rejection of earlier demands that patients adapt to social norms.

American Protestantism in the Age of Psychology

both have some good evidence and arguments on their side. Those concerned about atomization might look for, and be comforted by, evidence of discipline. Those concerned about psychology-bred conformity, meanwhile, might take comfort in the evidence of its promotion of radical autonomy.

The older antitherapeutic critical consensus paid insufficient heed to two other theoretical points. First, although much of the concern about the effect of psychology on faith builds on Tocquevillian observations about the social value of religion, Tocqueville himself argued that it would have to accommodate the dominant American passion for personal well-being.[81] And so it did. Although religion could not make martyrs or saints of such believers, it could gently "purify, regulate, and restrain" their most self-serving desires.[82]

Second, psychotherapeutic literature and practice itself offers many different visions of self, not all of which need be at odds with the cultural requirements of a liberal democracy. Clinician–theorists from Sigmund Freud through Carl Rogers and Abraham Maslow diverged quite sharply in drawing the boundaries of the self, identifying its fundamental drives, and assessing its capacities for good and evil. A related point is argued by philosopher Charles Taylor, who has traced the history of modern notions of "authenticity," which became closely bound up with the therapeutic in postwar America.[83] Taylor contrasts two models. In the older view, which Taylor locates in the eighteenth and nineteenth centuries, the individual achieved authenticity by choosing among a multiplicity of available traditions, each entailing its own identity, its own variety of selfhood. In the more recent understanding, an individual's "true self" stands in contradistinction to all existing traditions and commitments. Taylor sees the older vision as a senescent form he would like to revive.

---

[81] The fact that Tocqueville's insights originate in the 1830s pushes the prepsychological golden age of altruistic religious communalism into the ever-receding darkness of an unknown past. For those inclined to push it back to the Puritans, often the height from which American religious declensionist narratives begin, see Hall's fascinating account of how Puritans actually lived and experienced their faith, rather than how their erudite leaders formally wrote about it. Also, it makes more literary than historical sense to begin with the Puritans, rather than with the irreligious middle colonists, see Albanese, *America: Religions and Religion*; Finke and Stark, *Churching of America*; Hall, *Worlds of Wonder*.

[82] Tocqueville, *Democracy in America*, Vol. 2, Book I: chap. 5, Book II: chap. 9.

[83] Taylor, *Ethics of Authenticity*; Taylor, *Varieties of Religion Today*.

The Fall and Rise of Psychoreligious Cooperation

My research shows, however, that this model is stronger than believed, having retained (or regained) its viability among spiritual groups seeking to exploit the benefits of psychology in their outreach to the alienated. They fostered this older ideal of true selfhood – one gained by finding oneself within preexisting communities and traditions – rather than the more recent unencumbered one that critics condemn. As a paradigm that balanced the freedom of individual choice with transcendence and fellowship, this older ideal suited a democratic culture.

The three histories examined here were chosen because they all appeared to be "hard cases" that represented diverse expressions of the same phenomenon. Since the individualistic doctrinal and institutional structures of Protestantism have been seen as particularly vulnerable to the atomizing tendencies of the therapeutic,[84] I chose cases that emerged from the traditions of American Protestantism. Each group can be located within a different part of the Protestant spectrum that developed out of the conservative–modernist battles of the late nineteenth and early twentieth centuries. Clinical pastoral education began as a modernist movement among mainline denominations. Alcoholics Anonymous was probably the most widespread twentieth-century example of the transformation of some strands of American Protestantism into de-Christianized unchurched spiritualism.[85] And The Salvation Army was founded in the Victorian period as a modern evangelical church, committed to doctrinal orthodoxy.

Not only does each group find its home in a different part of the American Protestant spectrum in the twentieth century, but each emphasizes a different one of the three major facets of Christian life: ministry, fellowship, and evangelism. Clinical pastoral education offered a new vision of Christian ministry. Alcoholics Anonymous saw itself primarily as a fellowship. And The Salvation Army reached out to homeless men in order to evangelize them.

Although the groups did not often communicate directly with one another, they were all part of a cumulative and mutually supporting trend. Earlier efforts helped make later ones possible, and they came to overlap. This story begins with the movement to train seminarians and ministers in psychology not only because of chronological priority but

---

[84] Bellah, "Protestant Structure"; Heinze, *Jews and the American Soul*, 273–5; Hunter, "Beyond Individualism?"; Meyer, *The Positive Thinkers*, 325–30.

[85] Fuller's work provides the best history of this two-centuries long tradition; see *Americans and the Unconscious; Mesmerism;* and *Spiritual, but Not Religious.*

24   *American Protestantism in the Age of Psychology*

because the creation of a source of mental health providers who would act simultaneously as therapists and spiritual guides facilitated the activities of both AA and the army.

Each case comprises two chapters. The first traces the way the group contributed to the expansion of a therapeutic ethos in the decades after World War II. In each case, the group employed as therapists people outside the mental health profession, such as clergy or groups of alcoholics. Each group understood its programmatic activities as a new kind of therapy, such as seminars for chaplain interns or work in the salvage industry. Construing spiritual activities as therapeutic was part of this larger strategy. Then in the second chapter of each part, I demonstrate how this expansion of the therapeutic beyond its original professional and disciplinary boundaries allowed believers to harness it for their own religious and spiritual purposes. The therapies that the groups forged intentionally and successfully served as forums for ethical, social, and spiritual development. Under psychoreligious auspices, the pursuit of mental health was not the road to selfish individualism and disenchantment. Rather it was the path to faith and fellowship.

PART ONE

THERAPY AS MINISTRY IN CLINICAL PASTORAL EDUCATION

Introduction

A rift between Protestantism and psychology emerged from the scandals surrounding the Emmanuel Church movement and the demise of the psychology-of-religion movement in the 1920s. Had no one waded into the breach, the topography might quickly have come to resemble the chasm that opened between Protestantism and Darwinian theory in the same period after half a century of comfortable coexistence. Vitriolic and permanently divisive fights erupted in the 1920s as an atheistic emphasis on randomness replaced a religiously palatable teleological spin to evolution. After the Scopes trial, religious interpretations of historical biological change were permanently discredited among many educated Americans. A potential for similar ruptures in other fields, especially psychology, loomed.

Sensing danger, an unusual polymath named Helen Flanders Dunbar – medical doctor, scholar of theology and philosophy, and expert in psychosomatic medicine – warned in 1930:

[If] the priest who is coming to be suspect and ostracized from increasingly large social groups... is to be restored to his place in a populace which has imbibed deeply the scientific method, he must drink at the same well.[1]

Dunbar was eager to show clergy the way. The same year she issued her warning, she became the first director of a pioneering organization devoted to training Protestant clergymen in clinical psychology. Her

[1] Thornton, *Professional Education for Ministry*.

25

American Protestantism in the Age of Psychology

group called itself the Council for the Clinical Training of Theology Students.[2] Similar groups devoted to the same sort of pedagogy were soon formed. What they had to offer students eventually became known as clinical pastoral education (CPE) or clinical pastoral training (CPT).

But for many years, Dunbar and her colleagues convinced relatively few students of their dire need to imbibe the scientific method. Not surprisingly, the mavericks who agreed were either very troubled characters or hailed from the modernist fringe of the Protestant spectrum. Things picked up after World War II, however. And by the late 1950s, training programs successfully recruited large numbers of seminary students as CPE increasingly became a standard component of seminary curricula across a broad range of denominations. The social history presented in Part I is based primarily on personal files of students during their clinical pastoral education under the auspices of the oldest, most autonomous, and most radical of the training organizations – the Council for Clinical Training (CCT) – from its founding in the 1930s to the late 1960s.

Chapter 2, "The Priest Must Drink at the Scientific Well," details the training the CCT offered students. It usually enrolled them as chaplain interns in hospitals for one or more summer terms or academic quarters. There they were supervised by the institution's head chaplain. The CCT's most immediate goals were to improve students' self-awareness and maturity as well as their psychosocial astuteness and interpersonal warmth. It aimed to develop young clergymen's ability to counsel and emotionally nurture laity. Finally, it hoped students would emerge with a more sophisticated and personalized theology that made room for the anthropological insights of clinical psychology. The chapter concludes by discussing the experiences of the few for whom this deep drink at the "scientific well" was too deep. Those men generally drank on an empty stomach, and when they were done gulping, had little room for the rest of their religious education. But such men were in the minority.

Most students, while they sometimes became intoxicated by the scientific drafts, soon sobered up. Chapter 3, "Being the Love of God," examines the effects of CPE on the spiritual and religious lives of young clergymen. It demonstrates the way clinical pastoral education transformed them personally and matured them socially. It looks at

---

[2] In a failed bid to attract a broader range of students, the CCTTS soon shortened its name by dropping the last two words. For an institutional history of the early organization, see ibid.

Therapy as Ministry in Clinical Pastoral Education 27

students' vocational development during their internships. And it examines interns' attempts to integrate their theologies with the psychological paradigm they were learning. In the end, most found CPE a chastening but rewarding experience. Students emerged humbler and a bit shaken, but also wiser, more mature, and more confident ministers.

2

The Priest Must Drink at the Scientific Well

The Great Depression found Reverend Stephen T. Wood ministering to the inmates of an Illinois prison. Opening the hearts of convicts could not have been easy. So Wood searched for ways to equip himself better for the task. He had even begun studying under Chaplain Joseph Armstrong at a nearby psychiatric hospital. He hoped thereby to hone his ability to understand and aid difficult people. Armstrong welcomed students. He was so eager for them that he had recently helped start an organization – the Council for the Clinical Training (CCT) of Theological Students – which aimed to give ministers practice in dealing with the disturbed by employing them in psychiatric facilities.[3]

Another council founder, Reverend Arnold Dunshee, visited Wood at the prison in 1939. He was one of the nation's few fulltime, professional chaplains. He asked Wood about work with the inmates, probably because prison administrators had asked Dunshee whether they should hire Wood himself as a full-time, professional chaplain. The prison evangelist enthusiastically explained to Dunshee that he invited convicts into his office, where he could pray with them privately and talk to them about faith and the Bible. Wood's whole mission, he averred, was to "bring men to Christ."

Based on this exchange, Dunshee declared the man utterly unfit to be a chaplain anywhere.[4]

---

[3] The standard account is Thornton, *Professional Education for Ministry*.

[4] Arnold Dunshee, "Stephen Wood," August 12, 1939, RG 001, Box 148, folder 2262, Pitts.

The Priest Must Drink at the Scientific Well   29

What was the problem? Had Wood done anything unusual? No. And that was Dunshee's problem. Wood was thinking and behaving exactly as Protestant ministers had long done.

But Dunshee wanted clergy to act in a new way. He, along with many of the council founders, aimed to remake Protestant ministry in America. Pioneering council members understood the minister as a "professional" fundamentally concerned neither with the salvation nor succor of souls but rather with the maintenance of community health. It was therefore imperative that clergy have "first-hand knowledge of problems of physical health, mental hygiene, and penology." The council offered "supervised clinical training" in psychiatric facilities, hospitals, and prisons to provide just such first-hand knowledge.[5]

This was the education – which became known as "clinical pastoral education" – that Wood had sought from Dunshee's organization. But Wood wanted to use what he learned instrumentally. He did not imagine that psychiatric training should completely alter his role. He apparently assumed he would remain essentially an ambassador of Jesus. He probably also would have rejected the idea that the ideas of clinical psychiatry should make him rethink his theology.

But those who flocked to "clinical" training, especially the early rebels such as Dunshee, wanted precisely that. Edward Thornton, for example, began his training in 1950 in hopes of becoming a pastor completely different from the likes of Wood. He rejected what seemed to him the irrelevance, dishonesty, and coercion of the ministers he had known as a boy. He dismissed "the premillenial 'seer' of mysteries; the pietistic 'man of God'; and the evangelistic, 'soul winning' preacher." Instead, he dreamed of becoming a "person-centered" "professional" whose ministry was "informed by the behavioral sciences and shaped in the fire of human crises."[6]

This chapter examines the process by which the CCT taught clergymen such as Thornton to become person-centered professionals, whose pastoral interactions and religious duties were informed by the behavioral sciences. The CCT emphasized, first and foremost, the need for students to develop greater self-awareness and social savvy. It encouraged students to make pastoral counseling central to their ministries and trained them to draw on the ideas and techniques of psychological counseling. It asked

---

[5] "Council for Clinical Training," [brochure] n.d. [1940], RG 001, Box 1, folder 11, Pitts.
[6] Thornton, *Professional Education for Ministry*, 9–10.

them to take a "shepherding perspective" on all of their clerical duties, by which CCT educators meant adopting an approach that prioritized the individual emotional needs of those they interacted with. Finally, CCT educators urged students to rethink their dogmatic beliefs to ensure they did not conflict with the psychological understandings that clinical training fostered. In practice, this meant reinterpreting traditional Christian doctrines along existential lines laid down by theologians such as Paul Tillich, or replacing orthodox dogmas with Protestant modernist ones. After showing in this chapter the way in which the CCT immersed its students in a psychologically oriented reinterpretation of ministry, I look in the next chapter at the effect such therapeutic education had on them in their pastoral roles.

The CCT was soon joined by an growing number of other clinical pastoral education programs, all imitators or offshoots of the Council for the Clinical Training of Theological Students. They emerged in the decades after the original group was founded. They liked some of what the CCT aimed to do, but they deemed it too secular. These younger groups formed to offer a clinical pastoral curriculum that answered more closely the needs and concerns of seminary and denominational authorities. The proliferation and religious sensitivity of these new programs pushed CPE increasingly into the mainstream of theological education.

Even the CCT moderated its rebellious radicalism in the decades following World War II. This move was partly ideological; it was partly sociological, as ministers took over from the doctors who had dominated the early organization; and it was partly strategic since survival depended on seminaries' cooperation in sending their tuition-paying students along for training. The CCT remained, however, the most religiously modernist and autonomous of the national CPE organizations. It also remained a model and trendsetter in the field. By 1967, so few philosophical or institutional differences among the major CPE groups remained that they merged. The CCT, as an independent entity, ceased.

Part I is based on CCT archives throughout its existence, as well as the archives from the first few years of the newly merged organization, the American Council for Pastoral Education. I have drawn on histories of the movement and archival materials related to institutional and curricular development. However, I have focused most closely on a previously untapped source: the personal files of CPE students themselves.[7] These

---

[7] Access to these files is restricted. Therefore all names in private files have been changed.

The Priest Must Drink at the Scientific Well 31

files contain the applications, teachers' evaluations, self-evaluations, and supporting materials (e.g., theological essays) of students who pursued additional terms of CPE to advance up the ladder toward becoming CPE teachers themselves. It is from such students' vantage points that I re-create the most salient features of their psychological and religious education under CCT auspices.

This chapter and the next are in many ways the "hardest case" presented in this study. The men whose lives comprise its focus were unusual; most seminary students felt one term of CPE was adequate. But this study is based primarily on the experiences of those students who eventually became CCT and ACPE supervisors from the 1940s through the 1960s, an unusual group that chose chaplaincies over pastorates. By and large, they were generally vocationally weaker than their more typical peers. Private doubts or pains rendered them especially receptive to the siren song of psychiatry.

Furthermore, clergy who trained with the council trained with the most independent and religiously radical organization. As one seminarian who applied put it, he preferred the CCT to other CPE groups because it did not merely teach "pastoral techniques" but rather "shakes foundations."[8] How could such young men separate religious wheat from psychological chaff? Most of them ultimately could, as we will see in the subsequent chapter. Here, we examine how they performed this difficult winnowing.

Self-Awareness

By the time Thornton was pursuing his goal of becoming a person-centered professional in 1950, most of the council's students were seminarians whose training consisted of spending a summer break or academic term as interns under the supervision of a head Protestant chaplain at a psychiatric or general hospital. They occasionally worked at a prison or institution for the disabled. Students spent much of their time visiting patients and conducting religious services and activities. Each day interns would gather together in a seminar to listen to lectures on psychiatry or discuss their personal or theological concerns. Such concerns were pursued privately each week as well when interns met one-on-one with their supervising chaplains.

---

[8] C. Dale Weaver, [application], Folder 2218–2219, RG 001, ACPE archives, Pitts, Atlanta.

32 *American Protestantism in the Age of Psychology*

Supervisors used these activities to increase students' self-awareness. They wanted students to be able to recognize their own emotions better, especially the negative ones that seemed unbecoming a Christian and a minister. They wanted students to realize when they were communicating these feelings to others. Students were encouraged to connect important aspects of their own early lives to the way they felt and behaved as adults.

Such honesty and self-knowledge were seen as pathways to greater self-mastery and freedom of action. Ideally, for example, a minister would leave training capable of acknowledging the anger that a neurotic parishioner evoked in him. If he further recognized that the difficult woman reminded him of his mother with whom he'd had a troubled relationship, then he could overcome some of his hostility. He would be better equipped to handle the parishioner's concerns and treat her with the Christian love that she deserved.[9] As this example suggests, supervisors spent much of their time trying to increase the self-awareness of ministers in the performance of their clerical duties.

Supervisors met daily with their group of chaplain interns as well as one-on-one with them each week. Although such meetings were designed to discuss and analyze chaplaincy experiences, conversations could easily veer toward students' personal psychology. Supervisors sometimes had a therapeutic and analytic agenda for the young ministers in their charge. Sister Joan was encouraged to express negative feelings and develop a feminine identity, which her teachers believed had been squashed by convent life.[10] Although Joan must have stood out from her typically male and Protestant peers, students widely shared a discomfort with their own feelings of hostility, which their teachers aimed to overcome.

Often, teachers focused on exposing what they saw as students' hidden emotional rationales in their ministries. In one group, for example, seminarian Hugh refused to be drawn into a personal discussion despite appearing to want to participate. When Hugh finally spoke up, he raised theological rather than intimate concerns. In response, his teacher "accused him of having a 'last resort' God who was important to him because he wouldn't allow himself to get close to people."[11] A pair of novice supervisors refused to pray with a group of interns because

---

[9] James F. Crook, "[Self-]Evaluation After First Quarter of Training," to CCT, April 4, 1957. RG 001, ser. III, Box 136, folder 2069, Pitts.

[10] Clifford King, "Final Evaluation [of Sister Joan]," August 30, 1968, RG 001, ser. III, Box 150, folder 2289, Pitts.

[11] Gregory B. Perkins, "Running Summary of My Work with all Students Supervised," n.d. [1961], RG 001, Box 142, folder 2144, Pitts.

The Priest Must Drink at the Scientific Well   33

they believed their students wanted to "use" the prayer "neurotically."[12] Herb's supervisor similarly worried that he was misusing theology, noting that the student "conceives of man's chief sin as being the sin of self concern." This dogma primarily served the student as the "most usable vehicle for communicating the feeling that there is no good in him at all."[13]

Students sometimes resisted having their religious lives reinterpreted this way. One student, who seemed to have been forced into clinical training, possibly by his seminary's curricular mandates, complained repeatedly about supervisors' understanding of religion. He charged them with being antagonistic to theology and with relegating religious disciplines to mere compulsive psychological defenses.[14] An Anglican student, similarly suspicious of the training, believed "quite strongly that the 'free church' supervisors were out to undermine his religion."[15]

Nevertheless, many students sooner or later accepted one of the most basic lessons of clinical training – that psychological dramas can lurk beneath the facade of the most seemingly virtuous behaviors and discussions. They learned from their supervisors to be aware of the way underlying feelings and dramas could lead them to abuse religious resources and distort the religious messages they wanted to convey to those around them. Students reevaluated themselves, and began to make new choices. For example, head chaplain John noted that

A particular concern of mine was for him [the student] to look carefully at... his unspoken preference for avoiding the parish ministry in particular. Our conversations about this were quite meaningful for him and probably had something to do with his taking the parish job he now has.[16]

Many students reported their own new awareness and behaviors. One minister, when evaluating himself after a quarter of training, wrote: "I think I was insightful, aware of feelings and fairly open in the group. I did not intellectualize or theologize, which at times would have been

---

[12] CCT and Virginia Theological Seminary, "Joint Conference on the Relation between Clinical Pastoral Training and Theological Education," November 27–8, 1953, RG 001, Box 159, folder 2473, Pitts (11).

[13] Vernon Trollope, "Confidential Report," September 1, 1962, RG 001, Box 144, folder 2200, Pitts.

[14] John S. Thacker, "Candidate's Profile for Accreditation Committee," October 16, 1963, RG 001, Box 149, folder 2273, Pitts.

[15] James Rowe, "Report on Training [of George]," Summer 1959, RG 001, ser. III, Box 150, folder 2288, Pitts.

[16] John Thacker, "Confidential Evaluation of Assistantship," rec'd October 17, 1959, RG 001, Box 149, Folder 2270, Pitts.

34   *American Protestantism in the Age of Psychology*

tempting."[17] Even Jack Werden, a confident and capable minister, was taken aback to realize that his own niceness sometimes masked hostility: "I see other ministers operate this way and I hate it. It is jarring to me to recognize that this is the way that I have been operating."[18] Al Hart had not only absorbed the psychiatric perspective of the training but also its jargon when he confessed: "My over-concern about other people's problems was shown to be a concern about my own ego-status and this explained my identification and emotional involvement with the patients which left me useless to them."[19]

Students realized that psychological dynamics structured not only their daily interactions with others, but even the ways in which they performed their most traditional clerical duties. One, for instance, announced that training helped him realize that he had been "venting hostility in my sermons" and took measures to correct this.[20] Another more eloquent student articulated a similar discovery:

During and after clinical training, I concentrated on trying to answer the "universal needs" from the pulpit – those of anxiety, finitude, doubt, guilt, meaninglessness, loneliness, etc. – or fell back on an authoritarian concept of the preach and preached decision, challenge or discipline. Both types of sermons were attempts to tell the people what to "be" and how to "be" – especially in relation to me. The sermons I had thought were speaking to them were speaking at them – many times in judgment.[21]

One of the most poignant and compelling examples of the way clinical training could revolutionize the way students understood themselves was the case of Gary Pearson. Pearson entered training as a confident, popular mid-career minister of a fundamentalist church. While he chaffed a bit against the extensive restrictions his denomination put on its membership – against indulgences including dancing, watching movies, drinking, and smoking – he felt at home in it. Nevertheless, Pearson was open to the interesting things he was learning in training. He even contemplated leaving the parish to become a chaplain supervisor himself, prompted

---

[17] Carl Frick, "[Self-]Evaluation," Summer 1962, RG 001, ser. III, Box 137, folder 2083, Pitts.

[18] Jack Werden, "Evaluation of the Program in Clinical Training at the Patton State Hospital," Summer 1963, RG 001, Box 148, folder 2249, Pitts.

[19] Robert James, to Jack Herman, April 28, 1957, RG 001, Box 141, folder 2142, Pitts.

[20] Paul T. Haswell, "Application for Advanced Training," May 25, 1953, RG 001, Box 146, folder 2228, Pitts.

[21] T. Albert Williams, "Evaluation of Parish Ministry," rec'd July 17, 1964, RG 001, Box 138, folder 2107, Pitts.

probably in large part by his spouse, who was very unhappy living the life of a minister's wife. Her discontent put pressure on the marriage, which had grown contentious.

It was with a characteristically open-minded amiability that Pearson one day related a recent conflict he and his wife had to the other clergymen in his training group. He had been out of town when he had run into an old high school flame. The two had dinner and chatted about their lives. It was clear they felt their old attraction kindled, and, before parting after the meal, had shared a hug. Pearson confessed all this to his wife when he returned him. She did not take it lightly. Pearson confessed to his fellow interns that he felt bewildered by her pain and anger. The dinner had seemed relatively innocent to him, nor had he lied to her about it. But the other men had none of it. Had he told his wife merely to be honest about it? Or had he told her to hurt her? Pearson struggled against this second interpretation initially but then recognized its veracity. He had been deliberately mean.

Pearson was floored. Anyone might be taken aback by the sudden realization of one's own cruelty. But this realization had seismic theological implications for Pearson, whose denomination believed in a "second blessing" that freed some believers entirely from sin. As a Holiness minister, he had stood before his church as such a sanctified one. But the truly holy would not have lusted after a woman who was not his wife and certainly would not have wielded such feelings against his wife to deliberately wound her. He was not holy. And as he contemplated the other leaders and pious ones of his faith, he could not help but wonder if perhaps neither were they. And if none of them had received a second blessing, perhaps the dogma – a key dogma defining his church against other Protestants – was wrong. In anguish he asked,

Can a man be pure in his heart? . . . Is everyone deceived who makes such a testimony? These questions strike at the heart of my church. . . . Can I deny [holiness] and remain a [part of it]? Do I want to deny it? Can I yet be "clean clear though"? Can I leave the church in which I was cradled? Must I do that?[22]

It took Pearson a long time to absorb the implications of that small shock of self-awareness. But eventually he began to come to terms with it. An honest and humble man, he confessed his feelings and doubts to his church. He found surprising acceptance from his parishioners and

---

[22] Gary Pearson, "My Third Quarter of Clinical Training, Winter 1963," March 30, 1963, RG 001, Box 146, folder 2231, Pitts.

36   *American Protestantism in the Age of Psychology*

superiors. He remained part of his denomination. But he left the parish ministry, perhaps to his wife's great relief. And he became a full-time chaplain supervisor, able to direct other young ministers' eyes toward the hidden precincts of their own hearts.

Social Savvy

In 1961, a young seminarian named Larry encountered a student nurse crying in a hospital chapel. He himself had just begun a chaplaincy internship. Larry approached this troubled young woman with the best words of solace he knew. He told her that he could help her come to Jesus, the joy of whose loving embrace would presumably melt away even her greatest sorrows. When he later relayed the exchange to other ministers and seminarians working in the hospital, they criticized his audacity and cluelessness. They criticized Larry for assuming the nurse might be open to the Gospel without knowing, or taking the time to ask, a thing about her. He had not even bothered to find out why she cried.[23]

Larry's mistake seems to have been a common one. Thomas Taylor, a new Episcopalian intern, understood his task as "preaching and praying with every patient."[24] Dennis – another young student – would ask a few questions, wait for the patient to finish giving the answers, and then dive into "a short sermon and prayer or a brief lecture."[25] Concluding this, Dennis would take his leave. Even Fred, already a seasoned and successful minister when he began training, started to reassess his interactions with parishioners and patients: "I listened at the superficial level, being insensitive to man's real needs. I had just the right words of reassurance – love, mercy, forgiveness. I plied man with platitudes."[26]

When Dennis's teacher challenged his method, the student insisted firmly that "'spreading the Gospel'" "was what he had been taught."[27] Whereas such bold avidity in explaining the Gospel might have been esteemed in seminaries and churches, it was frowned upon in clinical training. The clergymen had been taught to pray, to preach, to instruct

---

[23] Gregory B. Perkins, "Running Summary of My Work with all Students Supervised," n.d. [1961], RG 001, Box 142, folder 2144, Pitts.

[24] James Rowe, "Report on Training [of Thomas Taylor]," Summer 1959, RG 001, ser. III, Box 150, folder 2288, Pitts.

[25] Fred Putnam, "V. Specific Issues Suggested For Exploration," n.d. [1966], RG 001, Box 144, folder 2190, Pitts.

[26] Fred Putnam, "III." [theory of CPE], n.d. [1966], RG 001, Box 144, folder 2190, Pitts.

[27] Fred Putnam, "V. Specific Issues Suggested For Exploration," n.d. [1966], RG 001, Box 144, folder 2190, Pitts.

parishioners in church doctrine. But clinical training supervisors believed ministers usually wielded such religious resources clumsily, knocking over possibilities for communication and even communion. Supervisors held that before students could effectively impart Jesus' message to someone, they had to be sensitive to how that person was feeling and thinking. They had to have a sense of how that person saw the world and what he or she needed to get from it.

One of the trickiest and most important lessons supervisors wanted to teach young ministers was that even traditional religious acts were not always what they seemed. Valuable information into the state of patients' minds and souls might be hidden inside their prayers or theological questions. Ministers needed to glean that information to assess the situation before they dived into a sermon. William F. Hunter became aware that when patients expressed religious doubts, they were testing him. His rush "to reassure them prevented more meaningful communication" and left them feeling that he was not really interested in them personally.[28] Along a similar vein, Archie Haig discovered he had to pay attention to patients' "feelings and not just their ideas."[29] A vivid example of this was relayed by Vincent Conway who came to recognize the submerged hostility in a woman who – although meek and mild-mannered – talked a great deal about the punishment that awaited sinners at Judgment.[30]

In their eagerness to rectify the students' psychological obtuseness in their use of traditional religious acts, teachers were themselves sometimes religiously obtuse. One supervisor-in-training came to regret the fact that he had not encouraged or even permitted his student ministers to worship together. He had been concerned that it was an attempt at "avoiding direct communication" with one another. Later, however, he realized that although "this still might be true, it has become apparent that some opportunity throughout the quarter should be provided for the students to worship together."[31]

Some supervisors' religious myopia made the training more bewildering and confrontational than it should have been. It could leave students

---

[28] "Accreditation Review, Wayne Moore" October 5, 1966, RG 001, ser. III, Box 150, folder 2281, Pitts.
[29] Archie Haig, "Self-evaluation," August 18, 1968, RG 001, ser. III, Box 150, folder 2289, Pitts.
[30] "Supervisory Interview Notes," June 18–August 27, 1954, RG 001, Box 149, folder 2273, Pitts.
[31] Kenneth Raschke, "Topic: Evaluation of Training Program," 1958, RG 001, Box 142, folder 2153, Pitts.

38   *American Protestantism in the Age of Psychology*

reeling. Some returned to their seminaries with their heads full of a psychological jargon and dogma unrelated to their religious training. One student's vivid recollection demonstrates the unchristian ends to which training could be put:

The middlers at Seminary last year [who had completed internships]... led me to believe that the whole Program was little short of demonic. Some of them were attempting lay-analysis of the new students on the basis of twelve weeks introduction to psychology.... Our distrust of the program was fortified by suggestions that the Supervisors were out to extract personality problems of the students in order to warn our respective deans. The way some of them talked[,] the seminars were little more than uncontrolled groups of students who spend many hours a week probing into each other's feelings with a motive somewhat short of charity.... [S]ome of my friends... had fallen into the trap of believing that in twelve-weeks they had found the sovereign panacea to man's problems. One of them specifically told me: "Bob.... [original ellipses] this is the real Gospel!"[32]

Nevertheless, a simple substitution of a Christian paradigm by a psychiatric one was not the goal. The better teachers helped students use their new psychiatric insights to expand rather than contract their understanding of what was happening in religious settings. Students were encouraged to perceive psychiatric dynamics as currents that ineluctably flowed through religious activities, rather than as the bedrock that defined them. A good example of this when it was effective are revealed in the reflections of Philip R. Brewer, an advanced student, after he spent a quarter interning in a general hospital:

I was impressed in this experience with the use to which some patients put the religious symbols such as prayer, Scripture, and worship. It was easier to talk about death in the context of the 23rd Psalm for one person and for another she was able to use the 19th chapter of Revelation. Some patients wanted prayer for the reason of manipulation while others used it for expression of thankfulness and alleviation of anxiety. An older man saved his first day to be out of bed to come to Sunday worship in the chapel. Chapel service represented not only his personal accomplishment of improvement but an expression of thankfulness.[33]

Clinical training not only helped students understand other people better, but it helped them to interact more sensitively in their ministry. Sometimes this corrected a serious problem. Oliver entered training as an awkward, distant, and socially clueless minister whose frustrations in the

---

[32] Robert James, to Jack Herman, April 28, 1957, RG 001, Box 141, folder 2142, Pitts.
[33] Philip Brewer, [advanced first quarter self-report, n.d./1950s], RG 001, ser. III, Box 142, folder 2161, Pitts.

The Priest Must Drink at the Scientific Well

parish had led him to flee it as "unbearable."[34] No wonder. He often said hurtful and offensive things to people not out of sadism but a profound social clumsiness.[35] Over many quarters of training and intense work on this problem, he finally learned to avoid such costly and painful mistakes. His relationships improved markedly.[36]

Even when ministers were not in as dire a need of social correction as Oliver, training often improved their relationships to their parishioners. For instance, Roger Sykes's congregation liked the changes in their spiritual leader. Congregants found him "much more approachable" and "down-to-earth" than he had been. "He speaks more our language," noted one.[37] Neal Beasley was distant, domineering, and overly intellectual when he entered training. However, over many months, he learned to let his defenses down. He became warmer and more engaged. Neal was pleased to find that his new demeanor had helped him successfully reach out to his parish's lapsed members, some of whom began attending worship again after a hiatus of years.[38]

Counseling

Self-knowledge and social savvy enhanced ministry, but they did more than that. They were also prerequisites for effective counseling. And the pioneers of the clinical pastoral training dreamed of a day when all ministers could as readily and competently counsel as pray with a parishioner. For they envisioned ministry not so much as a quest to guide souls toward salvation but rather to nurture psyches toward wholeness.[39] Or rather they saw these quests as intertwined and inseparable. They did not imagine that a soul who inhabited a cracked psyche could be saved. And they saw in nurturing another toward wholeness a microcosm of God's tender

---

34 Oliver Frank, "Spring Quarter Evaluation," 1961, RG 001, ser. III, Box 138, folder 2099, Pitts.

35 George Black, "Confidential Report on Student [Oliver Frank]," December 27, 1960, RG 001, Box 138, folder 2099, Pitts; Jacob Fothergill, "Council for Clinical Training, Confidential Report on Student [Oliver Frank]," Spring Quarter 1961, RG 001, Box 138, folder 2099, Pitts.

36 Jacob Fothergill, "Council for Clinical Training, Confidential Report on Student [Oliver Frank]," Summer Quarter 1961, RG 001, Box 138, folder 2099, Pitts.

37 Vincent Conway, "Final Evaluation for Roger Sykes," June 1963, for CCT, RG 001, ser. III, Box 136, folder 2080, Pitts.

38 Robert Ryder, Jr., "Winter Quarter Clinical Training," rec'd March 21, 1957, RG 001, Box 146, folder 2225, Pitts.

39 See, for example, Dwight Bedford, "An Evaluation of Clinical Pastoral Training, January-June 1961," RG 001, Box 145, folder 2205, Pitts.

40 *American Protestantism in the Age of Psychology*

love for humans and the best demonstration of that love to a wounded soul.

This therapeutic model of pastoral care was deeply compelling to some students. They found counseling an exciting and meaningful way of relating to congregants. Eugene Simpson enthused:

Clinical pastoral training revolutionized my ministry. I found myself spending much of my time in the parish in counseling situations, and even my preaching tended to become centered on the type of problem arising out of counseling situations.[40]

Lutheran minister Douglas Price also counseled more at his church over the course of his training. He attributed this development to the fact that congregants increasingly sought him out and he allowed regular conversations to take more personal turns.[41] Meanwhile Peter Simmons became so therapeutically adept that he began "functioning quite comfortably as a member of the psychiatric team." His supervisors proudly boasted that he was "the first resident (chaplain) on this [hospital] unit to whom patients have been assigned for follow-up counseling. He is the first chaplain resident to have a psychiatric resident ask him to see a patient regularly in conjunction with the resident."[42]

For some clergy, the allure of this new interpretation of ministry was that it made giving and receiving therapy integral to their vocation. In the hospital setting, students were counseled by their teachers and peers during their intense daily meetings. CPT pioneers had by the late 1940s also created a new clerical specialty – the chaplain supervisor – who was called upon to counsel both patients and students. And becoming educated to occupy such a role required much time spent in self-examination.

The earliest students, who sought training when it was still a rare cutting edge pedagogy, were usually eager for the guided self-examination it demanded. This was unusually clear in the case of Dean Davis, an unhappy and emotionally troubled minister. In the 1940s he had sought help from a psychologist, and then from a psychoanalyst. The analyst encouraged Dean to enroll in clinical training because it would provide

---

[40] Eugene Simpson, "Additional Background Information," n.d., RG 001, Box 143, folder 2171, Pitts.

[41] Doug Price, "Clinical Pastoral Training Evaluation Answers," rec'd February 15, 1960, RG 001, Box 147, folder 2240, Pitts.

[42] Jacob Fothergill for the Georgia Association for Pastoral Care, Atlanta, GA, to CCT, Winter 1965, re: confidential report on full time student [Peter Simmons], RG 001, ser. III, Box 137, folder 2088, Pitts.

him with "an opportunity for growth."[43] A few years later Thomas D. King's supervisor allowed him to use their personal conferences to examine difficulties he had with his parents. This had not only improved his relationship with his parents, but also with patients. Thomas was so pleased and impressed by this development that he began to seriously consider becoming a supervisor himself.[44] Nor did the desire for therapy ever entirely abate from some students' motivations in seeking CPT: In the early 1960s, Dale Harris acknowledged that he was applying for a second quarter of training "with the object of therapy as my primary goal."[45]

This was so common in the early phase of training that, at least through the mid-1950s, some students saw it natural to regard their clinical trainers as their therapists. Henry Fitzgerald, an assistant supervisor, noted in 1958 that "student-group relationships were characterized by an attempt of each of the students, at one time or another, to use the group as a means of receiving therapy."[46] In a different program in the early 1950s, Donald Adams had cherished the therapeutic role his supervisor had taken with him. So when he became an advanced student he noted his surprise and disappointment when his trainer now refused to oblige him: "I unconsciously, or maybe consciously, felt that the supervisor should continue in the role of therapist."[47]

As this last example suggests, however, the degree to which a supervisor could legitimately treat students as patients began to be contested by the mid-1950s. Increasingly, many in the movement came to discourage this. It could hardly have been appropriate for someone with so much authority over a student – as a teacher, boss, and evaluator – to act also as his therapist. When Donald Sheetz trained in the early 1960s, he tried to get his supervisor to help him come to grips with his unsatisfactory relationship with his father. But the teacher resisted repeatedly, believing it be

---

[43] Dean Davis, "Application for Clinical Pastoral Training," September 17, 1951, RG 001, Box 142, folder 2155, Pitts.

[44] Alfred Cooper, "Evaluation Report [for Thomas D. King]," Fall Quarter 1954, RG 001, ser. III, Box 137, folder 2086, Pitts.

[45] Dale Harris, "[Self-]Evaluation, Fall 1962," December 21, 1962, RG 001, Box 144, folder 2196, Pitts.

[46] Henry Fitzgerald, "Evaluation of Summer Program, 1958," Summer 1958, RG 001, Box 142, folder 2159, Pitts.

[47] Donald Adams, "Evaluation of Training," Summer 1955, RG 001, Box 143, folder 2165, Pitts.

42 *American Protestantism in the Age of Psychology*

untoward.[48] Because not all chaplains were as hesitant as Donald's was, advanced students hoping to become independent chaplain supervisors themselves were interrogated and criticized over the extent to which they treated their own beginning students as patients. In 1966 the committee tasked to decide whether or not to promote[49] Bert Foster, for example, expressed its concern:

We felt that there should be a stronger religious dimension in his training of students. It would be appropriate next year to see how he does with a real sharp student who is not in need of as much therapy as the one who was his intensive workup this year. This man has been in therapy for five years and has a tendency to approach the students with a therapeutic attitude.[50]

Over years, agreement strengthened that training rather than therapy should constitute clinical supervision. One student who resumed training in the early 1960s after having briefly begun it fifteen years earlier, noted the change: In the late 1940s there was

an emphasis on free association in supervisor-student relationships.... In a way, the experience in clinical pastoral training was a not-so-subtle attempt at individual and group therapy practiced by a chaplain. Training in the early sixties is quite different and has a focus on the pastoral role with some definite ideas of delineation of what is training as distinct from therapy.[51]

Although many supervisors appear to have conducted some modest therapy with first-quarter students, ministers and seminarians had to seek sustained therapy on their own. Those with deep problems – or who hoped to become supervisors themselves – were heartily encouraged to do so.

Despite the great value placed on psychotherapy in the movement, however, members did draw limits against it. Just as movement leaders began to recognize that it was inappropriate for people who played the

---

[48] Clark Anderson, "Full Notes on Individual Supervision with Donald Sheetz," Summer 1961, for CCT, RG 001, ser. III, Box 136, folder 2077, Pitts.

[49] Advanced CPE students who desired to become supervising chaplains sought positions first as assistant supervisors who helped seasoned chaplains teach new students. If CCT found these aspirants successful, and if they could secure their own chaplain positions, assistants were allowed to set up provisional training programs at their home institutions. The council directed students to them and closely scrutinized the experience at term's end. When such an "acting" supervisor demonstrated good pedagogical competence and psychological astuteness, displayed maturity and self-knowledge, and showed a commitment to the chaplaincy, he was promoted to supervisor.

[50] "Joint National Committee on Accreditation (ACPE)," October 15, 1967, RG 001, Box 142, folder 2158, Pitts.

[51] Lawrence Kerr, [1963 application], RG 001, Box 149, folder 2272, Pits.

The Priest Must Drink at the Scientific Well

role of teachers and supervisors to also play the role of therapist, they began to recognize that neither was the role of parish minister compatible with it. As advanced student Clark Anderson insightfully reflected in 1958:

I have wondered how much of the kind of depth counseling upon which training is focused, the pastor can actually utilize in his own congregation.... It seems to me there will be difficulties in doing "depth" counseling with members with whom the pastor has so many other social and congregational contacts.[52]

It was also becoming apparent that an education emphasizing intensive counseling was simply not well-suited to the needs of parish ministers, most of whom had little interest in or need to do sustained counseling.[53] The small minority, such as the previously mentioned Eugene Simpson, who felt counseling had revolutionized his ministry, often traded in their parishes for chaplaincy positions or even full-time pastoral counseling jobs. It is precisely these unusual clergymen whose experiences make up the backbone of these chapters.

A further way in which limits were drawn by the 1960s was the increasing clarity about the limits of therapy as a pastoral tool and a positive reappraisal of traditional religious practices. From the beginnings of the movement, counseling had never been synonymous with care, in either theory or practice, but the two concepts were frequently conflated. However, by the early 1960s, pastoral care became understood as a much broader ministry than counseling. A backlash against this reassessment came in the form of a minority of the movement forming in 1963, the American Association of Pastoral Counselors, which distinguished itself from the major pastoral care training groups by its focus on clergy who devoted themselves to providing intensive counseling services and teaching. Meanwhile, some pastoral professors began to tailor their courses to cover a broad array of aspects of care.[54] Publications in the field began to disaggregate the two terms, one broad and the other narrow, so that the *Journal of Pastoral Care* added *and Counseling* to its title. By 1990, when the movement finally produced a comprehensive reference work, the massive and magisterial volume was entitled the *Dictionary of*

[52] Clark Anderson, "Clinical Training Report and Evaluation, September 1958 through June 1959," n.d., RG 001, Box 144, folder 2183, Pitts.
[53] Roger Bell and others, "The Clergy as a Mental Health Resource: Parts I and II," *JPC* 30, no. 2 (1976): 109; Bob G. Fulmer, "Educational and Counseling Survey of Southern Baptist Pastors" (PhD, Southern Illinois University at Carbondale, 1975).
[54] Rodney Hunter, interview.

44   *American Protestantism in the Age of Psychology*

Pastoral Care and Counseling. All of this reflected the gradual realization that the intensive training in counseling was not, by and large, useful for most ministers.

Shepherding Perspective

Although few mid-century clergy found it useful to don the role of the therapist, many found it useful to adopt a therapeutic outlook. For a student in CPE, this meant first establishing a rapport with patients. It entailed helping patients articulate their feelings and concerns without judging them. It meant helping them find solace and solutions according to their own values, preferably ones that did not contradict a liberal Christian view of the world. CPE tried to teach clergy to draw others into this sustaining spiritual embrace through means drawn both from ancient Christian tradition and the new client-centered psychotherapy. Clinical pastoral supervisors regarded the establishment of a warm connection with a patient, or parishioner, as a prerequisite for any effective ministry.

Sometimes such a relationship, marked by a nonjudgmental nurturing concern for the person, could constitute itself the entire ministry. For a relationship of loving acceptance was understood to incarnate God's love for his children. Such a relationship was understood to speak louder than any words of either Christian or psychotherapeutic dialogue. This was poignantly exemplified by the approach of Luke Carter to a five-year-old boy who spent the summer of 1966 lying in a hospital bed dying of cancer: "Luke's ministry had been simply to hold this boy and love him and to show him physical warmth." The little boy clearly appreciated and returned the student chaplain's affection.[55]

The power of warm human attention was discovered by Peter Brill, who was already an accomplished minister although relatively new to CPE. He described in 1960 his regular visits to a teenaged girl hospitalized for weeks from complications from an abortion. While she was still weakened, Peter had read her "comforting words of the Bible" and recited prayers. Once she had resumed some strength, he tried to engage her in discussions about her feelings and personal concerns, as he had been training to do. But to his surprise and initial dismay, Peter found that she did not want this. Getting over his feeling of rejection, he realized,

[55] William Kirby, "Evaluation Report [of Luke Carter]," August 12, 1966, RG 001, ser. III, Box 150, folder 2281, Pitts; C. D. Weaver, "Evaluation Report [of Luke Carter]," August 26, 1966, RG 001, ser. III, Box 150, folder 2281, Pitts.

that this was not the important element in our relationship. More important was that I had been with her in the struggle and came to accept her as a person, although I did not really know her. I became a "pastor" in the real sense of the word for the first time.[56]

Establishing rapport with the laity required spontaneity and flexibility. A clergyman could be neither morally nor aesthetically rigid. William Hunter, for instance, was disturbed by the lack of order and dignity in the hospital ward hymn sings that he ran. After consulting his supervisor about this several times, Will eventually began to believe that the patients found a meaningful spiritual experience through the sings despite their lack of decorum and no longer felt the need to discipline the sings.[57] Tom's supervisor and training peers advised him that he was alienating others with "his rigid religious stance."[58] Although Tom defended the integrity of his theological position, he came to agree that he needed to "learn to express himself religiously in less 'pious and judgmentive [sic] ways.'"[59]

Supervisors also felt that establishing rapport required refraining from pressing some Christian ideas of morality, at least those in the process of being shucked off by liberal mainline Protestants. Clergy from "fundamentalist" backgrounds were frequently disciplined for this. For example, Frank Albrecht, a seasoned Mennonite minister, was shocked when during his first week of training a patient asked him for a cigarette. He had later exclaimed to his fellow interns, "Imagine... asking *me* for a cigarette!" Presumably he eventually learned what an effective icebreaker the small gift could be, and by quarter's end had begun carrying a pack around with him at all times. His supervisor praised this change as "real progress."[60] When Catholics began training with the CCT toward the end of the 1960s, they ran into similar pressures from their teachers.[61]

---

[56] Peter Brill, "Clinical Pastoral Training: A Learning Experience," [December 1959], RG 001, Box 145, folder 2214, Pitts.

[57] "Accreditation Review, Wayne Moore" October 5, 1966, RG 001, ser. III, Box 150, folder 2281, Pitts.

[58] Joel Graham, "Presenter's Report [on Walter Jessup.]," September 6–7, 1968, RG 001, ser. III, Box 150, folder 2292, Pitts.

[59] Mark Barnwell, "National Certification Meeting, ACPE," January 10–12, 1969, RG 001, ser. III, Box 150, folder 2292, Pitts.

[60] Ed Moriarty, "Summary Paragraphs on the other Three Students," New York Protestant Episcopal City Mission Society, Protestant Chaplain's Office, Bellevue Hospital (1956?) CCT, RG 001, ser. III, Box 136, folder 2071, Pitts.

[61] Catholics had begun adapting secular psychological ideas and techniques in their own pastoral training in the 1950s; see Gillespie, 60–1, 90–3.

46 *American Protestantism in the Age of Psychology*

Sister Joan, for instance, "became quite anxious and defensive" when issues of abortion and euthanasia were discussed. But her supervisor clearly hoped that the confrontations left her "more tolerant of moral concepts contrary to hers."[62]

Adopting a therapeutic outlook extended beyond informal conversations and chaplain visits. Since clinical pastoral educators felt the values and goals of therapy were essentially pastoral, they wanted their students to apply them to all of their religious activities. Educators believed all ministries could be enhanced if ministers made warm connections with the laity and if they gave laity the freedom to pursue their own spiritual development. Advanced student Hugh Bigsby articulated this lesson when he said, "In essence the pastoral task *in any setting* [emphasis added] is to relate openly and warmly without fear to a parishioner whose needs can be felt and understood so that that which is distorted and destructive can be recognized and dealt with."[63]

One important setting was the pulpit. Students often had a chance to preach during their internships, and they would discuss their ideas for this in their daily meetings. Supervisors evaluated interns on the degree to which their talks reflected an understanding of their listeners and offered emotionally helpful messages. Paul T. Haswell, for example, entered training as a poor preacher. But after about a year of training, his teacher commended him for his homiletical improvement:

In the last sermon preached here at the Hospital he evidenced marked feeling for the needs of the mentally ill patients and was able to achieve a high degree of meaningful communication, so that he was satisfyingly able to share with them helpful Christian understandings.[64]

Meanwhile, Glenn garnered similar praise from his supervisor, who wrote,

One [of Glenn's] sermon[s] titled, Out of the Pit, was particularly meaningful.... Glenn both struggled creatively with the despair that he felt as a result of confrontation with himself in the training program and at the same time spoke very helpfully to the feelings of despair and futile meaninglessness experienced by the patients.[65]

---

[62] Clifford King, "Final Evaluation [of Sister Joan]," August 30, 1968, RG 001, ser. III, Box 150, folder 2289, Pitts.

[63] Hugh Bigsby, "Key Issues in CPE," rec'd October 8, 1966, RG 001, Box 147, folder 2246, Pitts.

[64] S. Shorter, to Seymour Elliott, May 2, 1955, RG 001, Box 146, folder 2228, Pitts.

[65] Jacob Fothergill, "Confidential Report on Student, Fall and Winter Quarter 1958–1959," RG 001, Box 144, folder 2194, Pitts.

Religious education was another aspect of ministry that students frequently strove to rework along therapeutic lines. In 1954, Vincent Conway ran a religious discussion group in the hospital that met biweekly for, as he described it, "the purpose of supportive and mildly expressive therapy in a religious setting."[66] John, an intern who ran a Bible study class in a psychiatric ward, was similarly affected by his training. After reading one of Jesus' parables together, the group talked about what it meant to them, raising both personal and religious questions. At first, John tended to reply with the correct dogmatic response. But after learning more about group therapy techniques, he changed his method. He offered fewer answers, so the patients would be forced to struggle with their questions.[67]

Such techniques were also sometimes tried outside of hospital settings. Ernest Sprague, a Methodist minister, who continued activities in a parish during his training, used what he learned as an intern to help him train Church School workers, who were mostly parents in his congregation. He hoped that "in our program of religious education we could do a more adequate job of relating the educational process to the basic process of personality growth."[68] Alan Bell also worked part-time as a pastor while in training. He began to try to use a group therapy model in mid-week worship services. He initiated a congregational discussion series in which he talked about what he was learning in CPE. He encouraged participants to raise questions and issues of concern to them. Summers felt this a great advantage to his flock because "Due to a stilted cultural situation, the members had hardly ever experienced an opportunity to 'air out' some of their feelings, to bring up their doubts."[69]

Theology

Clinical pastoral educators wanted students to think differently not only about people but also about God. Clergy were encouraged to incorporate their new personal insights and psychological ideas into their theology.

---

[66] Albert Sutton, "Vincent Conway," Summer 1954, RG 001, Box 149, folder 2273, Pitts.

[67] John Westerveldt, "Six Months Evaluation of Clinical Pastoral Training," Sept. 11, 1961–Mar. 2, 1962, RG 001, Box 145, folder 2209, Pitts.

[68] Ernest Sprague, "Application for Advanced Training," rec'd March 23, 1955, RG 001, Box 137, folder 2090, Pitts.

[69] Alan Bell, "II" [application for further training], rec'd May 9, 1961, RG 001, Box 147, folder 2248, Pitts.

48 *American Protestantism in the Age of Psychology*

Chaplain supervisors wanted their students to approach the project of theology in a new way.

Students' first task was to purge their own theological commitments from any unrecognized or immature psychic problems. An extended example of this appears in the file of James Crook, an unhappy Lutheran minister. Crook had suffered as a child under a self-righteous and domineering mother who may have abused him. She stood aloof from the rest of the family, whom she taught her son to regard as wicked. In CPE Crook became aware of the ways his strange mother had hurt him and dominated his religious imagination. With a deep sense of liberation, he came "for the first time . . . to feel God as someone apart from my mother."[70]

Only when students became aware of the ways theological doctrines might perform certain psychological functions for them, could they assess a doctrine on its own merits. CPE saw this as a kind of intimate religious emancipation. Although historically freed from the religious tyranny of a prince or church, students might yet be slaves to their own subconscious. For example, Herbert O. Freshwater, a young Baptist man who began training in 1962, "conceives of man's chief sin as being the sin of self concern. Man fails to acknowledge his dependency on God. Herb goes on to state that all of his abilities and talents come from God." His supervisor expressed concern about Freshwater's elaboration of this doctrine, as he noted, "While there is some theological validity in this particular position, for Herb this understanding of man's problem and his proper place before God is his most usable vehicle for communicating the feeling that there is no good in him at all."[71]

The legitimacy of any dogma was not to rest on the authority of Scripture, church fathers, or any denominational creeds. The truth of a dogma rested on its ability to describe something profound about a clergyman's lived psychological and interpersonal experience. Clinical experience was to make concrete and immediate that which had been abstract and distant in the classroom. These ideas appealed greatly to the students of CPE, generally young men who, of course, had little life experience. As Clifford eagerly put it:

In the seminary classroom a theologue [seminarian] may learn concepts or doctrines of sin, guilt, forgiveness, love, incarnation, etc. In CPE a student becomes

---

[70] James Crook, "[Self-]Evaluation, Second Quarter of Training," for CCT, January 7, 1958, pp. 3–5. RG 001, ser. III, Box 136, folder 2069, Pitts.

[71] Vernon Trollope, "Confidential Report," September 1, 1962, RG 001, Box 144, folder 2200, Pitts.

The Priest Must Drink at the Scientific Well   49

involved with people who are estranged, alone, guilt-laden, seeking acceptance, love, and forgiveness, struggling to find meaning and purpose for their lives.[72]

Similarly, Norman Muncy articulated clearly his efforts to use his training to make sense of "the great doctrines of the Christian faith." "At the end of one seminary year," he explained, "my appreciation of them was at best not very profound, and largely theoretical." But he was evidently pleased to find that "As a result of this summer's [CPE] experience I am tempted to say that I have come to some understanding of what in reality and in experience these symbols represent." For example,

I have come through experience to known a little about fellowship.... I have seen and experienced acceptance and love, both on a giving and taking basis.... Redemption is another thing which I can understand more concretely.... Insofar as the various therapies are applied towards enabling the person to become more positive and more constructive, I can sense redemption in action.

And yet because Muncy had no psychiatry corollary to the doctrine of atonement, he admitted that "I do not yet understand [it] except in a very shallow theoretical way."[73]

Supervisors also wanted students to revise their understanding of specific doctrines. A good example is the way psychological insights were brought to bear on the doctrine of salvation.[74] Traditionally, the important part of a person that was saved was their soul. But people in the CCT almost entirely dismissed an immaterial soul[75] (along with spiritual–material dualism generally).

---

[72] Clifford King, "Essay: Clinical Pastoral Education," Fall 1968, RG 001, ser. III, Box 150, folder 2289, Pitts.

[73] Norman Muncy, "Impressions of the Program," n.d., RG 001, Box 143, folder 2168, Pitts.

[74] Gotfred C. Jacobsen, "An Evaluation of the Clinical Training Experience for Lutheran Seminarians" (BDiv, Gettysburg Theological Seminary, 1957), 71, RG 001, Box 200, folder 2930, Pitts; Kenneth Wayne Wanberg, "The Expectations and Realizations of Clinical Pastoral Training" (PhD, Iliff School of Theology, 1962), 8, RG 001, Box 161, folder 2497, Pitts.

[75] There are almost no discussions of "soul" in the CCT and ACPE supervisor files, the *Journal of Pastoral Care* between 1950–1980, and other major CCT publications from these years. When the word appeared in these files, it tended to be in the phrase "cure of souls" used as a synonym for pastoral care and was not itself subject to any elaboration. One notable exception was Rev. James B. Ashbrook, "The Functional Meaning of the Soul in the Christian Tradition," *JPC* 12, no. 1 (1958): 1–16. The lack of interest in the soul in CPE circles is further evinced by the goal of this article: to resurrect for therapists (and implicitly for those engaged in Protestant pastoral psychology) the idea of the divine soul as the center of a person.

50   *American Protestantism in the Age of Psychology*

This inattention to the soul was not an oversight. Rather it was part of a larger critique of many traditional understandings of salvation, which supervisors along with many pastoral and existential theologians saw as authoritarian or distorted.[76] David Roberts, whose 1950 book *Psychotherapy and a Christian View of Man* was a pastoral classic for decades, argued against a "static" view of salvation, which contrasted God's potency to man's impotency in effecting "inward regeneration."[77] He proposed instead a "dynamic" view of salvation as a "condition of wholeness which comes about when human life is based in openness (i.e., with 'self-knowledge') upon the creative and redemptive power of God. This condition is reached *by means of* man's freedom, and constitutes an enhancement of that freedom."[78] Miles Renear, a chaplain at Metropolitan State Hospital in California, agreed: "Our training has led us to be sensitive to the patient-parishioner as a person, not as a blank slate on which we can write the formula of salvation."[79] The influence of such views on those undergoing training is apparent in the words of a student whose three quarters of CPE training had led him to reevaluate what it meant "to confront people with the Christian gospel": "the use of authoritative language whereby the 'sinner' can 'conform' and be 'saved' loses much of its realistic value as far as assisting one to accept and adjust to life is concerned."[80]

Pastoral caregivers saw themselves as helping to save not souls, but rather *persons*. People were understood as multifaceted creatures whose spiritual aspect was inextricable from their physical, psychic, and social dimensions. This view led sometimes to a sophisticated and nuanced interpretation of salvation. But it also occasionally led to a reduction of salvation to psychic health and earthly well-being, or even, by the mid-1960s, to existential self-fulfillment. One supervisor at Milledgeville

---

[76] Tillich considered the idea that salvation was reserved for a small group of believing individuals, whereas the rest of humanity was doomed to "exclusion from eternal life," to be a "demonic distortion" of the kerygma; see Tillich, *Systematic Theology*, vol. II, 167.

[77] David E. Roberts, *Psychotherapy and a Christian View of Man* (New York: Charles Scribner's Sons, 1950), 125.

[78] Ibid., 132. As late as 1973, Roberts' book was still among the top ten most frequently assigned books in pastoral care and counseling classes; see Stokes, *Ministry After Freud*, 113–14.

[79] Miles Renear, "The Mental Hospital Chaplain: A Protestant Interpretation," *JPC* 9 (Summer 1955): 100.

[80] Dwight Bedford, "An Evaluation of Clinical Pastoral Training, January-June 1961," RG 001, Box 145, folder 2205, Pitts.

State Hospital in Georgia seemed to believe that ultimate deliverance could be found "on the couch": "[Ministers] have taken their 'sins,' their 'lostness' to the therapist's office. And in the working through of these deficiencies, they have experienced redemption, grace and salvation."[81] This message must have been echoed in some pastoral psychology courses. One CPE applicant said such classes led him to discount the "legal steps" to salvation taught by his denomination: "I now believe salvation to be integration of the personality, or wholeness."[82] In 1966, a supervisor-in-training insisted that "[W]e must have the integrity to state clearly to the church that authentic personhood is another way of saying saved by the blood of the lamb."[83]

But some influential CCT educators attacked this hermeneutical maneuver. Supervisor Knox Kruetzer publicly criticized the equation of salvation with health as utterly inadequate, and supervisor Wayne Clymer, in the *Journal for Pastoral Care*, ridiculed such incommensurate mappings of theological and psychological terminology.[84] The aspiring supervisor mentioned previously who equated being "saved by the blood of the lamb" with "authentic personhood" had a tough time before accreditation committees, which slowed down his promotions.[85]

While psychological theory did shape pastors' understanding of salvation, it did not necessarily do so in a way that wedged religion into the narrow borders of health. CPE pioneer Seward Hiltner, in *Preface to Pastoral Theology*, one of the most commonly used CPE texts, wrote that healing of body, mind, and soul were interrelated but cautioned that they were not equally important. Salvation was not "synonymous with ideas such as adjustment, maturity, or any possible content definition

---

[81] Henry Close, "A Second Look at Pastoral Counseling," *JPC* 19, no. 2 (1965): 89.

[82] Stephen Walton, "Application for Clinical Pastoral Training," March 15, 1955, RG 001, Box 146, folder 2230, Pitts.

[83] Hugh Bigsby, "Key Issues in CPE," rec'd October 8, 1966, RG 001, Box 147, folder 2246, Pitts. For a larger discussion of the emphasis on authenticity by young Christians during the 1960s, see Rossinow, *The Politics of Authenticity*, 53–84.

[84] Knox Kreutzer, "Some Observations on Approaches to the Theology of Psychotherapeutic Experience," (paper delivered at Fall Conference of Supervisors, CCT, Washington, DC, October 27–31, 1958) p. 2, RG 001, Box 160, folder 2486, Pitts; Wayne Clymer, "Can the Counselor Be a Prophet?" *JPC* 10 (Autumn 56): 150–60.

[85] Hugh Bigsby, to John S. Thacker, April 21, 1966, RG 001, Box 147, folder 2246, Pitts; "Candidates Profile for Accreditation Committee," 1966, RG 001, Box 147, folder 2246, Pitts; Hugh Bigsby, "A Statement of Faith and Identity," 1966, RG 001, Box 147, folder 2246, Pitts; Hugh Bigsby, "Key Issues in CPE," rec'd October 8, 1966, RG 001, Box 147, folder 2246, Pitts.

52   *American Protestantism in the Age of Psychology*

of functional wholeness. Healing is not everything."[86] Theological Paul Tillich made a cognate point when he argued that although "[t]heology had to learn from the psychoanalytic method the meaning of grace, the meaning of forgiveness as acceptance of those who are unacceptable," the acceptance of the psychotherapist was only "preliminary and easily can become permissiveness." Ultimate acceptance was possible only in the name, and through the power, of "the New Being."[87] Tillich's exegesis of the doctrine of salvation was very influential. Its key terms – essential goodness, existential estrangement, and reconciliation – appear frequently in CPE students' writing and pastoral publications.[88]

Wayne Clymer, professor of practical theology and director of fieldwork at the Evangelical Theological Seminary in Illinois, further clarified the subordinate place of psychology in soteriology. Psychotherapy was a path to salvation insofar as it helped a patient overcome determining influences to be able to make free and responsible choices. Such freedom was essential to salvation since only those who had attained it could meaningfully submit themselves to Jesus' cosmic and moral authority.[89]

Thus, psychotherapeutic revisions of soteriology ranged from believing that one must become self-aware and self-determining to be saved, to believing that once one was self-aware and self-determining, one was already saved. CCT supervisors tended to lean toward the former, but few could bring themselves to condemn outright the latter. They would have thought it a violation of the theological freedom and tolerance they cherished to dub it heresy altogether.

Why Accept Freud's Determinism But Laugh at Calvin's Predestination?

There was a problem with a psychiatrically infused vision of ministry, however. It appeared unnervingly close to a job that was already

---

[86] Hiltner, *Preface to Pastoral Theology*, 100–1.

[87] Paul Tillich, "The Theological Significance of Existentialism and Psychoanalysis," 93; and "The Theology of Pastoral Care," p. 128, both in Tillich, *The Meaning of Health*. "The Theology of Pastoral Care" was delivered at the 1956 National Conference of Clinical Pastoral Education.

[88] See, for example, T. Albert Williams, "My Philosophy of Clinical Pastoral Training," rec'd July 17, 1964, RG 001, Box 138, folder 2107, Pitts; [anon.], "Claude R. Gunn," n.d., RG 001, Box 145, folder 2213, Pitts; Carol R. Murphy, "Toward a Modern View of Man: Suttie, Sullivan, and Rogers," *JPC* 8, no. 2 (1954): 88–92; Hiltner, *Preface to Pastoral Theology*, ch. 6.

[89] "Can the Counselor Be a Prophet?" *JPC* 10 (Autumn 56): 150–60.

The Priest Must Drink at the Scientific Well

taken – by psychotherapists. Many religious people during the early and mid-twentieth century saw this fact as proof enough that the new vision was fatally flawed. But CPE leaders believed the opportunities and insights that the behavioral sciences held for clerical and religious revitalization were too great to forgo despite the complications that taking advantage of them entailed. They were deeply aware of the potential problems involved in what they were doing and sometimes spoke of them in spatial metaphors. They witnessed firsthand the worst cases: Religious miners of the depths of the human psyche became so fascinated with the artifacts below that they never re-emerged. They mistook the subterranean caves for the totality of the cosmos, and imagined mastering the dark labyrinth would reveal to them all the truth they needed to know.

But even those who kept above ground faced difficulties. Mid-century theological workers in the vineyards of psychoreligious integration labored under the shadow that was cast by the immense intellectual stature of psychology in the 1950s and 1960s. Many of the nation's most respected intellectuals did not doubt the scientific validity of psychoanalysis.[90] Academic psychology's repute was such that the United States established a covert multimillion-dollar effort to predict the political trajectories of Third-World nations through behavioral science.[91] Although psychology had been denounced by orthodox religious thinkers, it had not yet come under attack from a secular standpoint or been epistemologically called into question by members of the social science and intellectual establishment. Thomas Szasz, R. D. Laing, Michel Foucault and his epigones, and others of their ilk did not begin crafting the weapons with which psychology's critics readily armed themselves in the latter decades of the twentieth century. Their suspicions were not entirely absent at mid-century. Indeed, one prescient writer in 1952 had wondered,

Does it not seem strange that people will accept with alacrity the Oedipus complex as being an intelligible pattern of human experience, but just cannot see anything at all in the story of the Garden of Eden? Why do we accept Freud's determinism so easily and laugh at Calvin's predestination as if it were ludicrous[?][92]

But the author did not develop this insight, and it withered like seed sown on rocky ground.

[90] Stokes, *Ministry after Freud*, 164.
[91] Herman, *Romance of American Psychology*, ch. 5–6.
[92] Samuel Miller, "Exploring the Boundary Between Religion and Psychiatry," *JPC* 6, no. 2 (1952): 3.

54   *American Protestantism in the Age of Psychology*

There were many forces that made it difficult for students to integrate psychological ideas and processes into their ministries without compromising its fundamentally religious character. The shock and fascination with a whole new world – an entirely new vision of themselves and the way they related to the world – that was revealed to them in clinical education overwhelmed many students, at least temporarily.[93] Norman Muncy wrote after his first quarter of training that "I was thrown early in the summer into a state of self-preoccupation, soul-searching, I haven't been so preoccupied with myself since I can remember."[94]

This danger, which was intrinsic to the power of the psychological vocabulary to reveal and name what had been invisible or inchoate to students, was exacerbated by the kind of people who were attracted to clinical pastoral education in the first place. Although from the 1950s onward, CPE was increasingly recommended or even mandated by seminaries, many students sought out training because they wanted it. Many who were drawn to CPE, especially at the advanced level, had long felt plagued by some unease or pain that faith had not solved, were particularly interested in personal growth, or had experienced or anticipated disappointment in the parish.[95] In other words, a disproportionate

---

[93] Foucauldian-inspired critics of the therapeutic imagine the language of psychology to be an unnecessary and pernicious invention. But the social construction of knowledge does not amount to the social construction of reality. Those involved in CPE would have lacked a psychological perspective if the discipline had not been invented, but there is no evidence that they would have lacked a psychology. The best evidence for this is the experience of those students who came to CPE who suddenly became shamefully aware of how often they had told themselves they were ministering to others when really they were filled with resentment, anger, and contempt for them. This might have escaped the ministers' notice, but it surely did not escape that of their congregants. This is exactly what CPE folk wanted to prevent through psychological training. For those who seem to believe that selfishness and self-centeredness itself could be transcended by abolishing psychological discourse, see Cushman, *Constructing the Self*; Levine, *Constructions of the Self*; Pfister and Schnog, *Inventing the Psychological*; Rose, *Governing the Soul*; Rose, *Inventing Our Selves*. Useful correctives are offered by Battan in "The 'New Narcissism'"; Lasch, *Culture of Narcissism*, 32.

[94] Norman P. Muncy, "Impressions of the Program," n.d., RG 001, Box 143, folder 2168, Pitts.

[95] These findings emerge in studies of students as well as supervisor comments, files, and publications. See Thomas Klink, "Goals and Content of Advanced Clinical Pastoral Training," October 28, 1959, RG 001, Box 161, folder 2489, Pitts; Charles Gerkin, "Identity of the Pastoral Supervisor," in *Pastoral Supervisor and His Identity*, CCT and Institute for Pastoral Care, 1966 Fall Conference, October 17–20, 1966, Atlantic City, NJ, RG 001, Box 163, folder 2510, Pitts; John R. Johnson, Jr., "Clinical Pastoral Education and Student Changes in Role Perception," *JPC* 21, no. 3 (1967): 140–1; Kenneth E. Reed, "The Council for Clinical Training and the Institute of Pastoral Care:

The Priest Must Drink at the Scientific Well

number of seminarians and ministers who sought out clinical training lacked pastoral confidence or skill.

The difficulties were compounded by the fact that clinical pastoral educators taught clerical students – some of whom were weak or in crisis over their calling – this challenging new paradigm of ministry in the most inauspicious of locations: in state hospitals and psychiatric facilities, in prisons, and homes for delinquent youth. They were smack dab in the middle of the secular professionals whom they were trying to emulate without merely imitating or duplicating. And they were doing it outside of the church, that is, outside of the institutions and communities that authorized their role. They were trying to do it, in the words of one attendee at a pastoral education conference, in "somebody else's institution."[96]

This exerted a constant pressure on chaplain supervisors and interns to justify themselves in secular terms.[97] Sometimes this pressure was economic and institutional: Many chaplaincies were funded by the institutions that hosted them.[98] Other times the pressure was subtler if no less forceful: Chaplains had to demonstrate their utility in terms of the institutions' secular missions to the rest of the staff in order to be included

A Comparative Study" (1963), 38. There are many examples of troubled students in the archives. A few examples include Joseph Stover, who was illegitimate and abused (files from RG 001, Box 143, folder 2180, Pitts); Louis Smith, whose father killed himself (files from RG 001, Box 143, folder 2166, Pitts); Lawrence Wampler, who was plagued by depression (files from RG 001, Box 146, folder 2221, Pitts), as was Summers, *Hunkering Down.*

[96] Peggy Way, fourth respondent to Richard John Neuhaus, "Certification Versus Freedom for Ministry," in *ACPE Conferences 1978–1979* (New York: ACPE, Inc.), p. 57, RG 001, Box 166, folder 1979, Pitts.

[97] This issue was frequently discussed, see, for example, Charles R. Jaekle, report, in CCT, "Annual Conference of Supervisors," October 17–21, 1955, Atlantic City, NJ, RG 001, Box 159, folder 2476, Pitts; Jervis Zimmerman, "Why I Left the Institutional Ministry," presentation at the National Conference of the Council for Clinical Training, Inc., October 30, 1957, Atlantic City, NJ, RG 001, Box 160, folder 2483, Pitts; Frederick Proelss, "What Makes Clinical Experience Pastoral," presentation at the National Conference of the Council for Clinical Training, Inc., October 30, 1957, Atlantic City, NJ, RG 001, Box 160, folder 2483, Pitts.

[98] Other chaplaincies were funded by local faith groups. For discussions of funding, see Ernest Bruder, "Basic Issues Affecting Saint Elizabeth's Hospital and Council for Clinical Training, Inc., Relationships," paper delivered at the Fall Conference of Supervisors, St. Louis, MO, October 26–29, 1959, RG 001, Box 35, folder 451, Pitts; "Are you satisfied with the present Council fee structure?" n.d. [circa 1960], RG 001, Box 35, folder 453, Pitts; A. R. Gilmore, "Pastoral Counseling, Economics of," in Hunter, ed., DPCC; Morris Taggart, "AAPC Membership Information Project," *JPC* 26, no. 4 (1972): 239, hereafter DPCC.

56   *American Protestantism in the Age of Psychology*

in discussions on treating or rehabilitating residents. To be taken seriously, they had to avoid invoking the language of faith and Christian metaphysics or anthropology. The lure of secularity while ministering in such a context, especially ministering in a way that drew heavily on psychology, was well known – if not always avoided – by people in the pastoral care movement. One chaplain wrote of the familiar "phenomenon of the chaplain–supervisor who has 'gone overboard for psychiatry.'"[99] The power of context on self-definition was evident in one small study that found that seminarians' identities were elastic. They could be pulled either toward secular or religious directions depending on the environment in which they operated while completing internships.[100]

It is not surprising then that working in secular institutions stretched a few practicing and student ministers beyond the breaking point. This usually happened among those interns who began training with an apprehension or experience of grave doubt, dissatisfaction, or failure in carrying out the traditional duties of the parish ministry.[101] They started their internships finding it difficult to believe themselves to be or to act as representatives of God. The training did not substantially help them resolve these issues.

Students often went through much or even all of their first quarter of training without being able to relate psychology to religion on the conceptual level at all. Some schools complained that seminarians returned from training "with a psychiatric knowledge and a lingo that is unrelated to their religious knowledge and understanding."[102] One student who underwent a common "shake up" experience early in his training noted that, "I have come to hold all of the articles of theology less firmly than ever before, and in a sense have become almost a skeptic."[103] Another student confessed when strongly challenged by his supervisor, "I was pretty well oriented to the attitudes of psychotherapy and social work, e.g., I was most interested in the purely human aspect of relationships

---

[99] Jervis S. Zimmerman, "A Christian Theological Approach to Clinical Pastoral Training," *JPC* 7, no. 2 (1953): 62.

[100] John R. Johnson, Jr., "Clinical Pastoral Education and Student Changes in Role Perception," *JPC* 21, no. 3 (1967): 129–46.

[101] For a discussion of this finding and my methodology, see chapter 3, especially footnote #2.

[102] Reuel L. Howe for the Committee on Council-Seminary Relations, "Report," n.d. [circa 1955], RG 001, Box 34, folder 444, Pitts.

[103] Oliver Frank, "A Quarter's Evaluation," Winter Quarter 1961, March 23, 1961, RG 001, Box 138, folder 2099, Pitts.

The Priest Must Drink at the Scientific Well 57

and I tended to drag God in as an afterthought.... The fact was that I was and still am confused about what I really believe about life."[104]

Edward Moriarty, for example, had spent a few years as an Episcopalian minister but was clearly interested in changing careers and becoming a therapist. He was so intent on becoming a therapist that he was extremely upset when assigned to a general hospital. Apparently he needed work in a psychiatric clinic to complete a certificate as a lay analyst, and so he refused to conduct pastoral visits to the patients.[105] He later asserted that "I am not personally so concerned, as some of my fellow-supervisors and students seem to be, about the distinction between pastoral care or pastoral counseling and psychotherapy. I am not at all sure that fundamentally there is any difference or distinction between the two."[106] The accreditation committee was concerned about his lack of pastoral identity and functioning, and this was a factor in delaying and possibly ultimately denying him promotion to full supervisory status. Although the evidence does not suggest that clinical training lured men away from the ministry altogether, familiarity with cases such as Moriarty's generated anxiety about the possibility.[107]

The most egregious example of the potential corruptions of a psychological perspective was the case of Russell Marsh, who trained during the mid-1950s. The case was extreme less for the pastoral but clearly idiosyncratic failings of Marsh, than for the way his case was handled by the CCT. A seminary whose students he had taught when he was a supervisor-in-training had complained that his approach was inappropriate and counterproductive.[108] This may have been what prompted

---

[104] "Council for Clinical Training Report to Seminaries, Summer Quarter 1953," September 4, 1953, RG 001, Box 137, folder 2092, Pitts.

[105] Seymour Elliott, "Edward Moriarty," Summer 1950, RG 001, Box 141, folder 2142, Pitts.

[106] Edward Moriarty, [untitled description of relationship with a student], 1954, RG 001, Box 141, folder 2142, Pitts. John Johnson found those who least distinguished between therapeutic and pastoral roles evinced the greatest shifts toward a secular role perception after clinical training, John R. Johnson Jr., "Clinical Pastoral Education and Student Changes in Role Perception," *JPC* 21, no. 3 (1967): 140–1.

[107] Bruder and Barb, "A Survey of Ten Years of Clinical Pastoral Training," 69–71; Edward Thornton, "Ministerial Drop-Outs: A Note," *JPC* 13, no. 2 (1960): 117–18; Allen P. Wadsworth, "Dropout from the Pastorate: Why?" *JPC* 25, no. 2 (1971): 124–7.

[108] Merton Zwillman, to Christopher D. Hornberger, October 5, 1954, RG 001, Box 148, folder 2249, Pitts. Their complaints probably stemmed in part from the fact that Marsh was one of the few supervisors who became a devotee of the titillating ideas of Wilhelm Reich, a Viennese psychoanalyst. Reich's early work focused on the

58   American Protestantism in the Age of Psychology

the accreditation committee to slow down Marsh's promotions and to challenge his religious understandings and pastoral commitments. Nevertheless, it ultimately made him a full supervisor in 1957. This was in spite of the fact that – in the words of a committee member – Marsh found it "difficult to speak of his religious position in . . . traditional symbols. He has substituted a clinical vocabulary for the traditional religious vocabulary."[109] The committee forgave this lapse given that it found evidence that Marsh was "moving toward a maturing religious faith that was expressed in warmth toward people" and that he "was positive in his statements about moving toward the church."[110] At least one committee member did appear to have had deep misgivings about what Marsh's positions implied about the quality of his own CP education.[111] But to the extent that members accepted the legitimacy of the idea that the reality to which both theology and psychology pointed was unitary, and the idea that the languages were interchangeable, they had little ground on which to demote a man who had followed this logic to its ultimate conclusion.[112]

Conclusion

This discussion must end where it began, however, with the Reverend Dunshee. Readers will recall that he stood in harsh judgment over the Reverend Wood, having declared the man unfit to be a chaplain anywhere. Wood was, in Dunshee's opinion, too eager to share the Gospel. He showed inadequate concern with the psychological states and needs of the prisoners under his ministry. Dunshee, as a founder of the Council, was deeply interested in such matters. So deeply interested, in fact, that

---

importance of orgasm for psychic health, and his later work argued that the human nervous system was composed of units of cosmic energy that could be captured in a special box.

[109] Harold Nichols, "Accreditation Committee Action," October 28, 1957, RG 001, Box 148, folder 2249, Pitts.

[110] Ibid.

[111] See the handwritten note appended to: Timothy Lovejoy, "Marsh, Russell," Winter, Spring, Summer 1954, RG 001, Box 148, folder 2249, Pitts.

[112] For other evidence of this problem, see Royal Garrison, "Re: Francis Z. Noel," 1948, RG 001, Box 142, folder 2150, Pitts; Jacob Fothergill, "Accreditation Summary [for Jonathan S. Clampitt]," October 1960, RG 001, ser. III, Box 138, folder 2113, Pitts; Shirley C. Guthrie and Tom P. Malone, "Relational Learning in Theological Education and Psychotherapy" (paper presented at the ACPE Conference: Clinical Education: Heresy and Orthodoxy, Atlanta, GA, 1974), 14.

The Priest Must Drink at the Scientific Well 59

he eventually left the ministry altogether. He became a full-time therapist and supported himself by opening a private practice.[113]

And yet, neither Dunshee, nor Marsh, nor Moriarty represented the bulk of CPE students. The likes of them stood, in fact, as a warning to other clergy. Most of whom, as we will see next, used their lessons in psychology to strengthen their ministry.

[113] "Arnold Dunshee" in DPCC.

3

Being the Love of God

How did the psychiatric education detailed in the previous chapter ultimately affect most young ministers? Did it usually lead them astray, as it appeared to do to Edward Moriarty? Did it leave ministers such as Reverend Dunshee – who later left the ministry for a career as a therapist – to stand in judgment of ardent evangelists such as Reverend Wood? Did the clinical pastoral education (CPE) students find, as did Charles Clayton Morrison, editor of the *Christian Century*, that after having "baptized the whole Christian tradition in the waters of psychological empiricism," "what I had left was hardly more than a moralistic ghost of the distinctive Christian reality"? Morrison continued:

It was as if the baptismal waters of the empirical stream had been mixed with some acid which ate away the historical significance, the objectivity and the particularity of the Christian revelation, and left me in complete subjectivity to work out my own salvation in terms of social services and an "integrated personality."[1]

Morrison wrote that in 1939, at the movement's beginning. A shared CPE curriculum and standards were not yet in place. The pioneering Council for Clinical Training (CCT) was in its most radical stage, independent of religious institutions and answerable, in part, to doctors. However, chaplains and ministers soon took over the group. Furthermore, CCT's need for students and financial sustenance eventually forced it to forge closer ties with seminaries, to which it became increasingly responsible. Whereas the earliest students tended to be unusually rebellious

[1] Quoted in Meador, "Psychology's Secularizing of American Protestantism," 269.

Being the Love of God

and sometimes emotionally broken men, later generations represented a broader and healthier spectrum of aspiring clergymen. Would these changes make it safe to drink from the well of psychological empiricism, as CPE pioneer Helen Flanders Dunbar had urged?

Yes. Most men who imbibed the sour waters found them not a poison but rather an acerbic tonic that left them stronger ministers. Analysis of the files of the 45 CCT students (1940–1968) that provide enough evidence to assess pastoral identity and competence over the course of training found that four out of five – thirty-six in all – were strengthened by it.[2]

---

[2] I examined each of the files to determine whether, over training, the students came to feel more or less at home in their pastoral roles. First, I looked for whether their relations with others were more or less frequently characterized by qualities they and their congregants believed suited a Christian minister, such as maturity, kindness, integrity, generosity, and sensitivity. Did changes in their interpersonal interactions improve their ministries? I also looked for development in their ability to adequately fulfill traditional pastoral duties, such as delivering sermons, leading prayers and worship, and communicating Christian messages. I tried to determine whether they increased or decreased their efforts and success in nurturing people spiritually. Did they, over the course of training, relate to people more and more as a secular therapist rather than as a pastor? Finally, I was particularly interested in determining whether chaplains increasingly invoked psychological concepts and language to the exclusion of religious ones. Although none of the areas targeted by CPE – psychosocial, professional, and theological development – can be sharply distinguished from each other, various students demonstrate particular growth in one area or another. No file contained evidence to resolve all questions, but all files in the sample suggested an answer to at least one of the questions.

Three things should be noted about the methodology. First, this study is based on CCT supervisors, which is a "hard case." Supervisors often began training with weak pastoral identity and functioning. For example, out of a sample of forty-five pastors for whom vocational trajectories over the course of training can be gleaned, roughly half began weak. Many of those who ultimately sought to become chaplain supervisors as an alternative to more traditional ministries did so because they had been – or anticipated being – dissatisfied or unsuccessful in the parish. A sizable minority had felt torn between medical and ministerial careers. Furthermore, they obtained training under the aegis of the organization that was most psychiatrically and least religiously oriented. Of the four major groups offering training, the CCT had the most tenuous ties to the institutions that could best "domesticate" and neutralize the secularizing potential of CPE: the seminaries and denominations. Thus, CCT supervisors began their clinical educations with weak pastoral identity and/or functioning and were particularly vulnerable to learning to see the world and their role in it through a psychological lens. Second, these trajectories are not for the life of the minister, but rather for his time during training (where documentation ends). Third, a few of the pastors whose files are included in the Pitts chaplain supervisor collection may not have made it to supervisor status.

Learning to Be the Love of God

First and foremost, clinical pastoral educators hoped to cultivate greater psychosocial awareness and intelligence in their interns. This was because educators saw making a personal connection as the primary pastoral task and the prerequisite for all others. Indeed, ministry was an intensely social calling. A minister's ability to convey the Gospel depended greatly on his ability to cultivate rapport, to demonstrate loving concern, to sway. He had to learn to "be the love of God." A minister was also often a church's highest administrator and leader, and those roles demanded extensive interpersonal savvy as well. Educators believed that social limitations impeded a minister's ability to fill his role. Immaturity and personal limitations were obstacles to vocational success. But on a deeper level, given the essentially social nature of ministry, personal growth *was* professional growth. Student Dale Harris showed how deeply he had taken to heart this lesson when he said, "It is the relationship that counts and not the words."

Students did develop qualities that American Protestants wanted from their religious leaders: maturity, leadership, poise, warmth, sympathy, sensitivity, and honesty.[3] Some CPE students entered training already mature and socially adept. Others were not. Both groups improved.

Clinical pastoral education made the profoundest difference for those who least intuited its values. Many who sought out advanced CPE were psychologically wounded people whose interpersonal interactions were distorted and limited. Some were terrified at the prospect of taking on a pastorate. Others had taken on one with either little success or with a nagging sense of failure.

Some men entered CPE as extremely damaged individuals. From the details revealed in the archives about their relationships with patients and peers, it is easy to imagine the great difficulties their personal problems would have or did cause in the pulpit. An extended example of this appears in the file of James F. Crook, the unusually unhappy Lutheran minister who was mentioned in the previous chapter as having been liberated by CPE finally to conceive of "God as someone apart from my mother."[4]

---

[3] Merton Strommen, "CPE and Readiness for the Ministry," in *ACPE Fiftieth Anniversary of Clinical Pastoral Education* (ACPE: Minneapolis, MN: 1975), 50–8, RG 001, Box 166, folder 2542, Pitts.

[4] James Crook, "[Self-]Evaluation, Second quarter of Training," for CCT, January 7, 1958, pp. 3–5, RG 001, ser. III, Box 136, folder 2069, Pitts.

Crook had entered training after many years as a minister, husband, and father. And yet an introductory clinical pastoral education class had led him to recognize that something was very wrong:

I became more and more aware of my feelings of hate, and fear, and hostility, and guilt. I am beginning to realize a little how my relationships to God, my wife, my family, and my people [parishioners] are conditioned by these feelings. I don't love God, I don't love people, I don't love myself, I don't want to be this way. I feel I need help to learn to live and to relate to people in love.[5]

Indeed, Crook's outspoken hostility was his most outstanding characteristic, even to men who hardly knew him. As an adult, Crook recognized that even his most intimate family relationships were warped by anger and dishonesty. Not surprisingly, the Christian idea of Jesus as a God of love and mercy were mere words to him.[6]

Crook's saving grace was a capacity to reflect on his shortcomings with honesty and even humor. This allowed him to make use of what CPE had to offer. He was slowly able to "los[e] interest in myself" so he could become for the first time really interested in others. He began to feel some of the tenderness toward others he had longed to feel. Bit by bit, his relationships with patients, parishioners, and his family improved.

Furthermore, the training allowed him to air his resentment against his conservative church and even his own vocation. Venting and then coming to terms with his rebellion enabled him eventually to begin to renew his ties to his fellowship. When some of his congregants wrote to his church president to complain that he was not preaching "true Lutheran doctrine," he explained his position to the president without defensiveness. The president praised Crook, in fact, for his newfound empathy, warmth, and sincerity.[7]

After almost two years of making steady personal strides – which allowed him to behave more in a manner expected of a clergyman –

---

[5] James Crook, "Application for Training," to CCT, January 9, 1957, RG 001, ser. III, Box 136, folder 2069, Pitts.

[6] Ibid.; Arthur Smith, "Screening Report to the Council for Clinical Training," January 12, 1957, p. 3, RG 001, ser. III, Box 136, folder 2069, Pitts; James Crook, "[Self-]Evaluation After First Quarter of Training," to CCT, April 4, 1957, RG 001, ser. III, Box 136, folder 2069, Pitts.

[7] Arthur Smith, "Screening Report to the Council for Clinical Training," January 12, 1957, p. 3, RG 001, ser. III, Box 136, folder 2069, Pitts; James Crook, "[Self-]Evaluation, Second Quarter of Training," for CCT, January 7, 1958, pp. 3–5, RG 001, ser. III, Box 136, folder 2069, Pitts; Arthur Smith, "Confidential Evaluation on James Crook," to CCT, January 16, 1958, RG 001, ser. III, Box 136, folder 2069, Pitts.

64   *American Protestantism in the Age of Psychology*

Crook was prepared to embrace his calling anew. He brought more religious language to his discussions with patients than previously. And he began to speak frequently of his "ministry" for the first time during his training. Although his counseling skills were improving markedly, he singled out instead "praying the Lord's prayer with a dying patient" as one of the "finest experiences" of his advanced training. Although Crook had occasional setbacks and decided to leave the parish for the chaplaincy, his transformation was undeniable. One supervisor commented, "in a heart-warming manner I believe he has discovered, or re-discovered, his vocation."[8]

Peter Simmons's problems were different than Crook's, but no less crippling. And yet CPE transformed Simmons as much as it had Crook. Young Simmons's shy passivity before training struck one interviewer as "effeminate." He was deeply distressed about his wife who was suffering psychiatric difficulties and soon divorced him. The poor young man clearly needed therapy, which he sought out to good effect. His strengths were his personal insightfulness and sympathetic warmth. He immediately signed up for additional quarters of training, although he found his relationship with his supervisor challenging: "I wanted a friend on whom I could be dependent – and he resisted, which gave me good material for therapy." Simmons left CPE for a couple years to continue his clerical development in other arenas – probably aware that he would be required to have spent three years in a parish even if he ultimately dreamed of becoming a chaplain supervisor himself. And he did indeed complain in subsequent years that the "ordinary church is too frustrating." He found a stint as a Presbyterian minister less satisfying than his institutional work, and this prompted him to seek out advanced CPE training.

After a few more years of training, Simmons finally began to mature past his old detachment and passivity. His work with patients was praised for being "a lot better than average" and Simmons began to assert himself. He persistently pursued getting an office for himself to demonstrate his status vis-à-vis the other hospital professionals and successfully overcame their objections to having each new patient evaluated religiously. Despite the skepticism and casual contempt he encountered from his secular colleagues initially, over time he demonstrated his skills and the value of his

---

[8] James Crook, "[Self-]Evaluation, Third and Fourth Quarter [of training]," for CCT, May 29, 1958, RG 001, ser. III, Box 136, folder 2069, Pitts; Arthur Smith, "Confidential Evaluation on James Crook," to CCT, January 16, 1958, p. 3, RG 001, ser. III, Box 136, folder 2069, Pitts; Henry Fitzgerald, "Notes on Supervision of James Crook," rec'd September 23, 1959, by CCT, RG 001, ser. III, Box 136, folder 2069, Pitts.

relationship with patients. His colleagues came to respect his work, even making him the first chaplain on the unit to whom patients had ever been assigned follow-up counseling.

Simmons's new leadership abilities were tested to the limit when his conscience called him to ally himself with an African American social worker fighting to integrate the racially segregated ward in which he worked. Going up against powerful opposing figures in the hospital caused him no little anxiety, but he stayed committed. The integrationists triumphed. And ten years after he timidly began his training, the CCT finally deemed Simmons sufficiently self-possessed and clear about his clerical calling to promote him to full chaplain supervisor.

Joseph Stover well demonstrated the way that personal growth both constituted and facilitated vocational development. He was forty-five when he began CPE, older by decades than most students in the 1960s, who were more likely to be young seminarians. Stover had already served many years in the parish. He had, it appeared, two weaknesses in that role. First, for a seasoned minister, he showed a marked disinterest in religious matters, having read almost nothing about theology since his graduation from seminary. Instead, he avidly consumed best-selling psychological self-help works by Norman Vincent Peale, Rabbi Joshua Loth Liebman, and Smiley Blanton. Secondly, he clearly suffered internal distress from a sad and abusive childhood. He did not recognize the pain, hatred, and anger that lingered within him from such early mistreatment. But he did find himself suffering strange symptoms, such as a severe pain around his heart when preaching to his congregation.

Clinical pastoral education – especially the therapeutic private sessions Stover had with his supervisor – came like a thunderbolt in his life. Early on he enthused that the meetings:

have been the most rewarding experiences of my life.... I feel that I have been apologizing for living, however, now I feel that I can have feelings and opinions of my own.... Now I have a more realistic opinion of others and myself.... Now I feel that any day I do not learn something about myself is a loss.[9]

He felt an intense sense of gratitude for "these personal encounters with my Supervisor" in which he felt "permitted" for the first time in his life

to discuss my being an illegitimate child who was raised by relatives who were ashamed of me and rejected me as a human being who had feelings [including an instance of extraordinary abuse],... [so] I [could] beg[i]n to resolve the basic

---

[9] Joseph Stover, "Evaluation of Spring Quarter 1963," June 3, 1963, RG 001, Box 143, folder 2180, Pitts.

66 *American Protestantism in the Age of Psychology*

cause of my hostilities and feelings of inferiority.... I will never forget the day that you told me that I had a lot of hate in me and then you offered me an opportunity to let it out.[10]

The excitement over the discoveries Stover was making in CPE – combined with his theological liberalism and initial disinterest in religious matters – led him to become extremely therapeutically oriented for a couple of years. He seemed confused about the difference between training and receiving therapy, and between ministry and therapeutic counseling. Slowly, however, he began again to come to appreciate the fact that a human being was "inherently a religious being" and that the patients he saw often needed ministry as well as counseling. God was clearly important to Joseph, which was atypical of his theological liberal fellow students; and he found himself increasingly confident in his ability to convey divine love to his listeners. His heart pain while preaching disappeared. Eventually, Stover had progressed enough personally as well as vocationally that the CCT promoted him to full supervisory status.

A Call to Ministry?

Many students who entered CPE were unsure whether they were cut out for the ministry at all. This was especially true for the young seminarians who flooded the movement once it became a mainstream component of Protestant theological education beginning in the late 1950s. They did not suffer from pervasive psychosocial problems as did James Crook or Herbert O. Freshwater, as we saw earlier. Instead, they had a developmentally appropriate set of concerns about whether they had indeed been called.

For example, Vincent Conway claimed during his initial screening interview in the mid-1950s that he enjoyed his parish work and looked forward to more. Nevertheless, the young Methodist soon dropped this pretense. After enrolling in CPE, he admitted that he felt he had not succeeded despite winning his congregation's approval. Furthermore, he confessed that he was not sure what a "call to the ministry is" and that the theological concepts he studied as a seminary student meant nothing to him. He harbored deep doubts that his own interests and abilities matched those he imagined appropriate to a parish minister.[11]

---

[10] Joseph Stover, "Clinical Pastoral Training Evaluation, Summer Quarter," August 26, 1963, RG 001, Box 143, folder 2180, Pitts.

[11] "Supervisory Interview Notes," June 18–August 27, 1954, RG 001, Box 149, folder 2273, Pitts.

Being the Love of God 67

Vince was hardly alone. His personal doubts prompted a lively and broadly fruitful discussion in his group seminar about clerical callings.[12] The archives evince a noticeably high number of future CPE supervisors who were themselves the scions of clergy or intensely religious families. Parental pressure sometimes steered these sons into the ministry regardless of their individual interests and abilities, leaving them insecure and resentful. Many with vocational anxieties were alienated from their roles or in rebellion against their churches. Such men sometimes hid their turmoil and doubt as Conway initially did, but many others failed to adequately fulfill key clerical tasks demanded of them.

CPE usually helped such students come to terms with their professional identity and responsibilities. It did this by giving students room to air and even act out their rebellious grievances, and *then* by guiding them back toward mature acceptance rather than merely resentful resignation. Henry Fitzgerald, an Episcopalian who trained in the 1950s, was not from a religious background. But he described eloquently and succinctly how repeated quarters of CPE helped him master his own sense of inner revolt:

the pastor as an official representative of the Christian fellowship is perhaps the most difficult role for me to accept in the ministry. I constantly rebel against what I consider its demands, but secretly I have begun to feel that I am a better representative of the fellowship to the world than I would like to admit and better than some of the brethren who now represent it. There was a time when I shed my collar at every opportunity, feeling that it symbolized my official role; however, I have become much less self-conscious of the self-imposed and socially-imposed demands of the ministry as an official function.[13]

For those whose interests and temperaments were hopelessly at odds with the demands of a parish post, CPE offered an alternative vision of ministry: The chaplain supervisor enjoyed far greater autonomy, fewer administrative and financial burdens, and great opportunities for intense, intimate encounters. But unlike a parish job, where competence mattered most, promotion to this role demanded that students accept in their hearts a sense of themselves as representatives of God's love and success in conveying this to those around them.

In assessing students' professional development, I studied their files for development in their ability to fulfill adequately traditional pastoral

[12] Ibid.
[13] Henry Fitzgerald, [self-evaluation, Winter 1958], 1958, RG 001, Box 142, folder 2159, Pitts.

68   *American Protestantism in the Age of Psychology*

duties, such as delivering sermons, leading prayers and worship, and communicating Christian messages. I tried to determine whether they were increasingly successful in sustaining, guiding, and reconciling people spiritually. I was particularly interested in determining whether chaplains related to people as a secular therapist or as a pastor.

Claude R. Gunn began his clinical pastoral education highly ambivalent about his career. He had been raised in a strict Presbyterian family, which presumably had been pleased when their son announced a call to ministry. But seminary came as a shock. His "Sunday school religion," as he called it, "crumbled," leaving him in rebellion against both his church and parents.[14] Gunn appeared to have struggled with faith itself. Nevertheless, he remained outwardly on the path he had begun. He even secured a junior clerical post in a Baltimore church after graduation. But his inner upheaval and doubts weakened his performance. Gunn was a poor and unenthusiastic preacher, and seemed more interested in discussing psychiatric matters than religious ones in his clerical calls. Enrolling in CPE seemed a natural choice for him, but raised the possibility of serving as a bridge out of his clerical profession and into a therapeutic one. The latter career initially held great allure for him.

Gunn's supervisors were concerned about his lack of commitment to the ministry, despite his "meaningful contacts with patients." But over time he improved. After many quarters of training, he began to demonstrate that he did "get religious facts and feelings" and was capable of leading "meaningful religious services... [and] discussion group[s]." His preaching began to improve slowly. His stilted religious style gave way to a stilted psychiatric style that eventually gave way to a more sincere and engaging "sharing of his own faith." By the time he was promoted to a full supervisor, Gunn was deemed to have the potential to be "a quite superior rather than good preacher" and was able to articulate the religious elements of his interpersonal work. He pleased the accreditation committee with his assertion that "God's spirit is apparent in human relationships.... It is in relationships... that I may know and be known, may become reconciled to myself, to my neighbor (who is always my potential enemy), and to God."[15]

[14] Claude Gunn, [application], rec'd February 13, 1958, RG 001, Box 145, folder 2213, Pitts.
[15] Stephen Walton, to Dean Curly, April 4, 1959, re: Evaluation and progress report, RG 001, Box 145, folder 2213, Pitts; Stephen Walton, to Dean Curly, January 5, 1959, re:

Being the Love of God 69

Albert Sutton was unusually explicit about his ambivalence and resentment about the pastoral road he felt he had been forced down. As his CPE screening interviewer relayed, "He is the son of a minister and his vocation was chosen for him; he has reacted against this, yet feels there may be valid reasons for his continuing in the ministry." Having found some relief in pastoral counseling for his problems sparked Sutton's interest in pursuing CPE himself.[16] In fact, he had smothered his own interest in clinical psychology out of obedience to his parents, who had expected him to go into the ministry. He had become "seriously unhappy in his parish work" – so unhappy that it had contributed to his becoming sick enough to require hospitalization.[17] During that stay, a chaplain had helped him acknowledge his deep resentment while nevertheless suggesting that Sutton "could rebel against his parents without fighting the church which had become the symbol for them."[18] Sutton decided to enroll in clinical pastoral training himself.

After a number of quarters, however, Sutton still wavered. As he began advanced training he told his supervisor, "I'm in clinical training because I feel, right now, as though I want to be in the ministry and I don't want to be in the ministry. CPT is sort of half way between."[19] The question for this student was whether CPE would serve him as a doorway out of ministry, or a liminal space where he might discover a calling on new terms.

Over years of training, Sutton did find a role he could embrace and flourish in as an institutional chaplain. His written work tended to emphasize the ultimate goal of emotional health and religion as a resource toward that end. But he argued that allowing patients to communicate their feelings – especially when there was no one else to listen – was

---

Evaluation report, RG 001, Box 145, folder 2213, Pitts; "Council for Clinical Training, Regional Accreditation Committee Meeting, Southeast Region," April 7, 1960, RG 001, Box 145, folder 2213, Pitts; John Brooks, "Student Evaluation," July 3, 1960, RG 001, Box 145, folder 2213, Pitts; John Brooks, "Chaplain Supervisor's Evaluation Report," October 12, 1961, RG 001, Box 145, folder 2213, Pitts.

[16] Christopher Brewer, "Report on Interview with Applicants for Training," February 20, 1951, RG 001, Box 141, folder 2140, Pitts.

[17] Louis Smith, "Report on Interview with Applicants for Training," November 19, 1951, RG 001, Box 141, folder 2140, Pitts.

[18] Ibid.

[19] Louis Smith, "Evaluation for Accreditation Committee," March 21, 1952, RG 001, Box 141, folder 2140, Pitts.

70   *American Protestantism in the Age of Psychology*

"a way of expressing the love of God."[20] He gave a vivid description of how he tried to "be to [patients] the kind of a person they need in the immediate crisis situation." This entailed a variety of interactions:

Holding his hand and letting him feel a dependence on you before the operation. To another it means a kind but firm refusal to take sides with her against the doctor who advises something she does not like. To another it means granting their request to read the Bible and pray with them. To another it means listening to their bitterness toward the church. To another it means gentle encouragement to express her anxieties until she realized that she is finding it difficult to accept old age. To another it means listening to him express his feelings about dying until he is able to accept it without fear or guilt.[21]

Personal growth was the gateway to vocational growth for a number of CPE students. When Luke Carter entered CPE, he seemed destined for failure. Not only was he a wounded and repressed man who confessed that dealing with people made him intensely uncomfortable, but he hardly seemed to grasp theological matters. Carter had pursued the ministry after he had understood "a great unburdening of... feelings and thoughts" to a close friend as a "religious experience." Speaking of his feelings was unusual, and he did not speak readily about religious subjects at all. His first pastorate had been, in his own words, unsuccessful.

After a quarter of CPE, Carter had begun to speak about himself more openly and he successfully pursued a pastorate in a small town. His new openness was not yet matched, however, by new interpersonal sensitivity, as his supervisor noted:

Luke is a guy who has a whole lot of problems that hang out all over the surface. He is free to talk about them and free to discuss them. When he came back from his first quarter of training into parish life, he was quite open and began to share this stuff with the congregation, and it scared them half to death. They since have learned to love him in a way, and they kept him on as their pastor.

Despite this step forward, Carter still had a long way to go. But he plugged at it, year after year. His progress in the program was slow, as his supervisors continually worried that he remained too self-absorbed, immature, and vocationally adrift. But his hard work to develop into a chaplain and minister of substance finally began to show. Carter earned promotion up the ranks toward chaplain supervisor. He played a role

---

[20] Albert Sutton, "Application for Advanced Training," February 27, 1953, RG 001, Box 141, folder 2140, Pitts.

[21] Ibid.

Being the Love of God

in comforting a young child dying of cancer by visiting him regularly to "hold . . . and love him," an affection that was deeply reciprocated.

Carter also embraced his clerical role. He got himself hired at a country parish and seemed to enjoy it. As an assistant supervisor, he happily raised sermon topics and theological questions with his students. He read a book on theology, which one senior minister who knew him quipped was like "Billy Graham reading a *Playboy* magazine!" But it reflected Carter's own new theological engagement and refinement. This final stage of Carter's education, in which he demonstrated both great personal growth as well as an enthusiasm for and comfort with the role of minister, led finally to his promotion to chaplain supervisor.[22]

Does Dynamic Psychology Answer Theological Questions?

One of the original goals of CPE was to enable ministers to meet the religious challenges of modernity, particularly its intellectual challenges. As Helen Dunbar announced at the dawn of CPE, ministers had to drink at the scientific well if they were to understand the tastes that were tempting their flocks. Educated seekers such as Helen needed the guidance of sophisticated ministers who could help them navigate their own beliefs after many years of acculturation in institutions of higher education that divested them of their religious missions and curricula. By the late nineteenth century, the life of the mind was an increasingly secular one.[23]

---

[22] William Kirby, "[evaluation of] Luke Carter," September 22, 1960, RG 001, ser. III, Box 150, folder 2281, Pitts; C. Dale Weaver, "Confidential Report [on Luke Carter]," January 24, 1964, RG 001, ser. III, Box 150, folder 2281, Pitts; Luke Carter, "[Self-] Evaluation," Fall 1963, September 22, 1960, RG 001, ser. III, Box 150, folder 2281, Pitts; C. Dale Weaver, "Confidential Evaluation [of Luke Carter]," September 15, 1964, RG 001, ser. III, Box 150, folder 2281, Pitts; Timothy Hamm, "Accreditation Summary [of Luke Carter]," October 13, 1964, RG 001, ser. III, Box 150, folder 2281, Pitts; "Accreditation Summary [of Luke Carter]," March 1965, RG 001, ser. III, Box 150, folder 2281, Pitts; Ernest Sprague, "Regional Accreditation Committee Report [for Luke Carter]," February 20, 1965, RG 001, ser. III, Box 150, folder 2281, Pitts; William Kirby, "Evaluation Report [of Luke Carter]," August 12, 1966, RG 001, ser. III, Box 150, folder 2281, Pitts; C. Dale Weaver, "Evaluation Report [of Luke C.]," August 26, 1966, RG 001, ser. III, Box 150, folder 2281, Pitts; Philip Brewer, "Summary Notes for National Accreditation Committee [on Luke Carter] October 1966," RG 001, ser. III, Box 150, folder 2281, Pitts.

[23] Casanova, *Public Religions in the Modern World*; Conkin, *When All the Gods Trembled*; Croce, *Science and Religion*; Marsden, *Soul of the American University*; White, *Science and Religion*.

72   *American Protestantism in the Age of Psychology*

CPE pioneers believed their new training would permit ministers to keep up. Did it?

CPE did help. It gave students a forum in which to rescue their own childhood faith from their own rebellion and from the common stresses of seminary shock. In the years after World War II, many Protestants were religiously on the move.[24] The ethnic boundaries of various denominations became increasingly porous through intermarriage and ecumenism. This allowed believers to find the best religious product for themselves, but it left some with feelings of anxiety, guilt, and cognitive dissonance. Many young men in CPE had not intended to rebel, but they ended up struggling with the same feelings brought on by seminary itself. Even when a young man attended a school affiliated with the church in which he had been raised, he often found the breadth and interpretation of academic theology at odds with what he had been taught in Sunday school.[25] These more supple understandings of cherished doctrines left many students reeling. CPE created a space in which to grapple with these interlaced intellectual, emotional, and spiritual confusions.

However, CPE caused its own problems, too, for it sometimes served as young ministers' introduction to a secular, critical, and alternative paradigm to the faiths of their childhoods. This was integral to the CPE project of revealing the psychological baggage that some students brought to the theological enterprise. But the procedure sometimes led students astray before it guided them back to a faith tempered through testing and trial.

Mark Shields was a young theologically roiled minister who found answers in CPE after being temporarily tormented by it. His case also demonstrates the way that personal, professional, and theological development were sometimes inextricably interwoven in clinical pastoral education. As a young man, Shields had rebelled against his upbringing in a strict, conservative church he described as "a rabidly fundamentalist group with the idea of authority and obedience predominant."[26] This rebellion had left him ill at ease spiritually and personally. So he pursued college and seminary degrees in order to "straighten myself

---

[24] Ellwood, *The Fifties Spiritual Marketplace*; Finke and Stark, *Churching of America*; Wuthnow, *Restructuring of American Religion*.

[25] Finke and Stark, *Churching of America*.

[26] Mark Shields, "Initial Application," rec'd April 7, 1958, RG 001, Box 146, folder 2224, Pitts; Roy Kellogg, "Screening Interview," April 17, 1958, RG 001, Box 146, folder 2224, Pitts.

Being the Love of God 73

out theologically."[27] Deeply influenced by the writings of existentialist theologian Paul Tillich, Shields eventually became a Congregationalist minister.

Nevertheless, Shields had not solved either his personal or his religious troubles. He began his career with a sense of nagging guilt about his new theological liberalism as well as a sense of having been forced to take up the ministry by the need to find a livelihood rather than any sense of call.[28] Despite the intensity of his personal faith, his job was made even more difficult by his fear of social encounters and intimacy. Shields did not feel himself a success.[29] This was the context in which Shields initially applied for CPE.

The training worked at first on many levels. Shields appreciated the way it had

increased my self-awareness.... Most important, training has given me a deeper and more immediate experience of the gospel through the pastoral care and supervision of the Supervisor. I am more aware of my own dynamics, of my strengths, of goals, and of my orientation in the Christian Faith.

He hoped in further training to enhance his understanding "of psychodynamic theory, of theology, but especially the greater facility to move towards people with love and understanding."[30]

But after about a year, Shields underwent a not uncommon shake-up. After having built his confidence and abilities for many months, he suddenly found himself incapable of properly fulfilling any of the facets of the chaplain's or minister's roles. He confessed that he did not himself feel in communion with God and could not therefore serve as a conduit for divine forgiveness, blessing, or love.[31]

Fortunately, and typically, this period was only a temporary set back. Shields' hard-won confidence returned and he showed himself again adequate to his pastoral duties.[32] His supervisor, pleased with the student's success, encouraged him to apply for a supervisory assistantship, which

---

[27] Ibid.

[28] Ibid.; Mark Shields, "Critical Autobiography, Summer Quarter 1958," rec'd December 3, 1958, RG 001, Box 146, folder 2224, Pitts.

[29] Ibid.

[30] Mark Shields, "Application II: *For Further Training*," n.d., RG 001, Box 146, folder 2224, Pitts.

[31] Mark Shields, "Evaluation, Winter Quarter" December 1959-March 1960, RG 001, Box 146, folder 2224, Pitts.

[32] Mark Shields, "Evaluation," May 25, 1960, RG 001, Box 146, folder 2224, Pitts.

74   *American Protestantism in the Age of Psychology*

he got. After a few years, the supervisor noted with pleasure that "Mark Shields has moved from being a very talented person who was practically immobilized to becoming a very talented person who is increasingly able to function helpfully, insightfully and with personal satisfaction and reward." In 1964, he was accredited as a full chaplain supervisor.[33]

The experience of Mark Shields was not an anomaly. Even less promising perhaps was Herbert O. Freshwater, who began his training in 1964. Freshwater was the student whose supervisor believed he used the theological idea that God alone can confer dignity on human life to emphasize his own sense of personal worthlessness. Freshwater sought training because he felt he needed therapy.[34] This was not uncommon among entering CPE students, but Freshwater's neediness stood out. Concerned about the young man's self-absorbed unhappiness, his supervisor worked to make him understand that

if one was preoccupied with oneself and one's feeling and past problems it was pretty difficult to be a minister. We were able to focus on the fact that one needed to be able to think about the patient or the parishioner first and only deal with their own feelings as a secondary matter in order to be a minister.[35]

Freshwater came to recognize the truth in what his supervisor said. He sought therapy privately, which was typically recommended to advanced students. He began to focus his energies on his vocational development. He got himself hired at a local church and turned his advanced CPE training time to enhancing his pastoral abilities. At first, Freshwater felt he was "almost two different persons as a pastor, one in the local community and one in the hospital." The community pastor acted as a traditional Methodist minister, whereas as a chaplain intern he operated like a therapist.[36]

Studying classic works of pastoral care helped Freshwater begin to see himself and behave in truly Christian ways in the hospital. He began to

[33] John Thacker, "Report to the Accreditation Committee, CCT," October 11, 1960, RG 001, Box 146, folder 2224, Pitts.

[34] Vernon Trollope, "Confidential Report," September 1, 1962, RG 001, Box 144, folder 2200, Pitts.

[35] Albert N. Sutton, "Confidential Screening Interview," March 25, 1963, RG 001, Box 145, folder 2200, Pitts.

[36] Herbert O. Freshwater, "Clinical Pastoral Training Evaluation, 1st Quarter," rec'd March 30, 1964, RG 001, Box 145, folder 2200, Pitts; Herbert O. Freshwater, "Clinical Pastoral Training Evaluation, Summer Quarter 1964," rec'd October 15, 1964, RG 001, Box 145, folder 2200, Pitts; Herbert O. Freshwater, "Clinical Pastoral Training Evaluation, 2nd Quarter," rec'd March 30, 1964, RG 001, Box 145, folder 2200, Pitts.

Being the Love of God 75

realize that a therapeutic approach to patients was not necessarily the most pastoral. After many months as an advanced student, Freshwater was pleased to find himself finally able "to assimilate this feeling of being a pastor, a representative of God." For example, he drew simultaneously on psychological and theological knowledge when he visited Larry Pruett. Freshwater was able to discern that behind Pruett's verbosity and Scriptural search for predictions of the apocalypse lay an intense fear of death. Freshwater decided it most useful to the man "to get a Bible and work with him through the Bible," which he "would not have even considered doing" previously in his training. Similarly, when patient Neal Stoll asked him if he thought God might forgive his sins, Freshwater was alerted to Stoll's sense of guilt. But he deemed it less useful to ask the patient to expatiate on those than to answer the question theologically. Freshwater was proud and delighted with the new sense of pastoral identity and competence these exchanges had brought him: "I felt at these points truly a representative of God seeking to improve the relationships with men and God."[37]

Although Freshwater still had a lot of maturing to do in his vocation, his advances were not in his head. He evinced a more profound understanding of the relationship that should exist between his work in the hospital and the work of the surrounding Christian community. He undertook a project to foster closer ties between the mental hospital and local clergy. Among other things, this aimed to help patients experience their hospitalization not as an isolation from Christian fellowship but as a continuation of it. He organized Bible studies that aimed to be not merely therapeutic but also religiously educational.[38]

CPE was theologically useful even to students who struggled less in their vocation than Mark Shields or Herb Freshwater. Glenn Maddox

---

[37] Herbert O. Freshwater, "Clinical Pastoral Training Evaluation, 2nd Quarter," rec'd March 30, 1964, RG 001, Box 145, folder 2200, Pitts; Albert Sutton, "Evaluation Report, Fall Quarter 1964," December 30, 1964, RG 001, Box 145, folder 2200, Pitts; Albert Sutton, "Evaluation Report of Clinical Pastoral Training, Summer 1964," rec'd October 15, 1964, RG 001, Box 145, folder 2200, Pitts; Herbert Freshwater, "Clinical Pastoral Training Evaluation, Fall Quarter 1964," RG 001, Box 145, folder 2200, Pitts; Albert N. Sutton, "Evaluation Report," March 10, 1965, RG 001, Box 145, folder 2201, Pitts.

[38] Albert N. Sutton, "Evaluation Report of Clinical Pastoral Training, Summer 1964," rec'd October 15, 1964, RG 001, Box 145, folder 2200, Pitts; Herbert O. Freshwater, "Clinical Pastoral Training Evaluation, Fall Quarter 1964," RG 001, Box 145, folder 2200, Pitts; Albert N. Sutton, "Evaluation Report," March 10, 1965, RG 001, Box 145, folder 2201, Pitts.

76   *American Protestantism in the Age of Psychology*

began training after initial pastoral success but burdened by great doubts. Like Shields, he had been raised in an independent fundamentalist church. This intense upbringing had filled his Korean War draft service with anguish. How could a true Christian kill? Longing to serve not state but God, he entered the seminary when he was released from the military. He described it later as "three years of hell" as he had "the emotional 'rock' I stood on threatened and crushed." In an experience not uncommon to many seminarians recorded in council files, Maddox was both exhilarated and deeply unsettled by the ideas he encountered in seminary. Even the most conservative seminaries offered a breadth of vision that startled young Christians reared in fundamentalist churches.[39]

Maddox's entry into clinical training only exacerbated his confusion. He began to look at "long-cherished theological tenets . . . in the light of reality." Finding them wanting, he reported "losing much of my interest in theological questions." The doubts and new personal insights into himself wrought by training provoked in Robert a period of angry rebellion. Perhaps he did not want to be a minister after all. What truths could Christianity teach him that would not sink under the weight of scholarly inquiry and psychoanalytic examination? Maddox struggled even to fulfill his duty as a loving Christian pastor to the hospital patients he visited. After many months, Maddox's mutiny collapsed into a period of despair and guilty self-deprecation.[40]

And then after half a year, a new light shone on Maddox's heart. Still wistful for the "perpetual Garden of Eden" of his youthful faith, he nevertheless preached a powerful sermon entitled "Out of the Pit." He drew on his own recent despair to speak to his congregant-patients' sense of futility and meaninglessness. He began to accept the burden of pastoral leadership again and to do it well. His battered confidence revived. Grateful for the help of CPE in "becom[ing] a little wiser," he also had finally come to realize that "dynamic psychology, although an invaluable and indispensable tool for understanding Man . . . does not, in itself, answer the theological questions." And he strongly asserted that

Having said there are psychological dynamics that were going on with me which could be explained in scientific terms however, does not negate my conviction

[39] Glenn Maddox, "Application Answers," rec'd June 13, 1958, RG 001, Box 144, folder 2194, Pitts; Jacob Fothergill, "Confidential Report," February 9, 1962, RG 001, Box 144, folder 2194, Pitts; Glenn Maddox, "[Self-] Evaluation for the Clinical Year, Sept. 15, 1958-August 31, 1959," RG 001, Box 144, folder 2194, Pitts.

[40] Glenn Maddox, "[Self-]Evaluation for the Clinical Year, Sept. 15, 1958-August 31, 1959," RG 001, Box 144, folder 2194, Pitts.

Being the Love of God 77

that ultimate and theological battles were being waged in the battle of life. There *was* a struggle of light with darkness, God and the Devil.

Although Maddox was still struggling when the training file leaves off, he clearly had made great strides. With his hard-won knowledge and skills, he took on a congregation in crisis and managed to reunite them after having been split by their former contentious minister.[41]

Conclusion

From the literature on the therapeutic alone, one might have expected CPE to secularize ministers. For a small group of weak seminary students and ministers, it did. But for most, it did not. Instead, it strengthened ministers.

CPE improved clergy's interpersonal interactions and made them better people in innumerable small ways. They became more sensitive to others, more honest about themselves, and more sympathetic. It did this by deepening students' practice of critical introspection and teaching them to apply some of the basic concepts of clinical psychology.

CPE also made students more competent and confident ministers – better preachers, more socially savvy leaders, and more sensitive pastors. Perhaps almost any internship that put young ministers in challenging situations could have done this. But few other situations would have tuned them into the flood of unspoken messages sent by parishioners. Other internships might have better honed seminarians' theological exposition or their homiletic delivery, but none would have devoted so much time helping them analyze what their listeners actually *heard*.

Finally, CPE equipped seminarians to handle better the doubts provoked by their own theological educations as well as the metaphysical claims of authoritative secular professionals. It tried to help students integrate secular expertise into an intellectually rigorous and fundamentally religious whole. This was the weakest facet of clinical pastoral education, but it did allow students to articulate and confront doubts – a process that philosopher Charles Taylor has argued is inextricable from faith in a modern, secular age.[42]

These personal and interpersonal improvements were possible because the pioneers of CPE were right – twentieth-century Protestant ministry was a profoundly social endeavor. Ministers who alienated their flocks

[41] Ibid.; Jacob Fothergill, "Confidential Report on Student, Fall and Winter Quarter 1958–1959," RG 001, Box 144, folder 2194, Pitts.

[42] Taylor, *A Secular Age*.

78   *American Protestantism in the Age of Psychology*

through insensitivity, or who withdrew from them in fear and awkwardness, could not be effective religious leaders. Greater psychosocial sophistication helped ministers be better at their calling. This was especially true for rebellious, theologically confused, and emotionally wounded clergymen. CPE cultivated a maturation that not only paved the way for vocational growth, but sometimes even constituted it.

But what about Morrison's lament? *Christian Century* editor Charles Clayton Morrison found his Christian faith badly damaged by its baptismal dunk in the "acid" of psychology. Indeed, as we have just seen, clergymen did not exit the font unchanged. Some led Bible studies less like catechisms and more like group discussions; others innovated liturgically. More serious perhaps were the theological changes. Gary Pearson found it difficult to maintain absolute belief in Holiness doctrine; James F. Crook was criticized for abdicating true Lutheran dogma; and Frank Albrecht decided it impractical to condemn smoking.

So why were these changes not more devastating, as others have feared? Because the pH of clinical pastoral psychology turned out to be closer to that of vinegar or lemon juice than to that of hydrochloric acid. Sigmund Freud and his heirs may have hoped their ideas would corrode faith; Carl Rogers may have hoped his would replace it. But the CCT wanted no such thing. So it compounded a different psychological formula for its students.

It did this in many ways. Although Protestant ministers drew heavily on Carl Rogers, they downplayed his emphasis on patients' self-realization. They amplified instead the importance of counselors' nonjudgmental positive regard. Such regard was a secular version of the ideal of Christian love, a redemptive and altruistic concern for another human being regardless of his or her sins. Rogers taught therapists how to take an analogous approach,[43] perhaps drawing inspiration from his own intense religious upbringing and seminary education. His advice thus helped teach clergymen how to "be the love of God rather than [just] talk . . . about it."

Unlike secular therapists, ministers valued fellowship over autonomy. As we saw earlier, for example, supervisor-in-training Ken Raschke realized he had erred when he stymied his student chaplains' attempts to worship as a group even if his stonewalling did enhance their psychosocial growth. Glenn Maddox used his skills from psychiatric training to reunite a fractured church. Herb Freshwater used it to forge closer ties between free and institutionalized Christians.

[43] A. V. Campbell, "Love," in Hunter et al., DPCC.

Finally, clergymen understood therapy far more broadly than secular practitioners ever did. Souls had to be healed along with psyches. Relationships to God and Christian fellowship were as important as those to one's family and friends. Healing required an array of techniques beyond merely helping the troubled articulate and ventilate their feelings. Freshwater realized it was more useful to guide Larry Pruett through a close reading of the Bible than to talk about his fear of death. Peter Brill found praying with and reading Scripture to a sick and miserable girl the best nurture he could offer despite his therapeutic skills.

The longer ministers steeped in the psychological font, the more its sour waters mingled with – rather than ate away – the base of Christian tradition. This neutralized the liquid. The resulting psychospiritual brew *was* distinct from the traditional Protestant baptismal waters. But it was no longer the caustic acid that had depleted Morrison's faith. As we saw, a few traditions were transformed or even dissolved by their bath. But many were nourished anew. Some clergymen transformed utterly. But most emerged a bit more honest and humble, rather wiser and more confident, better men and stronger pastors.

PART TWO

THERAPY AS FELLOWSHIP IN ALCOHOLICS ANONYMOUS

Introduction

Unlike the pioneers of the Council for Clinical Training (CCT), the mid-century members of Alcoholics Anonymous (AA) had little admiration for psychiatrists and psychologists. Having little to offer people who were struggling against a chronic compulsion to drink, such professionals seemed more like quacks than wise scientists. The AA pioneers believed they had to create their own therapeutic knowledge and practice. Their distance from the assumptions of the behavioral sciences left them free to revive nineteenth-century traditions of lay healing that blended spiritual and psychotherapeutic goals.

Chapter 4 examines AA's development of democratic lay-led group therapy as the preeminent treatment for compulsive drinkers. Pioneers' own experiences and beliefs about community, cosmology, and human nature shaped their praxis. In the group's early years, it rejected therapeutic professionalism. Members decided that hierarchical and commercial relationships did not heal; only egalitarian friendships could. Furthermore, the multiplicity of group bonds were more efficacious than those between mere dyads (e.g., doctor–patient). An early friend to the movement declared that: "A. A. has proved that democracy is a therapy. The monarchic and aristocratic principles never cured alcoholism."[1]

Although AA therapy differed from that developed by psychologists and psychiatrists, it was quickly accepted as a legitimate therapy for chronic inebriation. In fact, in less than twenty years, it became the

[1] Edward Dowling, to Bill [Wilson], November 5, 1945, file 18.2, New York, NY GSOA.

preeminent therapy for compulsive drinking in the United States. Chapter 4, "Democracy Is a Therapy," examines this history. Since it differed from professional psychotherapy, however, AA engaged a half-century-long debate about its relationship to it. Precisely because the group was so democratic, it was very open to larger social and cultural trends. Therefore, most members in the decades after World War II emphasized the differences between (and superiority of) what they did and professional psychotherapy. But by the last third of the century, more and more members saw professional therapy and AA as two facets of a united process. Nevertheless, AA therapy lost neither its distinctive character nor its civic and cultural entailments.

Essential to AA's treatment was "the spiritual side" of the program. The vast majority of long-term AA members came to believe that human nature was multifaceted, containing within it a spiritual aspect. Therapy that denied or sidelined this fact was bound to fail. Furthermore, it was foolish. This spiritual element enabled people to connect to a strong benevolent force that could be tapped. Since most drinkers were religiously alienated, long-term members coached recruits through an ecumenical spiritual education. Chapter 5 describes this process. Most members – whatever their backgrounds – increased their religious practice and moved at least a few steps closer to faith over the course of their participation in AA. In some sense, then, they "Came to Believe," which serves as a title both for the chapter and a collection of spiritual testimonies that the organization published to encourage others.

AA enshrined community, self-improvement, and God-seeking at the heart of its therapy. In so doing, it created a formidable civil social institution through which, over the course of some sixty years, millions upon millions of Americans have passed. In becoming the paradigmatic treatment to deal with compulsive behaviors, it forged a greater arena for acknowledging spiritual concerns and for the unique values of community within the heart of clinical psychology itself. And as an important agent in the spread of a therapeutic ethos in postwar American society, it spread a vision of self and society, humanity and deity well-suited to the cultural needs of its democracy.

4

Democracy Is a Therapy

The situation that New York businessman and habitual drunkard Bill Wilson faced one Saturday afternoon in 1935 was a relatively new one in his drinking career. He found himself standing in a hotel lobby staring pathetically at a lively, patron-filled bar. The sounds of intoxicated hilarity sorely enticed him as he desperately tried to master an almost overwhelming urge to buy a drink. He had a half year of sobriety under his belt, but none of his other bouts of dryness had ever lasted very long during his two decades of destructive drinking. Thus, he was in for a struggle – one he had never won before. To make matters worse, he was in Akron, OH, far from friends and home. He was there pursuing a business opportunity in the hopes of salvaging his shattered financial and professional life.

A man in Wilson's shoes had few places to turn in 1935. In the first half of the twentieth century, a variety of institutions housed alcoholics – psychiatric asylums, hospitals, sanitaria, inebriate farms and colonies, skid row missions, and prisons – but few did more than help a drunk dry out temporarily. No one seemed to know how to keep someone like Wilson on the wagon for good.[2] Wilson himself had done numerous stints in hospitals, to no avail. After each release, he had returned to drinking sooner or later. Physically impeding access to alcohol via confinement or geographical isolation was the alcoholic's main hope. A treatment that restored the sufferer to health in society had not been discovered.

Wilson knew the odds were against him, and he was desperate. On a pay phone, warily eyeing the lobby bar, he dialed a random number from

[2] McCarthy, "Early Alcoholism Treatment"; White, *Slaying the Dragon*.

84 *American Protestantism in the Age of Psychology*

a list of local clergy. He hoped to find a member of the Oxford Group, a Protestant revival movement he had involved himself with in New York in his bid to stay straight. The Oxford Group had a side interest in reforming drunkards. He was looking for another boozehound like himself, one he might try saving and thereby talk himself out of his own urge. One call led to another, and before long he found himself deep in conversation with Dr. Robert Smith, an Akron proctologist and habitual inebriate, who had himself joined the Oxford Groupers in his own futile bid to lay off the liquor. Smith soon invited Wilson to move in with his family. Deeply impressed that the New Yorker had not had a drink since December 1934, Smith hoped that Wilson might help him achieve such a feat himself. By the end of the spring, he had. The two men spent the summer living, talking, and praying together in a mutual commitment to helping one another stay dry. Their vision transcended their friendship, however, for they both saw in it a seed of an idea for how others, too, might kick the alcohol habit.[3]

Creation of a Psychospiritual Therapy for Alcoholism

Wilson and Smith's efforts to nurture other drinkers sprouted in a few years time into a society of dozens of reformed drunkards led by Wilson in New York City and Smith in Akron. Four years later, this sapling of a movement had grown to some one hundred former drinkers and began to ramify and fructify. Wilson drafted a book based on their experiences. It was in many ways a group effort. Everyone helped edit it, and they decided to publish it themselves. *Alcoholics Anonymous* traced the history, rationale, and program of the group, and it included an appendix thick with their testimonies. From the point of view of a social and cultural history, AA emerged as a social movement by the end of the year the book was published – 1939. By that point, the group had completely separated itself from its early ties to the Oxford Group, of which it had initially been part. It had issued a book-length statement of principles and mission, settling on the title as its own name. And it had birthed a new independent group, in Cleveland, which got off and running without supervision from either Wilson or Smith.[4]

---

[3] For the early history of AA, see *Alcoholics Anonymous Comes of Age*; *Dr. Bob and the Good Oldtimers*; and *"Pass It On": Bill Wilson and How the AA Message Spread*.

[4] *Alcoholics Anonymous Comes of Age*, 21; *Dr. Bob and the Good Oldtimers*, 164–5, 76; *"Pass It On,"* 144–206.

Democracy Is a Therapy

AA enjoyed accelerating growth over the next decade. Hospitals and clinics in New York and Ohio invited members to talk to alcoholic patients or referred patients to AA. To get the word out and help groups to stay in touch, a half-dozen members began to publish a small magazine, *The Grapevine*, in 1944. That same year, AA finally grew big enough to attract the attention of the national print media. An article in the *Saturday Evening Post* flooded the movement with new members and requests for help. Within a *week* of hitting the newsstands, the article spawned new groups. In the years after World War II, these groups spun off more groups, and readers of *Alcoholics Anonymous* formed groups on their own. Even Hollywood took note: It began frequently to feature AA as the solution in the genre of "alcoholic" movies that emerged after World War II.[5]

The program was, as its adherents liked to emphasize, simple. The basic structures that were developed in the early years remained in place throughout the rest of the century. *Alcoholics Anonymous* – fondly known as the Big Book because it had been printed on the heaviest paper stock available – was the core text. Although the testimonies were replaced with more up-to-date ones in each of the subsequent three editions, its main text was left intact. It laid out a path of twelve steps that it claimed members had followed and that almost any alcoholic could follow to reach a lifelong contented sobriety. The number twelve was intentionally religiously resonant without being specifically symbolic. Wilson described becoming convinced – as he revised for incorporation into *Alcoholics Anonymous* the six steps that the initial fellowship had been using in the mid-1930s – that there should be a dozen, equal to the number of apostles.[6] These steps encouraged alcoholics to admit that they could not return themselves to sanity and to turn to God for help. They declare the need to inventory, confess, and make restitution for their past wrongs. And the steps commit AA members to lives of spiritual growth, moral honesty and self-improvement, and service to other alcoholics.

Members encountered the steps constantly. They learned them from the "Big Book," AA-produced and oriented literature, informal discussion with other members, and AA meetings. They were also reissued with explanatory essays in the 1952 publication of the *Twelve Steps and Twelve Traditions*, known as the "*12 & 12*." The twelve legacies included traditions about AA organization and customs, such as the confidentiality

[5] Room, "Alcoholism and Alcoholics Anonymous in U.S. Films."
[6] *Alcoholics Anonymous Comes of Age*, 161.

86   *American Protestantism in the Age of Psychology*

with which members treated what one another said in meetings and the anonymity they maintained when representing themselves as members of the organization in public. Passages from both *Alcoholics Anonymous* and the *12 & 12* were read aloud at many meetings.

The syntax of the steps reflected the democratic nature of the entire enterprise. They were phrased not as commands, but rather as simple descriptive statements reflecting the grassroots experience of the hundred original AA members who had discovered a path out of their self-destruction. This grammar was highly deliberate. Wilson, Smith, and the other contributors believed that alcoholics as a group were temperamentally rebellious and individualistic. They would resist anything that smacked of authority or authoritarianism. Inevitably, members began to debate about whether they had to take every step, or whether they had to take them in chronological order. Nevertheless, devoted members who modified the steps did so cautiously because, while they were free to do as they pleased, they knew the experience of countless others to be probably a more trustworthy guide than themselves.

The freedom of the program underscores the fact that AA was fundamentally a democratic, voluntary civic association. It did not partake of any of the other far more coercive institutions to which alcoholics were subject, especially from the 1930s through the 1960s. It did not isolate or institutionalize the alcoholic; it did not speak down to him or her from the peak of expertise; it incarcerated no one.[7] Drinkers' participation in the fellowship was based solely on their willing identification as members.

Although a few geographically isolated individuals had to pursue the program alone, the vast majority affiliated with a group of other alcoholics devoted to the program. These groups met regularly, usually at least once a week, for an hour or two to talk about how to obtain and maintain sobriety through the program. Members reached out to potential recruits, mentored (or "sponsored") newcomers, and forged mutually supportive networks outside of official meetings. Such extracurricular contacts were very important: An informal social event after an official weekly gathering was referred to as the "meeting after the meeting." Calling other members between meetings when one needed extra support was referred to as "dime therapy" (the cost of a call from a pay phone) or "telephone therapy."[8]

---

[7] For a history of pre-AA treatments of chronic inebriation, see McCarthy, "Early Alcoholism Treatment"; White, *Slaying the Dragon*.

[8] Madsen, *The American Alcoholic*.

A number of different types of meeting formats developed in the decades after the war. Some admitted nonalcoholics (often family members), whereas others were open only to drinkers. Some focused on the steps or the traditions; some were devoted to sharing testimonials from members; others were organized around a invited speaker; and others focused on beginners.

Although few if any detailed descriptions of meetings from the mid-century remain, an ardent critic of AA who penned a composite description of a relatively recent meeting captures something of what many meetings were probably like. The settings in church basements or school auditoriums were often banal and homely. Caffeine and nicotine addictions (benign compared to alcohol) were amply indulged:

[Walk into] a large, dingy room reeking of stale tobacco smoke....

The meeting's secretary and the evening's speaker are already seated at the table, smoking cigarettes and slurping coffee.... Perhaps half the [40] chairs are taken when the meeting starts.

Many meeting introductions worked to set newcomers at ease. They stressed AA's friendly ecumenism and openness, its spirituality, and its autonomy and democratic ethos:

Precisely on the hour the secretary raps his gavel, introduces himself, and asks two pre-selected members to read the AA Preamble[9] and the Serenity Prayer ["God grant us the serenity to accept the things we cannot change, courage to change the things we can, and wisdom to know the difference"]. Then... everyone in the room introduces himself or herself and is greeted by the crowd.... The secretary then asks any newcomers with less than 30 days sobriety to introduce themselves.... One hand timidly goes up in the back row and... its owner introduces himself as 'Tom'; everyone else loudly echoes, "Hi Tom," and applauds....

One key to keeping people involved in the program was to encourage their sense of hope through identification with others who had been

---

[9] Currently the Preamble reads: "Alcoholics Anonymous is a fellowship of men and women who share their experience, strength and hope with each other that they may solve their common problem and help others to recover from alcoholism. The only requirement for membership is a desire to stop drinking. There are no dues or fees for AA membership; we are self-supporting through our own contributions. AA is not allied with any sect, denomination, politics, organization or institution; does not wish to engage in any controversy; neither endorses nor opposes any causes. Our primary purpose is to stay sober and help other alcoholics to achieve sobriety." For the Preamble and its history, see GSO, "The AA Preamble: Some Basic Information," available at www.aa.org.

88   *American Protestantism in the Age of Psychology*

successful on it. Speakers were therefore sometimes invited to tell their stories:

> The speaker rises... and launches into a history of his alcoholism, describing at length and with apparent relish some of his more lurid drinking episodes... [and] the degradation, humiliation, and hopelessness he felt when he finally realized what alcohol had done to him.... [He] recounts how finally, in desperation, he hesitatingly walked into an AA meeting despite fears about "the God stuff."... He lights another cigarette and continues, saying that once he overcame his doubts, began to work the Steps, and found his "Higher Power," his life has been transformed....

Because leadership and hierarchy were relatively weak, and openness to troubled drinkers was a cardinal principle, members exercised only informal authority over one another. A great deal of tolerance (grudging or gracious) for each other was required:

> [Then] the secretary throws the meeting open to questions and discussion. A hand goes up in the front row and a nearly incoherent but boastful drunkalogue [a recitation of drunken escapades] ensues for ten minutes.... The next member to speak, who has been chafing at the bit during the drunkalogue, takes off on a tangent and describes how by working one of the Steps he overcame his frustration after a car accident. One or two others take off on different tangents....

The meeting concludes with an effort to remind members, through slogans and gestures, of the group's solidarity and support. Group prayer reminds them that AA is a fellowship and of the support they can find in a "Higher Power." Most are drawn in by the attempt to forge spiritual connections, but a substantial minority (probably a mix of relative newcomers and a couple longer-term committed atheists) remains aloof:

> The secretary announces the fact [that its time to end the meeting] and everyone rises, joins hands, and most say the Lord's Prayer.[10] About a quarter, looking pained or disgusted, remain mute. After a moment of silence everyone chants, "Keep coming back. It works!"... About half of those present leave immediately, while... the rest stand around... chatting, two of them paying special attention to the newcomer....[11]

---

[10] The prayer is drawn from the New Testament. Although different Christian denominations use different translations and slightly different texts, one basic recitation of the prayer runs: Our Father who art in heaven, hallowed be thy Name. Thy kingdom come. Thy will be done, on earth as it is in heaven. Give us this day our daily bread. And forgive us our trespasses, as we forgive those who trespass against us. And lead us not into temptation, but deliver us from evil. For yours is the kingdom, and the power, and the glory, forever. Amen.

[11] Bufe, *Alcoholics Anonymous*, 13–15.

Although meetings varied over time and by type, they shared common structures from the beginning of AA's history. Each group was entirely independent. Anyone could start one. No charter, permission, or money was needed. Copies of some AA literature and a place to gather were sufficient. At each meeting, members dropped loose change or dollars into a collection plate to cover the cost of nonalcoholic beverages and the nominal rents some groups paid. AA members liked to joke that all one needed to start a new group was a coffee pot and a resentment. The democratic, grassroots nature of the movement, combined with low start-up costs, nurtured a productive factiousness. Groups could split over many disagreements, such as personality differences, interpretation of the steps, or fights over whether smoking should be permitted during meetings.

These myriad autonomous groups proliferated across the nation and together constituted the AA fellowship. American membership exploded during its first decade – from about 3,500 to almost 112,000 between 1941 and 1951. Interest then stagnated and even declined during the 1950s to a low of about 92,000 around mid-decade, but then exploded again in the beginning in the 1960s. In the early 1960s, AA in the United States regained its membership strength of the early 1950s, and by 1971 claimed some 181,500 members. Over the next decade, this membership increased by 250 percent and more than doubled itself again in the 1980s. Finally, growth cooled as membership numbers again stagnated in the 1990s.[12] It should be noted that the decentralized, democratic nature of AA meant that these figures significantly underestimated membership and participation. Members and groups did not have to register with anyone. Furthermore, anyone who said they were a member – usually someone who attended some meetings or otherwise participated in the program – was one. One highly rigorous study found that about *three* times the number of people AA claimed as members had attended meetings out of concern for their own drinking, and *twice that* number had gone out of concern for a family member or friend.[13]

Having skyrocketed in size over some fifteen years, by 1955 Wilson believed AA had outgrown its initial structures and spearheaded a new organizational form that remains in place today. All AA groups were still independent. Financially and institutionally they were no more beholden

---

[12] "AA Membership Estimates for the United States Based on Figures Listed in AA Directories," 1941–2000, GSOA, photocopy in author's files.

[13] Room and Greenfield, "Alcoholics Anonymous."

90 American Protestantism in the Age of Psychology

to anyone on earth than they ever had been. As they sometimes said, their only authority was God in Heaven. However, those who chose to could establish and support regional intergroup offices that listed affiliated groups, answered inquiries, and published recruitment and educational materials. Groups were also asked to help support a General Service Office (GSO) in New York, which functioned as an international intergroup office and held annual conventions, to which groups could elect delegates. Delegates approved literature for national distribution and voted for the board that sat at the head of the GSO. The GSO drafted new editions of *Alcoholics Anonymous* and worked closely with *The Grapevine*, which remained nominally independent. At the dawn of the twenty-first century, the majority of groups chose to support all this work.[14]

The middle of the 1950s marked not only what AA would refer to, when reflecting on its new structure, as its "coming of age" but also its ascendance as the most common way Americans tried to cope with problem drinking. When Wilson and Smith first met, two years after the repeal of Prohibition, the vast majority of Americans believed such men simply lacked sufficient virtue or willpower. Twenty years later, however, most Americans had rejected the analysis, believing instead that alcoholism was a disease.[15]

This transformation reflected the concerted efforts of a handful of educators and interest groups involved in research and public education about the causes and solutions of problem drinking. By the mid-1950s, they presented alcoholism as a singular and predictable disease whose recovery required lifelong abstinence and affiliation with AA. Thus, while AA was not the only treatment for alcoholism developed in the mid-twentieth century, it was and remained for decades the preeminent one.[16]

---

[14] *A. A. Fact File* (New York: General Service Office of Alcoholics Anonymous, n.d.), at www.aa.org.

[15] Petigny, "The Permissive Turn," 70–6; White, *Slaying the Dragon*, 178–98, 288.

[16] For example, a mid-1950s survey of 200 psychiatrists revealed that most referred alcoholics to AA instead of treating them directly, in Max Hayman, "What Psychiatrists Think about Alcoholism," *California Medicine*, cited in "Psychiatry and Alcoholism," *The Grapevine* (March 1956): 26. Ten years later, a study of state hospitals showed that the vast majority used AA as their primary therapy instrument and as primary follow-up modality, see Robert Tournier "Alcoholics Anonymous as Treatment and as Ideology" *JSA* 40, no. 3 (March 1979): 230–9. Although Tournier was writing more than a decade after this study was conducted, his controversial article attacked AA for being so therapeutically hegemonic that it had stifled adequate research and testing of other, possibly better or complementary, alcoholism therapies. White, *Slaying the Dragon*, 288.

Democracy Is a Therapy 91

This greatly bolstered the power of AA to build civil society by creating a mass, democratic "group therapy" organization.

AA as Therapy

AA was, first and foremost, a program that promised drinkers whose lives had become "unmanageable" to sober them up for good. Its primary goal was transforming inebriates into teetotalers. AA shared with at least a century worth of such efforts the intuition that such a transformation required faith in God. AA believed the only path to sobriety for most drunkards was the way of spiritual transformation. This analysis differed, however, from earlier church and missionary-based efforts to save alcoholics. These earlier attempts were based on an understanding of alcoholism as caused by a sinful disharmony with God. Thus, religious conversion would inevitably entail sobriety as well as Heaven; drunkards could be rescued from sin, strong spirits, and Hell simultaneously.[17] Their goal was ultimately salvation.

The founders and early membership of AA, however, almost never spoke of eternal souls or of destructive drinking itself as a sin.[18] It was understood as an irrational compulsion, a kind of insanity, against which mere willpower inevitably failed. Such drinking was portrayed as a multifaceted phenomenon that was best understood as a "mental, physical, and spiritual disease." Therefore – while many members related chronic inebriety to alienation from God, and believed that, while drunk, they sometimes sinned grievously – their analysis of drinking was medicalized compared to that of the missionaries and evangelists. Their goal was a medical one: Permanent sobriety came first and last; spirituality was the means.

---

[17] Ibid., 71–8.

[18] In the AA written record, I have found no references of habitual drunkenness itself as a sin, and almost no concern at all about the eternal salvation of souls. The few and far between examples of such references are the exceptions that prove the point. For instance, one member in the 1939 edition of the Big Book makes reference in his testimony to praying to God to have mercy on his soul after a belligerent rant against God and believers. The author of a booklet of essays produced in Connecticut from the mid-1960s does conclude a meditation on the eleventh step by noting that "as long as I stay in His home and work in His fields, all that He has is eternally mine"; see *Twelve Steps and the Older Member* (Cheshire, CT: Older Member Press, 1964), pp. 59–60, in Box II Pamphlets Distributed by Other AA Groups, file "Connecticut," GSOA. The few references I found were invariably oblique and evinced no concern to convince anyone else of the importance of eternal salvation.

92   *American Protestantism in the Age of Psychology*

Furthermore, despite the strong spiritual elements of the program, and despite the fact that AA considered itself a fellowship, it had strategic reasons for presenting itself as therapy. Its main mission was to help problem drinkers, few of whom were primarily concerned with their spiritual state. It wanted to present itself to them in as neutral a manner possible. For the early decades of the fellowship, most newcomers were recruited directly by others already involved. As we later see, evidence suggests that when older members pursued recruits they downplayed the spiritual element. One reflection of this is that introductory brochures emphasize AA as a therapy over its spiritual aspects to appeal to potential recruits and avoid repelling them.[19] Indeed, compared to such canonical literature as *Alcoholics Anonymous* and the *12 & 12*, such materials were some of the most secular the group produced.

AA's emphasis on its own therapeutic validity reflected not only members' spiritual alienation, but also their relatively high levels of education. The movement attracted drinkers from all sorts of backgrounds, but many had (or had had in the past, before chronic alcoholism set in) middle-class educations, professions, and lifestyles.[20] The national leadership from the early years – like Wilson and Smith – emerged from the haute bourgeoisie or, like wealthy socialite and national alcoholism educator Marty Mann, even higher. This may well have remained the case throughout much of the century. The high intellectual level of early issues of *The Grapevine* and the emphasis in its apologetics that spiritual belief was not an insult to

---

[19] For at least the first two decades of AA, the most commonly distributed brochures by far were "This is AA" and "AA – 44 Questions and Answers." A third, "Is AA For You?" was also massively distributed beginning with its publication in the late in 1950s. These hardly mentioned the spiritual side of the program. Beginning in 1962, AA began distributing a brochure to build relationships with clergy and encourage them to steer alcoholic parishioners in their direction. This carefully targeted brochure was not distributed to potential recruits. The GSOA houses a collection of locally produced brochures. These appear not to have been collected systematically but rather to have been donated by various individuals, and so the chance for sample bias is large. However, I have found these local brochures aimed at recruitment were – like the national ones – usually entirely or largely secular, particularly those produced in the Southern states, including Alabama, Arkansas, Georgia, and Kentucky. Introductory brochures published in California during the early years of the fellowship were more likely than most others to be religious. Possibly this is because a stronger religious climate in the Bible Belt meant that AA had to work harder to be distinguished from revival groups. See Box II Pamphlets Distributed by Other AA Groups, Box IIA Pamphlets Distributed by Other AA Groups, and Pamphlet Box 3, GSOA.

[20] Trice and Roman, "Predictors of Affiliation with Alcoholics Anonymous," 55; Ogborne and Glaser, "Characteristics of Affiliates of Alcoholics Anonymous"; Vaillant, *The Natural History of Alcoholism*, 205.

the modern educated intelligence (discussed at length in the next chapter) suggest that members felt a sincere desire to be members of an intellectually serious and medically respectable program.

The strategic advantage of an emphasis on the therapeutic was reinforced by another major route by which newcomers could be brought in: referrals by doctors and clergy, the two sets of experts to whom alcoholics turned for help. Therefore, these professionals had to be persuaded to send clients and parishioners AA's way. AA had to persuade doctors, and especially mental health professionals, that its program constituted a bona fide therapy, and not mere quackery or a revival movement. Furthermore, although some Protestant clergy might have preferred evangelism to therapy, priests did not. In fact, AA's origins in the Oxford Group – which the Catholic Church proscribed for its laity – may have initially impeded its expansion to Catholic drinkers. AA went out of its way to reassure Catholic authorities that it was in no way attempting to lure parishioners from the church.

Thus, the therapeutic interpretation of the AA program eclipsed all others and became hegemonic. This was in spite of the fact that a handful of Americans always insisted on seeing it as something else. During the 1940s and early 1950s outsiders hoped AA was a revival group or would advocate the reinstatement of Prohibition.[21] Beginning in the 1960s, some began to accuse it of being a cult or religious movement.[22] Such accusations culminated thirty years later in the legal declaration of AA as a form of religion.[23]

But in the second half of the twentieth century, American citizens were for many reasons by and large convinced that AA was a therapy. This was partly because in the years after World War II they became overwhelmingly convinced problem drinking was a medical illness.[24] It was also because AA was presented to them as a means of recovery through the mass media.[25] And ultimately it fit an old tradition of lay-led psychospiritual therapies to which many Americans were receptive.

---

[21] *Final Report: Second General Service Conference of AA* (New York: Alcoholics Anonymous, 1952), 13, GSOA.

[22] Cain, "Alcoholics Anonymous: Cult or Cure?"; Cain, "Alcoholics Can be Cured"; Alexander and Rollins, "Alcoholics Anonymous: The Unseen Cult"; Bufe, *Alcoholics Anonymous*.

[23] Spencer, "Religious Freedom Not an Issue"; Spencer, "Prison Condition a Religious Violation; Pines, "Judge Again Backs Atheist"; Hamblett, "AA at State-Funded Facility."

[24] Cited in Petigny, "The Permissive Turn," 70, 76.

[25] Room, "Alcoholism and Alcoholics Anonymous in US Films," 368; Alexander, "Alcoholics Anonymous: Freed Slaves of Drink."

94   *American Protestantism in the Age of Psychology*

AA was very much part of the renewal of this older tradition. The fact that AA was lay-led, group-oriented, and spiritual made it a therapy that seemed eminently sensible.

Although lay people readily accepted AA as therapy for alcoholism, its acceptance by the medical community is, in retrospect, a bit surprising. AA therapy represented a break from the practice of psychoanalysis and the psychiatric treatment of alcoholism in the first half of the century. AA relied on lay people in place of professionals; it emphasized the group over the dyadic relationship between physician–patient; and it hewed more closely to a behaviorist than a dynamic paradigm, recommending in place of a wide-ranging exploration of psyche and family a narrow self-inventory of personal failings. Although medical professionals took a while to agree that alcoholism was a compulsive disorder itself and not a symptom of another mental illness, AA soon embraced – for strategic and heuristic reasons more than anything – the idea of alcoholism as a disease. Nevertheless, doctors did come to accept AA because they realized that, by and large, their own expertise had failed to help their alcoholic patients. Thus, AA did not represent – as we saw in Chapter 1, the Emmanuel Clinic *had* – a direct threat to their bailiwick. An increasing number of doctors were willing to acknowledge that there might be something about the structure of psychotherapy and psychiatry that was not well-suited to treating alcoholism.[26] By the last third of the twentieth century this had become the common wisdom, and mental health professionals often refused to treat alcoholics until after they had gotten control of their drinking through rehabilitation or AA.

Because most understood or came to understand AA as therapy, they then soon wondered what its therapeutic mechanism was. Three main aspects of the program contended for that designation: the group solidarity, the spiritual submission (Steps Two and Three), and the moral inventory and confession (Steps Four and Five). Both AA members and medical researchers agreed that these three components were the engines of the program's success. Researchers debated about which of these components were the most important and how they related to each other. AA members tended to focus most on the group solidarity and mutual support that every newcomer could benefit from immediately, and on the spiritual submission and superhuman assistance that they believed members increasingly relied on to stay sober.

[26] Harry Tiebout may have been one of the first to argue this; see "Why Psychiatrists Fail with Alcoholics," *The Grapevine* (September 1956): 5–10.

Democracy Is a Therapy 95

Some writers focused on the spiritual aspect of the program. This was Steps Two and Three, which assert that alcoholics in search of sobriety realized that only a "Power greater than ourselves could restore us to sanity" and a consequent decision to "turn our will and our lives over to the care of God as we understood Him." As we will see in the next chapter, most members believed this to be a crucial part of the program and therefore worked very hard to "improve their conscious contact with God" (Step Eleven) and help others to do so, too. They believed such a divine resource could help them precisely because it existed outside the member or fellowship. Doctors, however, explained it entirely as a transformation within the self, an internal event with psychiatric consequences.

The psychiatric benefits of a conversion experience were highlighted in the first two medical articles about AA ever published. AA made its medical debut in a 1939 article entitled, "A New Approach to Psychotherapy in Chronic Alcoholism" published by Dr. W. D. Silkworth, a neurologist who worked at the drying-out hospital in Manhattan where Bill was repeatedly confined in 1933 and 1934.[27] Silkworth attributed AA's success to its sense of group solidarity, which fostered alcoholics' receptivity to "a simple religious proposal" that, in turn, helped trigger a "profound mental and emotional change."[28] A few years later Connecticut psychiatrist Harry Tiebout presented and then published an analysis of the "Therapeutic Mechanism of Alcoholics Anonymous." He refined Silkworth by arguing the therapeutic benefit of group solidarity was a secondary support to the central mechanism: the act of an alcoholic turning his or her will over to God, which deflated the "grandiosity" and "narcissism" that were the underlying causes of destructive drinking. Sincere and devoted religious belief, therefore, had the psychiatric effect of "changing the character structure that made [alcoholics] vulnerable to compulsive drinking in the first place."[29] Tiebout developed his argument in a series of articles he published in the 1940s and 1950s.

Others emphasized not the character transforming potential of Steps Two and Three, but rather the cathartic one of Steps Four and Five. Step Four was to make a "searching and fearless moral inventory" of oneself, and Step Five was to confess the results of such an inventory "to God, to ourselves, and to another human being."[30] Wilson himself presented

---

[27] Kurtz, *Not-God*, 15.
[28] Silkworth, "A New Approach to Psychotherapy."
[29] Tiebout, "Therapeutic Mechanism of Alcoholics Anonymous," 311.
[30] *Twelve Steps and Twelve Traditions.*

96   *American Protestantism in the Age of Psychology*

the phenomenon that took place when a member undertook Steps Four and Five as translatable into either a psychological or religious system: [while] "the doctor recommends a 'mental catharsis,' our pastor speaks of 'confession' or 'frank discussion.'"[31] *The Grapevine* editors agreed that taking personal inventory was profoundly relieving: "Psychiatrists call this a catharsis: a cleansing or purging of the mind. In any event, once the person analyzes himself honestly, he feels tremendously improved."[32] Some members agreed. One who had had, and benefited from psychoanalysis, wrote that a "psychiatrist, for example, will speak of a 'mental catharsis' being necessary in his treatment.... AA Steps Four, Five, and Eight which are in effect accomplishing the same ends without all the psychiatric fanfare called catharsis."[33] A few researchers even came to argue by the mid-1980s that the cumulative evidence pointed to the moral self-inventory and confession as constituting alone the entire therapeutic mechanism for AA.[34]

Everyone agreed, however, on the importance of group solidarity and mutual support. In this, AA represented and helped expand a larger trend. In the 1950s there was a revolution within the field of mental health that overwhelmingly refocused psychic exploration, diagnosis, and healing from the individual to the group.[35] The connection between AA and this larger trend was made explicit by a Chicago doctor in 1945, who noted that, "Group psychotherapy is all the vogue today. Its rationale and efficacy was never better demonstrated than in this mass movement known as Alcoholics Anonymous."[36] A year later, a doctor at the prestigious Mayo Clinic even claimed that "A.A. has taught psychiatry many things about the value of group therapy and has given suggestions for the treatment of other psychiatric disorders."[37]

---

[31] William G. Wilson, to Paul Deland, August 4, 1943, Box 18, file 4.1, pp. 34–6, GSOA.

[32] "On the 4th Step," [editorial], *The Grapevine* (February 1947): 2.

[33] P. K. in Peublo, CA, "One Cheer for Psychiatry," *The Grapevine* (December 1953): 18–20.

[34] D. R. Tuite and J. Wuiten, "16PF research into addiction: Meta-analysis and extension." *International Journal of the Addictions* 21 (1986): 303, cited in Emrick et al., "Alcoholics Anonymous," 56.

[35] Sheehy, "The Triumph of Group Therapeutics."

[36] D. B. Rotman, "Alcoholism: A Social Disease," *Journal of the American Medical Association* (March 10, 1945), excerpted in "Chicago Doctor Cites A.A.," *The Grapevine* (June 1945): 6. See also the assertion that "Alcoholics Anonymous is a widespread inexpensive form of group psychology" in H. D. Kruse, ed., *Problem Drinking and Alcoholism* (Albany: Advisory Committee on Alcoholism, New York State Interdepartmental Health Resources Board, 1957), p. 36, in Pamphlet Box 4, file "Miscellaneous Pamphlets," GSOA.

[37] W. C. H., "Rochester, Minn. Group Marks First Anniversary," *The Grapevine* (September 1946): 10.

Democracy Is a Therapy

97

Publications aimed at potential recruits and new members frequently spoke of AA as a form of, or including, group therapy.[38] One such brochure distributed in Chicago and Illinois explained that AA offered the newcomer "the heartening meat and drink of group support, group counsel, group therapy."[39] A pamphlet distributed in Ohio asserted that AA had demonstrated the efficacy of "spiritual group therapy" in curing alcoholism and character defects.[40] And throughout the mid- to late-twentieth century, members who wrote in to *The Grapevine* frequently referred to "group therapy" as one central component of AA. One alcoholic, for example, who had been institutionalized in a psychiatric hospital on the eve of World War II after having had a nervous breakdown, insisted on the inferiority of the occupational therapy he had received there to "AA group therapy."[41]

The emphasis on group therapy over other potential forms of therapy in AA served to harness its various aspects – psychology, religion, self, community, and Higher Power. As we saw with the psychiatrically trained chaplains and will see in the case of The Salvation Army, group therapy accommodates and links psychological and religious relationships by overlapping with the praxis of Christian fellowship. An intense, mutually concerned community of people who acknowledge a connection to the Divine while struggling to help each member improve him or herself can be easily understand either as a group therapy and as a fellowship. The ease with which the one phenomenon could be seen through either lens is made explicit in the appositive syntax employed by a member in

---

[38] For example, "Twelve Steps to Recovery" (Baton Rouge, LA: Mid-City Group, n.d. [1970–1976]), pp. 18–19, in Box IIA "Pamphlets Distributed by Other AA Groups," file "Louisiana," GSOA; "AA Is a Tender Trap" (Chicago: Alcoholics Anonymous [Chicago], n.d. [circa 1955–1975]) in Box IIA "Pamphlets Distributed by Other AA Groups," file "Illinois," GSOA; "The Secret Behind AA Recoveries" (n.p.: n.p., n.d.) in Box II "Pamphlets Distributed by Other AA Groups," file "Colorado," GSOA.

[39] "The Long Haul" (n.p. [Chicago]: Alcoholics Anonymous, n.d.) in Box IIA "Pamphlets Distributed by Other AA Groups," file "Illinois," GSOA. Also see, "Twelve Steps to Recovery" (Baton Rouge, LA: Mid-City Group, n.d. [1970–1976]), pp. 18–19, in Box IIA "Pamphlets Distributed by Other AA Groups," file "Louisiana," GSOA; "AA Is a Tender Trap" (Chicago: Alcoholics Anonymous [Chicago], n.d. [circa 1955–1975]) in Box IIA "Pamphlets Distributed by Other AA Groups," file "Illinois," GSOA.

[40] Jack A. H., "Surrender," *AA Central Bulletin* (Cleveland), Fall 1951, (reprint) in Pamphlet Box 3, file "Ohio," GSOA.

[41] A. T. in New York City, "The Joys of Occupational Therapy," *The Grapevine* (April 1955): 15–17. Also see, Leo C. in Portland, OR, "On the Subject of Dependence," *The Grapevine* (January 1948): 5; Doc. in Portland, OR, "Having One Primary Purpose," *The Grapevine* (November 1950): 20; Bill Mc. in Monterey, CA, "My Help Was Always There," *The Grapevine* (June 1953): 38–9; B. E. in Memphis, TN, "An Agnostic's Higher Power," *The Grapevine* (April 1973): 13–14.

98   *American Protestantism in the Age of Psychology*

Florida who described the process of AA's "psychological and spiritual program" in a 1947 letter to *The Grapevine*. R. W. wrote that after an alcoholic admitted the need for help, there "follows the group therapy, the fellowship of other alcoholics."[42]

AA Therapy and Psychotherapy

Despite the fact that people generally understood AA as a behavioral treatment for problem drinking, they disagreed about its relationship to professional psychotherapy. They disagreed about whether AA was better or worse than professional psychotherapy and psychiatry, whether the two were similar or different, and whether one was a prerequisite for or obviated by the other. The presentation of the relationship between the two approaches depended partly on who (AA, doctors) was speaking to whom (potential recruits, long-term members, larger public). But it was mostly a matter of sincere intellectual discovery and debate among members and mental health workers. Proponents of the various positions clashed repeatedly in a variety of forums, from meetings to counseling sessions, from private correspondence to lay and professional journals. As we will see, these conflicts were associated with alternate visions of cosmology and human nature.

Mental health professionals made their peace more quickly than membership did. By the 1960s, professionals began to figure out how to synergize AA and what they had to offer, generally through "Twelve-Step Facilitation Therapy" in rehabilitation centers – essentially a mix of psychotherapy and the first five steps. By the 1980s, they decided that AA, or at least sobriety (which often meant AA), was a prerequisite for viable psychotherapy.

Many alcoholics in the early years and decades of AA were skeptical or even hostile to the claims of psychiatry. Grace O., for example, a contributor to the fledgling *Grapevine*, thought sincere Christianity obviated psychotherapy: "Jesus Christ was the world's greatest psychologist. To understand the true meaning of the Sermon on the Mount is to find the answer to any personality conflict."[43] Although not many members put the matter in such explicitly Scriptural and religious terms, others echoed this repudiation of the validity and utility of psychological, especially

---

[42] R. W. in Daytona Beach, FL, "Modern Miracle," *The Grapevine* (April 1947): 9.
[43] Grace O., "The Pleasures of Reading" [book review of Ernest Ligon, *The Psychology of Christian Personality*], *The Grapevine* (June 1945): 3.

Democracy Is a Therapy   99

psychoanalytic, theory. At the group's First International Convention in 1950, AA cofounder Dr. Bob Smith, dying of cancer, delivered his final address. He declared to the thousands of rapt listeners, "Let's not louse up [the simplicity of our program] with Freudian complexes.... Our Twelve Steps, when simmered down to the last, resolve themselves into the words 'love' and 'service.'"[44] This dichotomy between a useful simplicity and destructive Freudian complexity was long remembered and repeated by AA members[45] and echoes distantly in the oft-repeated slogan, "Keep it simple." The influence of such a message still resonated later in the decade when John P. L., an old-time member and alcoholic trustee of AA, explained that his group's approach differed from the psychiatric one in that the important factor for a member was that he was alcoholic, not whether he was one "because he was locked in the closet as a small boy or because he was breast fed or wasn't breast fed."[46]

Such antipsychiatry was hardly confined to elites. It resonated with the membership at large. Beginning in the 1950s, some members wrote to *The Grapevine* to complain about the fact that when they had wanted to seek professional psychological counsel, fellow members had discouraged them from it.[47] This antipsychiatric tendency was sufficiently pronounced that Bill Wilson – who felt it harmed the well-being of individual members as well as AA as a whole – felt the need to refute it in an editorial. He urged greater cooperation between AA and psychiatry.[48] AA's headquarters, the GSO, believed the message still needed to be articulated in the mid-1960s, when it began issuing a pamphlet asserting the utility of psychotherapy for alcoholics.[49]

By the 1970s and 1980s, when cultural and social trends outside the organization converged with these internal efforts, the bias appeared to have subsided. This was due in part to the significant increase in members who had consulted psychological counselors of some sort before joining

---

[44] *Dr. Bob and the Good Oldtimers*, 337–8.

[45] Ibid., 337.

[46] John P. L., "Through the Looking Glass," *The Grapevine* (August 1957): 9–14.

[47] Bob in Salem, OR, "I Needed Psychiatry," *The Grapevine* (September 1953): 31–3; P. K. in Peublo, CA, "One Cheer for Psychiatry," *The Grapevine* (December 1953): 18–20; "Psychiatry and the Big Book," *The Grapevine* (June 1958): 47–9; RJC in Philadelphia, PA, "I Told It to Doc," *The Grapevine* (July 1958): 38–40; J. S. in Syosset, NY, "In Defense of Psychiatrists," *The Grapevine* (September 1970): 39.

[48] Bill W., "Let's Be Friendly with Our Friends... the Psychiatrists," *The Grapevine* (July 1957): 2–4.

[49] T. E. Dancey, "Are Psychiatry and AA Incompatible?" *The Grapevine* (October 1968): 28–33.

100   *American Protestantism in the Age of Psychology*

AA, or who had even been referred into the fellowship by them.[50] Beginning in the early to mid-1970s the issue of members entering AA because of a referral made in counseling and rehab emerged. Analysts of a 1977 AA survey of itself noted, that whereas there was still only a minority who had so entered, their ranks were growing sharply, from about 14–15 percent in the early 1970s to 24 percent. It continued to climb, therefore proportionately shrinking the main way that members had been recruited traditionally: by other members.[51] By 1989, only a generous third had traveled this old-time route, while the second largest group (30%) had been urged to attend while in or after rehab and another ten percent had been referred by counselors.[52] It is therefore hardly surprising that one mental health professional noted in 1979 that he rarely encountered the type of "old-timer" who had rejected psychiatric concepts out of hand.[53]

This antipsychiatric bias had multiple etiologies.[54] Some members had had disappointing or even harmful experiences with mental health

---

[50] Table 6, "Summary of a Survey of 11,355 Members of Alcoholics Anonymous (June-July 1968)," in file "Survey 1968," in box "AA Surveys, 1958–1978, Box I," GSOA; Table 6, "Defining the Universe," in file "Survey 1968–1971," in box "AA Surveys, 1958–1978, Box I," GSOA; "1974 Survey By Regions," in file "Survey 1974 II," in box "AA Surveys, 1958–1978, Box I," GSOA; John Norris, "Analysis of the 1977 Survey of the Membership of A.A.," paper presented to the 32nd International Congress on Alcoholism and Drug Dependence, Warsaw, Poland, September 3, 1978, Figure 8, in file "Survey 1977," in box "AA Surveys, 1958–1978, Box I," GSOA; "Analysis of the 1980 Survey of the Membership of A.A.," p. 2, in file "Survey-1980," in box "AA Surveys, 1980- , Box II," GSOA; "Analysis of the 1983, Survey of the Membership of AA," p. 5, in file "Survey-1983," in box "AA Surveys, 1980- , Box II," GSOA; [John Bragg], "Comments on A.A's Triennial Surveys," [1989], in file "John Bragg 1989 Survey Analysis," in box "AA Surveys, 1980- , Box II," GSOA.

[51] John Norris, "Analysis of the 1977 Survey of the Membership of A.A.," paper presented to the 32nd International Congress on Alcoholism and Drug Dependence, Warsaw, Poland, September 3, 1978, p. 5, in file "Survey 1977," in box "AA Surveys, 1958–1978, Box I," GSOA.

[52] [John Bragg], "Comments on A.A's Triennial Surveys," [1989], in file "John Bragg 1989 Survey Analysis," in box "AA Surveys, 1980- , Box II," GSOA.

[53] Robert A. Moore, [Response to Tournier], *JSA* 40, no. 3 (March 1979): 328.

[54] The predominance of men in the AA fellowship contributed to this bias. Women increased as a proportion of members until by 1980s they constituted roughly one-third – a proportion they have never surpassed. Men were probably less likely to seek professional mental health help. "The AA Member" (New York: Alcoholics Anonymous World Services, Inc., 1978), GSOA; John Norris, "Analysis of the 1977 Survey of the Membership of A.A.," paper presented to the 32nd International Congress on Alcoholism and Drug Dependence, Warsaw, Poland, September 3, 1978, p. 3, in file "Survey 1977," in box "AA Surveys, 1958–1978, Box I," GSOA; "Analysis of the 1980 Survey of the Membership of A.A.," p. 2, in file "Survey-1980," in box "AA Surveys, 1980- , Box II," GSOA; "Analysis of the 1983, Survey of the Membership of AA," p. 3, in file "Survey-1983," in box "AA Surveys, 1980- , Box II," GSOA; [John Bragg], "Comments on A.A's Triennial Surveys," [1989], in file "John Bragg 1989 Survey Analysis," in box "AA Surveys,

Democracy Is a Therapy

professionals.[55] The special bitterness reserved for the field of mental health may have arisen in part from the hopes it raised and then dashed among those seeking relief from their compulsion. When researchers surveyed over 1,000 members in New York City in the early to mid-1960s, they asked respondents about the helpfulness of professionals they had consulted before AA. Less than one-fifth of those who consulted psychiatrists found them helpful, whereas well over one-third found them utterly useless and a handful (6%) even felt the consultations had hurt them. Those who saw clergy or others kinds of doctors were less likely to have found them useful, but were also less likely to have found their advice worthless or pernicious.[56]

The antipsychiatric bias, however, also emerged from a sense that the psychological lens was cracked and could not provide a morally and metaphysically clear vision of humanity and the world. One member who in the early 1950s tried to incorporate into his AA testimonies the psychoanalytic ideas he had learned while institutionalized in a mental hospital reported that others in the meeting dismissed his ideas as "psychiatric baloney."[57] Others had a subtler analysis. The psychotherapeutic emphasis on explaining behavior could appear as an attempt to explain it away, thereby excusing it. In 1946, R. F. S. in New Jersey accused some alcoholics of looking for ways to excuse themselves through "the worship of false psychological gods."[58] This note was also sounded again when the editors of The Grapevine ran a piece by a psychologist who cautioned readers against the use of psychology as a blind for excusing unethical behavior.[59]

1980- , Box II," GSOA; AA World Services, "Alcoholics Anonymous 1998 Membership Survey" (New York: 1999), GSOA; AA World Services, "Alcoholics Anonymous 1992 Membership Survey" (New York: 1993), GSOA; AA World Services, "Alcoholics Anonymous 1996 Membership Survey" (New York: 1997), GSOA; AA World Services, "Alcoholics Anonymous Membership Survey" (New York: 1987), GSOA. Joint Commission on Mental Illness and Health, *Action for Mental Health*, 102.

[55] J. S. in Syosset, NY, "In Defense of Psychiatrists," *The Grapevine* (September 1970): 39; Whitley, "Life with Alcoholics Anonymous," 1977, 838; R. W. in Van Nuys, CA, "Is My Gratitude Grateful," *The Grapevine* (June 1963): 2–4; "Where Psychiatry Fits In," *The Grapevine* (November 1956): 13–14; A. T. in New York City, "The Joys of Occupational Therapy," *The Grapevine* (April 1955): 15–17.

[56] Bailey and Leach, *Alcoholics Anonymous*, 22–4.

[57] P. K. in Peublo, CA, "One Cheer for Psychiatry," *The Grapevine* (December 1953): 18–20.

[58] R. F. S. in Montclair, NJ, "When Alcoholics Come of Age," *The Grapevine* (March 1946): 4–5.

[59] O. Hobart Mowrer, "How 'White' Is a 'White Lie?'" *The Grapevine* (September 1962): 10–15.

102   *American Protestantism in the Age of Psychology*

But on an even deeper level, psychiatry's intense focus on the self and its disassociation from God was often seen as a profound, and even dangerous, misrepresentation. R. F. S. worried not that alcoholics abused psychological ideas, but that they would be led astray by them from the knowledge that Man was "'a nothing surrounded by God, indigent of God, capable of God and filled with God, if he so desires.'"[60] A few years later, Leo from Oregon echoed this sense of human emptiness and divine fullness when he worried that some people in AA were relying too much on each other to keep themselves sober: "God channels his power to us through other human beings, . . . until we recognize and acknowledge Him as the only true source of the help we receive in AA we shall always be more likely to 'resume drinking.'"[61] R. W. from California seconded this concern when he testified that his interest in psychology had eroded his AA participation and mental health, ultimately landing him in psychiatric care. A clergy member pointed out that the psychology books he was reading and professional psychotherapy he was participating in all put the self at the center. What he really needed, and had already committed to, was putting God at the center. Following this advice returned him to health.[62]

Despite the persistent antipsychiatric bias throughout some of the fellowship during the first half of its history, other fellows were downright enthusiastic about the ideas and techniques psychology had to offer. They constituted a minority early on, but one that grew in the final third of the twentieth century. Bill Wilson himself developed AA out of psychiatric discussions he had with his own doctors and those of other alcoholic friends. In a hoary and frequently retold bit of AA history, the very idea that the proper psychotherapy for alcoholism was a spiritual one was introduced to Wilson by his friend Ebby T., who had learned it from an alcoholic patient of Carl Jung. Jung had prescribed as the only effective therapy a "vital" religious experience that could utterly transform him. The patient had found this in the Oxford Group and had passed on what he had learned to Ebby. Ebby had shared it with a deeply impressed Wilson, who himself stopped drinking a month later after an extraordinary religious revelation while he was hospitalized in December 1934.[63] This was why Wilson immediately thereafter had joined the Oxford Group.

[60] R. F. S. in Montclair, NJ, "When Alcoholics Come of Age," *The Grapevine* (March 1946): 4–5.
[61] Leo C. in Portland, OR, "On the Subject of Dependence," *The Grapevine* (January 1948): 5.
[62] R. W. in Van Nuys, CA, "Is My Gratitude Grateful," *The Grapevine* (June 1963): 2–4.
[63] *"Pass It On,"* 111–15.

Democracy Is a Therapy   103

The interest in psychiatry was not confined to AA leadership. From the 1940s there was evidence of people in the fellowship who read and talked frequently in meetings about psychology. They invoked psychological labels and lenses, and identified themselves with psychopathological diagnoses. The earliest printed evidence dates from 1948, when *The Grapevine* published a cartoon entitled, "There's One in Every Group." Under a drawing of a pontificating man the caption read: "The ham psychiatrist – this type just discovered psychiatry six months ago and he thinks that it has done him so much good that he can't wait to pass the word around. He has wrecked many a 12-step enterprise with his constant misquotes of Strecker, Jellinek, Freud, AA, etc."[64] Such types had surely not disappeared a decade later when a member mused, "There's a kind of an inverse pride I sometimes detect in alcoholics who seize on all popular references in psychiatric literature and really take great pride in being thought a screwball."[65] A woman who complained in the early 1970s about the compulsion of some AA members to analyze each other while commenting on others' testimonials was obviously fighting an uphill battle.[66]

As is evident from these examples, AA itself furthered members' psychological educations despite the antipsychiatric attitudes of some members. Debates over psychology themselves must have served to draw attention to it. Meetings and the strong informal networks of members created social forums where people familiarized each other and inevitably discussed – and defended and attacked – psychotherapeutic ideas about human behavior. AA publicized and popularized psychiatric findings about alcoholics in its magazine[67] and brochures.[68] Most of this publicity

---

[64] "There's One in Every Group," *The Grapevine* (February 1948): 2. Strecker and Jellinek were prominent psychiatric alcoholism researchers.

[65] John P. L., "Through the Looking Glass," *The Grapevine* (August 1957): 9–14.

[66] D. B. in Gulfport, FL, "Amateur Analysts," *The Grapevine* (February 1973): 21–2.

[67] For example, Howard T. Blane, "The Alcoholic Personality," *The Grapevine* (June 1963): 32–7; O. Hobart Mowrer, "How 'White' Is a 'White Lie?'" *The Grapevine* (September 1962): 10–15; "Psychiatry and Medical Views," *The Grapevine* (February 1956): 7–8; Harry Tiebout, "What Takes Place in an Alcoholic's 'Spiritual Awakening'?" *The Grapevine* (April 1954): 30–5; Harry Tiebout, "The Pink Cloud and After," *The Grapevine* (September 1955): 2–7; Harry Tiebout, "Why Psychiatrists Fail with Alcoholics," *The Grapevine* (September 1956): 5–10; J. L., "Reality Therapy," *The Grapevine* (April 1968): 45; E. Deering, "Doctor, Why Can't I Stop Drinking?" *The Grapevine* (August 1970): 7–10.

[68] For example, "Twelve Steps to Recovery" (Baton Rouge, LA: Mid-City Group, n.d. [1970–1976]), p. 17, in Box IIA "Pamphlets Distributed by Other AA Groups," file "Louisiana," GSOA.

104   *American Protestantism in the Age of Psychology*

and education was measured in its tone and claims, despite a smaller contingent who appeared to have embraced psychiatry unabashedly. Those who protested to *The Grapevine*, or who argued the point with other members, usually believed that psychology could enhance the program by providing insights and guidance it could not. They were often simply trying to promote greater acceptance for the idea that some members needed more than AA to achieve sobriety and a little peace of mind.

Members' and outside commentators' understandings of the relationship between AA, on the one hand, and professional psychotherapy and psychiatry on the other, were shaped by what they saw AA itself as comprising. The most common position throughout its history, codified in its canonical literature and reiterated by its membership, was that it was a convergence of religious and psychological insights and techniques. This was often what was meant when members asserted that it was a spiritual program. This convergence was unusually therapeutically efficacious because it took into account with especial perspicacity – greater than either religion or psychology alone – the nature of cosmological reality, and the self, and the relationship between the two. Religion on its own could be too institutionalized to help the alcoholic, who could "go through the motions" without sincere belief or commitment. In that sense, religion did not emphasize the self enough. Organized religions were not therapeutically effective. They did not adequately guide people, at least broken people like alcoholics, *how* to transform themselves, how to put God at the center of themselves. AA members understood being spiritual as feeling and applying personally the truth of religion. As one member from Daytona Beach, Florida, succinctly expressed it in the late 1940s, "Ministers and priests are turning to psychology because faith is an act of the mind.... Faith must be built on our psychological experience."[69]

Thus, AA strove to create for members a "psychological experience" through its program that would generate both faith and recovery. Throughout the middle decades of the century doctors and members alike insisted frequently that AA was a successful therapy because it was good (or even superior!) psychotherapy, that is, because its program embodied an understanding of human nature similar to that of psychology. A. W. from New Jersey reported back in the late 1940s to other members after consulting some psychology textbooks that they demonstrated that AA's

[69] R. W. in Daytona Beach, FL, "Modern Miracle," *The Grapevine* (April 1947): 9.

methods were in perfect accord with the procedures of psychotherapy.[70] Wilson himself argued that professionals should study the AA model to improve group therapy, which did not sufficiently exploit the principle of identification or harness the therapeutic efficacy of spirituality.[71] Some doctors were inclined to agree with the high estimates of AA's harnessing or surpassing of the best psychological principles.[72] In particular, Wilson's psychiatrist, Harry Tiebout, who became an AA trustee, argued that AA was a superior form of psychotherapy for two reasons. First, it helped precipitate a religious conversion, which was the surest way to deflate alcoholic narcissism; and, second, AA embodied a form of behavior modification therapy that was more effective for alcoholism than etiological models that sought to ameliorate symptoms through exposing root causes.[73]

Although psychology on its own well explained some aspects of human nature and helped people make sense of themselves, it did not seem to recognize the inherently spiritual aspect of humankind. In 1946, a member explained that

human nature is tripartite, consisting of a spirit as well as of a mind and body.... The alcoholic has indeed a "split" personality, not so much ... in the strict schizophrenetic [sic] sense as in the fact that his body has got itself separated from his soul.... The function of AA is to help to reunite the elements that comprise man so that he may become an integrated individual.[74]

This was a view that many in AA shared throughout the middle decades of the twentieth century and, to a lesser extent, in its final decades. The program itself canonized it when it dubbed alcoholism an illness of the mind, body, and spirit. Personal testimony about the dire effects of a lopsided understanding of human nature was offered in the 1970s by a graduate student in counseling who had become morbidly introspective and highly psychoanalytical in a futile attempt to heal herself. Instead, it drove her to drink all the more. Finally, she finally joined AA, which

---

[70] A. W. in Jersey City, NJ, "An AA Discovers Psychiatric Therapy," *The Grapevine* (June 1948): 9.

[71] Bill Wilson, to Cleo Dieruf, January 14, 1954, Box 30, file 18.2, p. 104, GSOA.

[72] "Psychiatry and Medical Views," *The Grapevine* (February 1956): 7–8; Maxwell, "Alcoholics Anonymous," 1962, 582; Bailey and Leach, *Alcoholics Anonymous*, 4.

[73] Harry Tiebout, "What Takes Place in an Alcoholic's 'Spiritual Awakening'?" *The Grapevine* (April 1954): 30–5; Harry Tiebout, "The Pink Cloud and After," *The Grapevine* (September 1955): 2–7; Harry Tiebout, "Why Psychiatrists Fail with Alcoholics," *The Grapevine* (September 1956): 5–10.

[74] R. F. S. in Montclair, NJ, "When Alcoholics Come of Age," *The Grapevine* (March 1946): 4–5.

106 *American Protestantism in the Age of Psychology*

"has relieved me from that terrible bondage of self-analysis. Introspection is no longer an obsession, and God has replaced psychology as my higher power.... Now that I am no longer morbidly preoccupied with self, I can reach out to others and contribute to life."[75] Professional psychotherapy was therefore frequently indicted for overemphasizing the efficacy of the self, leaving little room for God's power. As a writer after World War II noted: "Psychologists are turning to religion because just knowing about ourselves is not enough. A man needs the added dynamic of faith in a power outside of himself on which he can rely."[76]

Indeed, many members, along with the canonical literature, argued that *every* aspect of the program had spiritual ramifications. This included those steps that were seen as the heart of the "good psychology" of the AA program: confession and restitution, as well as group participation and service. For example, during AA's first decade, in some areas, members taught new recruits about the AA program through a series of four introductory meetings. The one devoted to what was called the "spiritual phase" of the program comprised not only turning one's will over to God and seeking continual contact with the divine (Steps Two, Three, and Eleven), but also enumerating, readying oneself to transcend, and praying to be freed from one's "short-comings" (Steps Four, Six, and Seven).[77] One long-time member explained that his contact with God was impeded for years because he had been unwilling to have his short-comings removed and to pray that God do so (Steps Six and Seven).[78] Others focused instead on admitting one's wrongs: "Many an AA, once agnostic or atheistic, tells us that it was during... Step Five that he actually felt the presence of God. And even those who had faith already often become conscious of God as they never were before."[79] Yet others saw the most "sociological" step – recruitment – as fundamentally spiritual

---

[75] C. R. in Greenbelt, MD, "Keeping It Simple," *The Grapevine* (March 1979): 22–3.

[76] R. W. in Daytona Beach, FL, "Modern Miracle," *The Grapevine* (April 1947): 9.

[77] Penciled notes on both copies of a brochure in the GSOA suggest this may have been the practice in Washington, DC, Washington State, and Mississippi; Alcoholics Anonymous, "Alcoholics Anonymous: An Interpretation of Our Twelve Steps" (Washington, DC: The Paragon Creative Printers, 1944) in Box II "Pamphlets Distributed by Other AA Groups," file "District of Columbia," GSOA; Alcoholics Anonymous, "Alcoholics Anonymous: An Interpretation of Our Twelve Steps" (Washington, DC: The Paragon Creative Printers, n.d.) in Box II "Pamphlets Distributed by Other AA Groups," file "District of Columbia," GSOA.

[78] "Willingness" (Chicago: Alcoholics Anonymous [Chicago], n.d. [circa 1955–1975]) in Box IIA "Pamphlets Distributed by Other AA Groups," file "Illinois," GSOA.

[79] Alcoholics Anonymous, *12 & 12*, 62.

Democracy Is a Therapy

because of the altruism and fellowship it nurtured. J. F., for example, testified in 1961 that antireligious antipathy led him to put off turning his will over to God while working the rest of the program. Eventually, he was sent to "Twelfth step" a man on probation who had been praying that someone would come to help him sober up. J. F. was so startled and moved to discover that he himself was the answer to the probationer's prayers that he began to believe in a Higher Power.[80] Thus most AA members would have agreed that their therapy had an advantage over professional psychotherapy: It healed both psyche and soul.

AA, the Self, and Civil Society in the Last Decades of the Twentieth Century

While ideas of a "tripartite" (physical–spiritual–psychological) human nature never evaporated, the final third of the twentieth century witnessed a shift in the relationship between AA, professional psychotherapy, and ideas about the self. The distinctions between AA and professional psychotherapy blurred. One of the earliest bits of evidence pointing to a change came in a 1968 letter of protest addressed to Wilson. Some members in Seattle were upset about the introduction of new therapeutic techniques in AA groups in their area, specifically psychodrama, in which a member was supposed to "act out in pantomime the various things in his past which he or she feels caused his compulsive drinking." The letter writers held that "such 'therapy' has an odor of invasion of privacy, and...no man or woman should have to put up with this sort of nonsense."[81]

Although none of the occasional ad hoc borrowings from the proliferation of exotic therapies in the late 1960s and 1970s appeared to have become institutionalized in AA, more and more members appeared to adopt psychotherapeutic diagnoses and concepts when talking in meetings during the 1970s and especially the 1980s. Some members and doctors began advocating, protesting, or observing greater borrowings from

---

[80] J. F. in Mt. Rainier, MD, "No Place to Go but Up," *The Grapevine* (February 1961): 22–3. The sex of the author is unclear from the story itself, but given the mid-century predominance of men in the fellowship and concerns about "13th Stepping" (having an affair within the fellowship) it seems unlikely that a woman would have been sent to recruit a man on probation. I therefore refer to the anonymous author as "he."

[81] Austin M. and Violette M., to Bill [Wilson], Seattle, WA, June 18, 1968, Box 18, file 4.1, p. 288, GSOA.

108 American Protestantism in the Age of Psychology

professional psychotherapy in AA meetings.[82] This was inevitable given that more and more were entering AA from therapy and rehabilitation at institutions that included professional (and sometimes lay) therapy. Some new members must have begun their recovery careers with one or more short stints in a rehab that blended psychotherapy and AA, moved on after their release to regular AA meetings, and then sought out professional counseling on the side after they felt their sobriety was stable and that they were capable of dealing with other problems that had surfaced since they had stopped drinking. The tendency of some members with these experiences to blend psychotherapy and the steps in AA meetings, just as they had in rehab, bothered other members. For example, David A. in Michigan protested,

When we AAs speak more about our counselors and our therapists than our AA sponsors, when we describe our aftercare and family sessions as frequently as we speak about practicing the Steps and working with others, how does it appear to the newcomer? Are we saying to newcomers that they need a therapist and a counselor and aftercare and family sessions?.... When we talk about our counselors and therapists at an AA meeting, we imply that they are a necessary and vital part of our program. Some members openly state that their real help doesn't come from AA anymore, but from these people.

The writer thought this eroded newcomers' confidence that all they need for recovery was AA.[83]

Part of the attack on AA's view of the self was expressed outside rather than inside the fellowship. Because AA had become *the* therapy for alcohol abuse – and the model for a range of efforts to help Americans cope with substance addiction and other compulsive habits – it inevitably invited challenge. The fact that the paramount therapy for alcoholism and a host of other ills were at their core a "spiritual group therapy," appalled some devoted atheists and individualists. Attacks began with the *Harpers Magazine* publication of "Alcoholics Anonymous: Cult or Cure" in the early 1960s.[84] The 1970s and 1980s witnessed a rise of feminist and

---

[82] "A Psychiatrist Looks at AA," *The Grapevine* (February 1972): 45–6; Andrew Malcolm, "Advice to AA from a Psychiatrist," *San Francisco Secretary's News Letter*, October 1976, Local Newsletter Files, San Francisco, CA, GSOA; *Final Report: Twenty-Sixth General Service Conference of AA* (New York: Alcoholics Anonymous, 1976), 23, GSOA; D. B. in Gulfport, FL, "Amateur Analysts," *The Grapevine* (February 1973): 21–2.

[83] David A. in Ann Arbor, MI, "Talking the Talk," *The Grapevine* (August 1989): 8–9; Charlie Bishop, Jr. and Bill Pittman, *To Be Continued.... The Alcoholics Anonymous World Bibliography 1935–1994* (Wheeling, WV: The Bishop of Books, 1994), xi.

[84] Cain, "Alcoholics Anonymous."

secular sobriety groups that criticized the spirituality and self-deprecation in AA. Women for Sobriety was started in 1976 on the presumption that alcoholic women needed more, not less, self-esteem. The belief that it was absurd to claim that an alcoholic was inadequate without God spurred the formation of Secular Organizations for Sobriety, which began in 1985. Rational Recovery, formed a year later, went further and argued that alcoholics needed neither God nor others; the ties of fellowship were portrayed as merely a new form of addiction.

But these alternatives attracted relatively few. Most inebriates sought out AA. In fact, AA was flooded with new members in the 1970s and 1980s. But some of them wanted AA therapy to be closer to professional psychotherapy than it had been. The interrelated phenomena of a flood of new members and a conflation of AA with generalized group therapy sparked protest and unease among older members. In 1989 *The Grapevine* devoted an issue to what the editors clearly saw as a problem. People who were *not* alcoholics were entering AA in search of the kind of psychopathological identity and therapeutic fellowship AA offered. A man in Connecticut was bewildered and irritated by such "therapy junkies."[85] Gary in Michigan reported that the proportion of such junkies had gotten so high in a group he had started for gay alcoholics that he had stopped attending its meetings because it was no longer a useful way for him to talk about how to stay sober. Young newcomers had indeed often abused alcohol and drugs and been through substance abuse treatment, but because their primary problems were other than compulsive drinking, they turned meetings into "free-for-all group therapy."[86] Gary argued that this simply was not AA, which he described as a spiritual program aimed at helping alcoholics stay sober. Although there is not a lot of evidence that many AA groups were thus transformed, the conflation of AA with professional psychotherapy was pervasive enough to become a source of conflict.[87]

Some of this tension may have been relieved by a rapid proliferation of other groups that allowed nonalcoholics to participate in a twelve-step program without resorting to alcoholic identities that ill-suited them. On the other hand, the proliferation of twelve-step groups so altered the therapeutic universe in which AA found itself, that the new climate may have

[85] Dolph L. in Westport, CT, "Guys Like Louie and Me," *The Grapevine* (August 1989): 2–3.
[86] Gary R. in Fenton, MI, "Recovery Feels Better than 'Feeling Good,'" *The Grapevine* (August 1989): 4–5.
[87] Makela et al., *Alcoholics Anonymous*, 204.

made it more difficult to preserve AA's distinctive therapy. California, especially the parts centered around San Francisco and Los Angeles, may have been especially vulnerable to such a development. It was more spiritually experimental and more psychotherapeutically involved than most regions of the country. In the 1960s and 1970s, these areas attracted numerous Americans interested in experimenting with drugs and self-exploration. Sociologist Robin Room, after reviewing the development of a national market for recovery periodicals and books and studying letters to the editor in a San Francisco Bay area recovery magazine, argued that twelve-step group members had begun "to think of themselves as members of a more general phenomenon, a '12-step movement' or 'recovery movement' transcending AA or the other particular groups that they attended."[88]

Room worried about this because these twelve-step epigones differed in important ways from AA. They borrowed more heavily from psychodynamic views of human nature. Some were less spiritual. And they tended to emphasize self-care and self-sufficiency over AA's traditional emphasis on fellowship and the God-given inadequacy of the self. Nevertheless, Hazel Cameron Johnson, a doctoral student in sociology who observed hundreds of AA groups and meetings in the 1980s, primarily in southern California, where the recovery movement appeared to be strongest, did not find many meetings transformed into therapy groups. The feedback and exchange that is the key mechanism of group therapy, for example, was not permitted in AA meetings. However, she did note that groups differed from one another in many ways, and groups comprising primarily members with long-term sobriety spent little time talking about alcoholism per se. Rather they focused on how to cope with life stresses and difficulties without resorting to drink or drugs.[89]

Conclusion

In contradiction to those who see AA's self-help as merely another manifestation of the socially atomizing spread of a therapeutic ethos in American culture, it has helped build civil society since the eve of World War II. It achieved this by forging a convergence between the concept and practices of group therapy and fellowship. In AA, the therapy *was* the

---

[88] Room, "Healing Ourselves and Our Planet."
[89] Johnson, "Alcoholics Anonymous."

Democracy Is a Therapy   111

fellowship, and vice versa. Ultimately, AA enhanced civic life by democratizing the understanding of what constituted therapy and who was capable of delivering it, that is, by expanding the therapeutic ethos in American culture.

Of course any therapy that helped inebriates control their drinking and paved the way for them to reconnect with others could be said to have bolstered civil society. But AA's psychospiritual format allowed it do more than other therapies could. This psychospiritual synthesis enabled it to do more for civil society than merely treat alcoholics, that is, than merely assuage a potent source of alienation in Americans with substance abuse problems. The group itself *constituted* a formidable civil social institution – totally independent, self-supporting, grassroots, and democratic. AA's ecumenical openness to all problem drinkers allowed diverse Americans to come together and discover common bonds and a common identity inside the organization. Once there members formed friendships and social networks, contracted romances and marriages, found employment and business deals, and forged special fraternal religious and spiritual groups. Hundreds of thousands – millions over its seventy-year history – of citizens learned lessons in the importance and power of community; and of democratic participation, leadership, and responsibility.

5

Came to Believe

Alcoholics Anonymous did not believe that group therapy alone could turn drunkards into teetotalers. Nor could any other merely psychological or sociological phenomena exploited by Alcoholics Anonymous (AA). Most longer term members believed that the miraculous transformation of an inebriate into a sober citizen required "awakening" him to a "Higher Power" (which they usually called God). Thus joining AA entailed enrolling in a spiritual education, whether or not a newcomer wanted it. To help newer members overcome their spiritual reluctance, the fellowship developed a large body of oral and written advice encouraging emotional and intellectual openness to a Higher Power, prayer and meditation, the reading of religious and spiritual literature, the attendance of spiritual retreats and meetings, and apologetics. Most members did increase their level of faith and their participation in spiritual activities. Some, especially during mid-century, even returned or turned anew to conventional religious involvement.

The Tocquevillian Paradox

Whereas the "group therapy" of the program was immediately available to anyone who attended meetings, the "spiritual side" generally took more time and was more difficult to attain. In addition, the newcomers did not necessarily want to attain it. AA members usually went in spite of, not because of, AA's spirituality. As Bob A. in 1949 testified, "The new man has no religious creed. Nor does he want one," and may, in fact, be discouraged by the "religious fervor he may encounter."[1] The fact that drinkers joined AA to improve their own lives, and then discovered that the only way to do this was to improve that of others and to "find God" had been presaged by Tocqueville a century earlier.[2] In *Democracy in America*, he had argued that churches were only able to ennoble citizens after seducing them through earthly boons. Thoughtful Americans and AA members understood this idea. Indeed, the Reverend Sam Shoemaker, an early and long-time friend to AA, preached in *The Grapevine* in 1955, "Most of us. . . . come selfishly" to God, but then must mature by ceasing to try "to get God to do what [we] want," and beginning to ask God to show us "what He wants."[3]

This irony created a dilemma: Recruits, who were often intimidated or repulsed by the spirituality, had to be reconciled to the fact that they could not "work the program" without it. Public submission to God was, in fact, a prerequisite for membership in the earliest days, and quite possibly for many years after that in some of the more orthodox groups, especially those in and around Ohio and those that looked to "Akron style AA" as a model. During the mid- to late 1930s, when what would become Alcoholics Anonymous was still a subgroup within the Ohio Oxford Group, help-seekers were expected to get on their knees in front of the other members of the group and announce their submission to Jesus.

Many worried, however, that this evangelical style public submission threatened to deter newcomers, thus interfering with their central mission of "helping the alcoholic who still suffers."[4] Although there are almost no statistics from mid-century regarding the number of drinkers who abandoned AA after attending a meeting, by the late 1960s and 1970s, it appears that 50 percent of members left within the first four months.[5] Admittedly, this figure may well have been higher than in other periods due to the massive influx into the fellowship, including those mandated there by courts and prisons.[6] Nevertheless, it is clear that many drinkers

---

[1] Bob A., "Don't Tell Me – Ask Me!" *The Grapevine* (May 1949): 14–15.

[2] Tocqueville, *Democracy in America*, Vol. 2, Book I: chap. 5, Book II: chap. 9.

[3] Samuel Shoemaker, "The Spiritual Angle of AA," *The Grapevine* (October 1955): 2–7.

[4] This concern is frequently sounded throughout AA's historical record. It appears not only in their own literature, but also in meetings as recorded by members and as observed by researchers. See, for example, Whitley, "Life with Alcoholics Anonymous," 836; Wilcox, *Alcoholic Thinking*, 79.

[5] Emrick, "Alcoholics Anonymous," 59.

[6] For the increasing reliance of the state on AA in the 1980s and 1990s, see Nolan, *Therapeutic State*.

114   *American Protestantism in the Age of Psychology*

were scarcely ready to tackle sobriety yet, much less a public display of abject humility before God. Some, of course, would reject it even after achieving sobriety. Thus, members were often advised – by one another as well as official AA publications – to "soft pedal" the "spiritual aspect" of the program when reaching out to potential recruits. Introductory brochures tended to be the least religious literature AA produced. Although one can find the occasional religiously oriented brochure, most downplayed spirituality and emphasized the low threshold and versatility of the concept of the Higher Power. One brochure, for example, distributed in Ohio and California during World War II, reassured readers that

a lack of belief or faith in an orthodox religion is not a barrier to recovery through this program. All that is necessary is a sincere desire for and a willingness to accept aid from any power greater than one's self. If all that the pathological drunk can do is to say, with *honesty*, in his heart: "Supreme Something, I am done for without more-than-human help," that is enough for Alcoholics Anonymous to work on.[7]

The widespread use of the term Higher Power in *Alcoholics Anonymous* and other AA literature was itself partly an acknowledgment of how skittish newcomers might be when confronted with a program that seemed religious (and partly a compromise with those who remained skittish). As Bill Wilson explained to a priest who pointed out some Catholics' discomfort with the term,

the average Catholic or other denominationally trained person objects far less to the use of the term "Higher Power" than the average agnostic does to the word "God." As two out of three people coming into the A.A. Groups are agnostic or indifferent it was felt we must make this much concession to their sensibilities. In fact four years experience with them fairly shouted that we had to – so great was their abhorrence of God![8]

This pattern appears to have characterized on-the-ground recruitment as well. When dealing with a "baby" or "pigeon," a member might postpone an introduction of the Higher Power, focusing instead on telling his or her own drinking story and offering AA as a solution, without sketching what that solution consisted of in detail. Mid-century members

---

[7] "AA" [This Booklet....] (Los Angeles: Los Angeles Group of Alcoholics Anonymous, n.d. [probably 1942–1944]) in Box II "Pamphlets Distributed by Other AA Groups," file "California," GSOA.

[8] William G. Wilson, to Father [Marcus] O'Brien, March 10, 1943, Box 18, file 4.1, p. 42, GSOA.

Came to Believe 115

wrote into *The Grapevine* to caution other members about the importance of not coming off as a "crusader" or "Bible Thumper."[9] D. E. in Evanston, IL, testified to the efficacy of such an approach from his own experience: He was an agnostic when he was first introduced to AA and his sponsor "wisely" left the spiritual stuff for later, simply working with him on the first step and stressing the importance of the Big Book. Thus, he explained, he was able to enter AA without having to overcome the great resistance that he otherwise would have felt against religious folk. He recommended this tack for sponsors working with spiritually wary newcomers.[10]

However low the spiritual threshold was for entry – and in most groups, open hatred and revolt against God would not have barred entry – as soon as drinkers began affiliating with AA, they began their spiritual education. To assist younger members, the fellowship developed a large body of oral and written advice encouraging emotional and intellectual openness to a Higher Power, prayer and meditation, the reading of religious and spiritual literature, the attendance of spiritual retreats and meetings, and reasoning about God.

Shorter term members soaked up the advice around them, even when they could not or would not follow it immediately. "These people had something I lacked. And I wanted it!" recalled one member after her first AA meeting.[11] Many pored over the literature – most especially *Alcoholics Anonymous*, but also the *12 & 12*, *The Grapevine*, *Came to Believe*, and readings these books recommended, such as sections of the New Testament and William James's *Varieties of Religious Experience*. They turned to sponsors and older members privately and in meetings.

The Will to Believe

AA members sometimes told each other that they must have, as William James had said, the "will to believe." The importance of an integrated psychospiritual therapy was highlighted for AA members by a conviction

---

[9] Art S. in Vancouver, BC, [letter] *The Grapevine* (December 1949): 37; R.A.B. in Seattle, WA, "Me, A Crusader," *The Grapevine* (April 1957): 42–3.

[10] D. E. in Evanston, IL, "The Arena," *The Grapevine* (May 1950): 32–3. For other warnings against coming on too strong spiritually, see Elizabeth E. in Tulsa, OK, "'You're Welcome Here,'" *The Grapevine* (April 1988): 2–4. R.P.C. from Indianapolis, "Patience with the Spiritual Factor," *The Grapevine* (November 1946): 3, 5. C. C. in Bayside, NY, "Must We Throw Flying Lizards," *The Grapevine* (January 1949): 17–18. R.P.N. in Rochester, NY, "It's a Touchy Subject," *The Grapevine* (December 1968): 26–8.

[11] *Came to Believe . . .*, 25.

116   *American Protestantism in the Age of Psychology*

that certain emotions precluded faith, whereas others were prerequisites for it. Alcoholics were cautioned against intellectual and emotional postures that might make it difficult for them to work the steps, most especially the spiritual ones. Therefore, they were urged to cultivate emotions and outlooks conducive to belief, particularly humility, open-mindedness, and hope. Grandiosity, narrow-mindedness, and despair or cynicism were understood as common alcoholic traits that closed the mind and heart to awareness of the possibility of a supernatural order, of an extrasolipsistic source of intervening power. For example, R. S., who described his experience to *The Grapevine* in the early 1970s, had had great difficulty believing, which he attributed to being a veteran and former MENSA member (a society for people with high IQs). But it was clear to him in his desperation to stay sober and renew his life that those who had faith were better off for it. He sought out advice from older members. One pointed out that the "will to believe" was a prerequisite for faith. He finally achieved this, and after a year and a half in AA, he said he had begun turning his will and life over to the care of God as he understood him.[12]

The major AA literature, official and lay, was filled with admonitions about the importance of cultivating a psychology that would make possible intellectual, personal, and spiritual changes. Humility and an open mind went hand in hand. Resistance to AA's spiritual program should not be mistaken, as the alcoholic might be wont, for intellectual integrity, moral courage, or rationality. *Alcoholics Anonymous* and the *12 & 12* made the case that – given how low was the bar to entering the program, how impressive the visible results of others who had found salvation from inebriety through it, how open to each individual's own empirical experience and interpretation – reluctance to try it could only be due to "obstinacy, sensitiveness, and unreasoning prejudice."[13] Readers were reassured that the founding members "found that as soon as we were able to lay aside prejudice and express even a willingness to believe in a Power greater than ourselves, we commenced to get results."[14] Drinkers were warned against falling into the trap of denying God by pointing to the moral failings of religious people, which only served to artificially inflate their own egos and avoid looking at their own shortcomings.[15] A rather grandiose artist who shared his story in the first edition of the Big Book, explained his failure to find either sobriety or God until he became

[12] R. S. in Houston, TX, "The Will to Believe," *The Grapevine* (April 1972): 16–19.
[13] *12 & 12*; *Alcoholics Anonymous*, 60; Makela et al., *Alcoholics Anonymous*, 128–30.
[14] *Alcoholics Anonymous*, 58–9.
[15] *12 & 12*, 30.

Came to Believe 117

humble, upon which "an entire new world opened up for me." For the first time, he ceased to crave alcohol and began to recognize and repair his many personal and spiritual failings.[16] Thus, humility in all its forms – intellectual, moral, and personal – was necessary.

These messages were repeated not only in the official (and unofficial[17]) messages of the program, but they seemed to represent the actual personal experiences of many members through the fellowship's first half century.[18] The messages were therefore part of the personal advice given to new members. When the agnostic Teet C. in North Hollywood, CA, for example, asked older members how to find God, they told him to try seeking him sincerely and humbly, especially through prayer. They even recommended he try praying on his knees, since this position made it hard to be anything but humble.[19] Such humility did not always guarantee overwhelming effects, but it always facilitated change for the better. As R. C. in Alhambra, CA, noted in the early 1960s, as a youth he had rejected all forms of religion because he believed they were founded on ignorance, fear, and superstition. Priding himself on his atheism, he was initially appalled by the praying and talk about God in AA and so refused to participate in this part of the program. But eventually, as he became more humble, he began to join in, which had allowed him to stay in AA for eleven years, let go of his antireligious hostility, and open himself up to the possibility, if not the belief, in God.[20]

Those who entered with belief still found learning humility similarly transformative. One priest admitted that it was in AA that he realized he had thought he did not need God's help in much of his life work, such as leading his flock: "I used to think I was some kind of fountain or reservoir [for God]. All I was spouting forth was my own ego and selfishness."[21] Similarly, another member who, while drinking, had maintained that "there was a God of some sort," but did not think he needed him, found that it was not until he humbly called out to God for help, that he was freed from his craving.[22]

---

[16] "An Artist's Concept," in *Alcoholics Anonymous*, 384–5.

[17] For example, see *The Little Red Book*, 142; *Twenty-Four Hours a Day*, s.v. January 10.

[18] A large, international recent study of AA noted that by the mid-1990s, there was "a shift toward viewing aspects of pride (self-respect, self-confidence) as potentially virtuous" despite Bill Wilson's and the early fellowship's focus on it as the key vice through which the alcoholic falls. Makela et al., *Alcoholics Anonymous*, 128–30.

[19] Teet C. in North Hollywood, CA, "Finding a God of Our Understanding," *The Grapevine* (October 1975): 2–4.

[20] R. C. in Alhambra, CA, "From Atheist to Agnostic," *The Grapevine* (April 1961): 7–8.

[21] D. M. in Northbrook, IL, "Let Go and Let God," *The Grapevine* (April 1979): 7–9.

[22] "He took control" in *Came to Believe . . .* , 29–30.

118   *American Protestantism in the Age of Psychology*

In addition to striving to replace cynicism, prejudice, and grandiosity with an open-minded humility, newcomers were also encouraged to have hope. They were constantly reminded that the sober, sane people around them in the fellowship, many of whom had forged new lives of serenity, success, and joy for themselves, were once at least as miserable as they were. Change, renewal, and salvation was not only possible, but almost *guaranteed* for those who sincerely and diligently followed the program. In a much read and repeated chapter from the Big Book, readers are reassured that the only people who try AA seriously but fail are those unfortunate few who are "incapable of being honest with themselves."[23] New members found models of success in the program wherever they looked: at meetings, in informal socializing with sponsors and older members, in *The Grapevine*, and in the Big Book. The main text drafted by Bill Wilson of this classic never changed, but AA reissued it roughly every couple of decades to update the dozens of success autobiographies in which readers might identify, and therefore project themselves into the sober future of the writers. The rooms where meetings were often held were not themselves inspirational, often smoky and sometimes even dingy, but the walls were sometimes hung with encouraging slogans – such as, "Keep Coming Back!" or "It works!" – and these might be shouted in unison at the end of meetings, sometimes after members had physically symbolized their fellowship through standing or holding hands in a circle while reciting the Lord's Prayer.[24]

God Grant Me Serenity

Prayer was an important way of connecting to a Higher Power, or even to finding one. It was both promoted and demonstrated throughout AA. Most meetings in the United States began and ended with prayer.

---

[23] *Alcoholics Anonymous*, 70.

[24] Johnson, "Alcoholics Anonymous in the 1980s," 207. It is not entirely clear when and where the handholding custom began or how quickly it had spread. It may have started in the 1970s; it appeared to be common by the time Johnson was an observer in the 1980s. Also see *Final Report: Thirtieth General Service Conference of AA* (New York: Alcoholics Anonymous, 1980), 29, GSOA. References to group recitation of the Lord's Prayer dated back to the earliest years of the fellowship, probably because Oxford Group meetings in Akron ended with it; see *Dr. Bob and the Good Oldtimers*, 141, 48, 83, 261. References to standing in a circle while reciting it are also evident from the 1950s; see Fulton Oursler, "Charming Is the Word for Alcoholics" (Richmond, VA: Alcoholics Anonymous Richmond Group, n.d.) in Pamphlet Box 3, file "Virginia," GSOA; Bob T., "And the Dogs Quit Growling at Me" (Staunton, VA: Staunton Group of Alcoholics Anonymous, 1957) in Pamphlet Box 3, file "Virginia," GSOA.

Came to Believe 119

Sometimes these were spontaneous prayers designed for the occasion and setting, as is common among low-church Protestants.[25] Frequently, however, they were common ones.

The opening prayer was often what is known as the "Serenity Prayer": "God grant me the serenity to accept the things I cannot change, courage to change the things I can, and wisdom to know the difference." The petition's neo-orthodox tone well suited the outlook of AA, which emerged (without any direct connections) in the same period that the theological movement did. The prayer's brevity, eloquence, theological simplicity ("God grant"), and focus on the here-and-now resonated with AA members.

Beginning in the early 1940s, the AA office in New York City produced and distributed wallet-sized cards with this prayer inscribed on it. One woman, a "self-ordained atheist," received such a card at her first AA meeting and held on to it for "dear life" when the next day her husband entered a psychosis triggered by delirium tremens. He locked the two of them in the house for the better part of a week, while he raved and threatened her life. She attributed to the prayer, which she repeated like a mantra, her ability to get through the nightmare without a drink.[26] Few members sought out its modest encouragement in such dramatic or life-threatening situations, but the prayer became so popular that eventually it became a kind of unofficial AA motto and was reprinted in every language in which there is an AA fellowship.

Most, but not all meetings, concluded with a group recitation of the Lord's Prayer, often while standing in a circle holding hands.[27] This prayer probably worked well because it is so fundamental and simple; indeed Jesus taught it directly to his followers (Matthew 6:9–13). But it did not mention any doctrine of great theological specificity, such as eternal life. It also was a point of common ground for all Christians, allowing Protestants and Catholics to comfortably pray together. For the odd Jew and the frequent freethinker, the prayer offered no Christological referent. This practice apparently began early in the history of the

---

[25] For an example of such a prayer, see "Profanity Not Necessary," excerpted from the *Inter-Group News of Akron, Ohio*, in *The Brighter Side* (First Quarter, 1967) newsletter of Alcoholics Anonymous in Waterloo, IA, Newsletters, Box III, GSOA.

[26] "A Small White Card," *Came to Believe...*, 24–6.

[27] *Final Report: Twenty-Fifth General Service Conference of AA* (New York: Alcoholics Anonymous, 1975), 40, GSOA; *Final Report: Twenty-Sixth General Service Conference of AA* (New York: Alcoholics Anonymous, 1976), 25, GSOA; D. S. in Belmont, CA, "Call on the group conscience," *The Grapevine* (February 1975): 39–40.

120   *American Protestantism in the Age of Psychology*

fellowship and continued to be widely practiced throughout the rest of the century in the United States.[28] It was intentionally left out of *Alcoholics Anonymous*, probably because it seemed "too" religious.[29]

Clearly this simple and beautiful prayer appealed to a majority of AA members, for the radically decentralized nature of each group meant that each could have dispensed with it, and few appear to have done so. Although as committed atheists and non-Christians gained confidence within the fellowship in the last third of the century, more and more complaints that the prayer was too religiously specific emerged.[30] It is also from this era that *The Grapevine* began publishing some reflections on what this prayer meant to members. Don in the Bronx, who had enjoyed the much-coveted spectacular spiritual awakening but who had found that it had not been enough to keep him dry, discovered the prayer he learned in AA to be the real path to spiritual growth. He wrote,

I begin to know at last the Lord's Prayer, for I touch each word nightly, and feel the breath of AA blow through it. And I begin to know where the kingdom is – in the big table where I am renewed, in the friends I go out speaking with, in these basements in heaven where I feel daily the power of a handshake, the glory of a sober eye.[31]

Another member echoed this sense of the prayer as the heart of the AA program and as a kind of spiritual educator when she wrote,

The most important part of the prayer for me is the word that runs all the way through: "Our." I have heard people say they don't care what the words are, but they do care about the circle we form as we hold hands to pray, and they do feel the unity of the program at that moment. I can feel the energy in the room, too, as we say the words together: the feeling of solidarity and commitment, of mutual caring, the presence of higher power. It is the only time we speak in unison and

---

[28] M. L. in Rochester, NY, "Answer from [the] Genesee [AA Group]," *The Grapevine* (November 1945): 5; John C. Ford, S.J., to Bill [Wilson], Weston, MA, January 22, 1953, Box 30, file 18.3, p. 17, GSOA. It was not the custom in most other nations, where AA tended to be far more secular. See Makela et al., *Alcoholics Anonymous*, and *Final Report: Twenty-Sixth General Service Conference of AA* (New York: Alcoholics Anonymous, 1976), 25, GSOA.

[29] Father John Ford brought it to Wilson's attention, so its omission was clearly a choice and not an oversight. John C. Ford, S.J., to Bill [Wilson], Weston, MA, January 22, 1953, Box 30, file 18.3, p. 17, GSOA.

[30] D. L. in Oklahoma City, OK, "Prayers at AA Meetings," *The Grapevine* (June 1975): 42; E. E. in Tulsa, OK, "Not Allied with Any Sect or Denomination," *The Grapevine* (January 1985): 5–7; M. W. in San Francisco, CA, "On the Lord's Prayer," *The Grapevine* (April 1987): 17–19.

[31] Don N. in Bronx, NY, "Three Times I've Come Here," *The Grapevine* (April 1973): 9–13.

Came to Believe

touch each other. As we practice the Eleventh Step in the group, I learn to practice it on my own.[32]

In addition to this "public" education in prayer, members urged each other to pray on their own. They helped each other do this through instructions and suggested prayers in national publications[33] and newsletters,[34] and by recommending to one another commercially published guides geared toward AA members, such as *The Little Red Book* and *Twenty-Four Hours a Day*. The Big Book encouraged them to seek God spontaneously throughout the day when they needed inspiration or guidance. And it walked them through the steps of making a discipline of morning and evening prayer. This was how members could make and improve their "conscious contact" with God (Step Eleven). Doubters were often urged to "experiment" with faith by committing themselves to trying to pray sincerely. Older members apparently felt that such an experiment could hardly fail to succeed.[35] Newcomers who felt unsure of how to pray were reassured that they would get better at it as they matured personally and spiritually.

The vast majority did try prayer on their own. This was true even for the many who, due to skepticism or simple indifference, had not prayed for a long time prior to joining AA. For example, it was only in reluctant response to strong urging by a sponsor that A. W. in Oklahoma began to talk to God for fifteen minutes each morning. Eventually the conscious spiritual contact and moral self-examinations this achieved led A. W. to double the amount of time spent each morning in such meditation.[36] D. B. in Texas got off to a similarly rough start. His/her first attempts to pray began: "I don't know who or what you are or whether or not

---

[32] M. W. in San Francisco, CA, "On the Lord's Prayer," *The Grapevine* (April 1987): 17–19. The frequency of this experience is suggested in *Twenty-Four Hours a Day* (1975), which was not printed by AA but was one of the most popular "daily devotionals" used by members. The "Thought of the Day" for December 31 notes that "The Lord's Prayer has become part of my AA thoughts for each day," and reprints the prayer.

[33] *Alcoholics Anonymous*, fourth ed. new and rev. at www.aa.org (New York: Alcoholics Anonymous World Services, Inc., 2001), 85–8; *12 & 12*, 99–103; *Came to Believe...*, 21–6.

[34] See, for example, *Central Bulletin* [Cleveland, OH], Newsletters, Box III, GSOA. Not all newsletters published prayers. *The Grapevine* also made it a point of editorial policy not to publish any of the prayers that readers submitted; Santon, interview.

[35] The lesson that one should not wait for faith to pray, for indeed prayer could bring one to faith, was one frequently repeated in AA circles. See, for example, B. C. Revelstoke in BC, "An Answer without a Prayer," *The Grapevine* (April 1986): 5–6; J. C. in West Henrietta, NY, "'A Sometimes Painful Concoction,'" *The Grapevine* (July 1988): 8–13.

[36] A. W. in Enid, OK, "God's Time," *The Grapevine* (November 1962): 33.

American Protestantism in the Age of Psychology

you can hear me or whether you even care about me, but I need help in overcoming my drinking problem, and if it's within your power and desire to aid me, I will be forever grateful."[37]

Others had prayed even while drinking, but had done so infrequently or self-servingly. One woman in Tennessee reported that, even while drinking heavily, she had always prayed. However, her drinking prayers generally consisted of: "God, I'm checking in. I'm drunk." When she first entered AA, it grew to "God, please restore me to sanity." Eventually she began to express frequent gratitude in her prayers, and even (prompted by a song) asked for peace on earth and her own ability to be a channel of that peace.[38] Pete in Pennsylvania increased his occasional prayers to daily ones after a while in AA. He learned that it was important not only turn to God in "times of distress, fear and sorrow" but cultivate the relationship as a consistent part of his life.[39]

These latter examples point up a common piece of advice: Members urged each other to improve the quality as well as the quantity of their prayers. In particular, members were advised to make themselves less willful and selfish. Some members with only short-term sobrieties admitted they began by asking for all kinds of things, including success at work and to escape the consequences of their actions. They reported back to the rest of the fellowship that such prayer was not effective. Apparently, God was – in the words of one long-term member – no "errand boy."[40] Members learned that they could petition God for help in doing things that were in accord with his will, such as how to pray properly and to stay sober. But that was just the beginning. One long-term member confessed that it took him a lot of time to learn this. At first, he had "consigned God to a corner with a piddling task to perform [helping him stay sober] and orders to speak only when He was spoken to. It earned me a couple of years of fairly miserable dryness."[41] Such experience was probably common. Big Book readers were humorously reassured that

Being still inexperienced and having just made conscious contact with God, it is not probable that we are going to be inspired at all times. We might pay for this

---

[37] D. B. in Texas, "First Steps Out of Agnosticism," *The Grapevine* (April 1968): 9–10.

[38] "More than a Symbol," in *Came to Believe...*, 21–2.

[39] Pete W. in Carnegie, PA, "Time to Dust," *The Grapevine* (January 1958): 52–4.

[40] *Twelve Steps and the Older Member* (Cheshire, CT: Older Member Press, 1964), pp. 23–5, in Box II "Pamphlets Distributed by Other AA Groups," file "Connecticut," GSOA.

[41] "Willingness" (Chicago: Alcoholics Anonymous [Chicago], n.d. [circa 1955–1975]) in Box IIA "Pamphlets Distributed by Other AA Groups," file "Illinois," GSOA.

Came to Believe

presumption in all sorts of absurd actions and ideas. Nevertheless, we find that our thinking will, as time passes, be more and more on the plane of inspiration.[42]

AA members prayed for help in making psychological changes. AA literature and old-timers advised newer members that the best object of prayer was to replace such personality traits and feelings as compulsion, selfishness, dishonesty, and self-pity with faith, generosity, and caring. AA found that ancient spiritual wisdom of particular importance for alcoholics whose overblown egos were seen to have gotten them into trouble in the first place. Although the issue of alcoholic grandiosity seems to have been emphasized more in the early decades of the fellowship than the latter ones (and most especially by Bill Wilson), AA members demonstrated that they took all this advice very seriously and that it increased both the quantity and quality of their prayer. They testified that they slowly learned not merely to ask for things that they wanted, but to ask instead to realize God's will. In 1947, F. W. in Pennsylvania discovered, "I pray differently, too. I used to tell God I'd be good and do certain things if he'd do certain things for me. Now I ask God to help me so that I may help others."[43] Decades later, E. P. in Virginia reported that as she slowly stopped listing the things she wanted and asked instead to understand and accept God's will.[44]

Members did not have to become saints to make such a change. Many appeared to have found that the change brought its own intrinsic rewards. An anonymous writer in Ohio described the experience of a "friend" in AA who said he "used to pray – or thought I did – but I asked for the material things in life, the things *I* wanted for myself. And I worried, I fretted, I became annoyed and resentful because my 'prayers' weren't answered.'" But now when trouble came the man submitted himself to the will of God and to knowing his will and thus "'I find my help – right at the moment.'"[45] This experience was common enough to have made it into the Big Book. The experience of the authors promised that the same benefits could accrue to readers if they, too, improved their prayers:

As we go through the day we pause, when agitated or doubtful, and ask for the right thought or action. We constantly remind ourselves we are no longer running the show, humbly saying to ourselves many times each day "Thy will be done."

---

[42] *Alcoholics Anonymous*, 87.

[43] Scranton, PA, "A Newcomer Looks at AA," *The Grapevine* (February 1947): 10.

[44] E. P. in Alexandria, VA, "Divine Hot Line," *The Grapevine* (December 1977): 2–4.

[45] Anonymous in Warwick, OH, "Right at the Moment," *The Grapevine* (December 1949): 5.

124   *American Protestantism in the Age of Psychology*

We are then in much less danger of excitement, fear, anger, worry, self-pity or foolish decisions.... We do not tire so easily, for we are not burning up energy foolishly as we did when we were trying to arrange life to suit ourselves.[46]

The Big Book and the Good Book

Prayer was not the only way that AA members were encouraged to find and make contact with their Higher Power. They were encouraged as well to read the spiritual and religious literature with which they were surrounded. As with prayer, some of this exposure was private and other public. Not uncommonly, meetings started off with a reading from the Big Book or from the *12 & 12*. Some meetings were devoted to a specific step or tradition, and the relevant text was probably read. Some of the material in these works was spiritual, and AA members perused them for spiritual inspiration. Given that the vast majority of groups, in the mid-1960s, featured literature displays at meetings and either sold, loaned, or gave newcomers copies of the Big Book,[47] it is not surprising that most members at the time reported that they read AA books, pamphlets, and *The Grapevine*.[48] A good-sized minority of newcomers were also introduced to *Twenty-Four Hours a Day* and *The Little Red Book: An Orthodox Interpretation of Alcoholics Anonymous*, which were not published by the General Service Office (GSO) itself but were written for and by members. In the mid- to late 1960s, these books were distributed by a large minority of groups,[49] and well over one-quarter of members in 1965 reported that they supplemented AA material with such inspirational literature.[50] AA historian Ernest Kurtz reported that during the mid-century years, members read the cheap, portable *Twenty-Four Hours* at least as frequently as the heavy, expensive *Alcoholics Anonymous*.[51]

---

[46] *Alcoholics Anonymous*, 87–8.

[47] *Final Report: Sixteenth General Service Conference of AA* (New York: Alcoholics Anonymous, 1966), 22, GSOA.

[48] Bailey and Leach, *Alcoholics Anonymous*, 29–31.

[49] They were distributed by roughly one out of four groups, and one out of seven groups respectively; see *Final Report: Sixteenth General Service Conference of AA* (New York: Alcoholics Anonymous, 1966), 22, GSOA; *Final Report: Eighteenth General Service Conference of AA* (New York: Alcoholics Anonymous, 1968), 26, GSOA.

[50] Bailey and Leach, *Alcoholics Anonymous*, 29–31.

[51] "Hazelden-published *Twenty Four Hours a Day* turns 50, touch millions," *The Voice* (Winter 2004), at hazelden.org; Kurtz, *Not-God*, 347, footnote 13. Many AA members probably did not make sharp distinctions between materials produced by AA or outside publishers. And, in fact, a few delegates to the national conference reported in the 1970s that members did not realize *Twenty-Four Hours a Day* was not "official" AA literature

Both books emphasize the spiritual aspects of the twelve steps. *The Little Red Book*, first published in 1957, drew on early Oxford movement ideas.[52] Although the "orthodox" aspect of the book did not entail specific Christological references, it did portray the program as entirely spiritual and emphasized that aspect. The even more popular *Twenty-Four Hours a Day* was first self-published and distributed by its author, AA member Richmond Walker, in 1948. The GSO apparently found it too religious to take over publication when Walker offered it to them in the mid-1950s. But the alcoholic rehabilitation facility Hazelden, which became both one of the nation's premier substance abuse treatment facilities and a major publisher of recovery literature, leaped at the chance.[53] It has remained in print ever since. Over nine million copies have been distributed.

Twenty-Four Hours a Day has often been published to look like a small black prayer book, with a page for each day. Each date offers a paragraph-length mediation, "thought for the day," and a prayer. Its major themes are the importance of faith, turning one's will over to God, staying sober, becoming an altruistic person, and service to the AA fellowship and other alcoholics. Although it avoids doctrinal or Christological references, it frequently invokes or cites verses and phrases of the Bible to talk about the relationships between humans and God.[54] For example, at the height of May, readers found Psalm 40:2, "He brought me up out of a horrible pit, out of the miry clay, and set my feet upon a rock and established my goings."[55] In early fall they read Isaiah 32:17, "The work of righteousness shall be peace and the effect of righteousness shall be quietness and assurance forever."[56]

---

and read it at meetings. (See *Final Report: Twenty-Seventh General Service Conference of AA* (New York: Alcoholics Anonymous, 1977), 20, 26, GSOA.) Hazelden began to distribute such materials to patients in their programs. Since Hazelden was the archetype of the "Minnesota model" that was imitated by treatment facilities across the nation, it is not improbable that the importation of such "recovery" literature into twelve-step programs expanded in the final third of the twentieth century.

[52] *The Little Red Book.*

[53] *Final Report: Eighteenth General Service Conference of AA* (New York: Alcoholics Anonymous, 1968), 27, GSOA.

[54] Other examples include, "Behold I make all things new" (August 21); "There is a proper time for everything" (June 26); "He that heareth these sayings and doeth them is like unto a man who built his house upon a rock" (June 12); "Except ye become as little children, ye cannot enter the kingdom of heaven" (July 2); "Blessed are they that hunger and thirst after righteousness, for they shall be filled" (July 3).

[55] *Twenty-Four Hours a Day*, s.v. May 19.

[56] Ibid., s.v. October 3.

126 *American Protestantism in the Age of Psychology*

In the early period of AA, members encouraged each other to turn to incorporate Bible reading into their spiritual activities. Newcomers clearly followed this advice. They were directed in particular to concentrate on the Sermon on the Mount, First and Second Corinthians, and the Book of James.[57] A number of the contributors to the first edition of *Alcoholics Anonymous* described returning to or beginning to read the Bible regularly in their testimony.[58] For instance, A. J. R. in Chicago was a mid-century member who discovered the Bible for the first time after joining AA. With the excitement of an explorer, he reported to the fellowship that he had already found useful and interesting passages in Proverbs and the Sermon on the Mount.[59]

Although most of the textual evidence for private Bible reading dates to the 1940s, this probably reflects the way that AA's published sources began quickly to filter out anything that seemed too distinctly religious and "churchy" at least as much as it reflected a decline in Bible reading among members. Publications occasionally printed members' testimony about their increased scriptural reading after the 1940s, but this was not the norm.[60] Evidence from much later dates surfaced when AA was trying to curtail any explicit links between their group and Scripture. Clearly some members as late as the 1970s and 1980s were gathering together for regular Bible study.[61]

Calling the Higher Power by Name at Retreats and Eleventh-Step Groups

Another activity Anonymous Alcoholics pursued to deepen their conscious contact was to attend, in addition to AA meetings, retreats and specialized spiritual recovery gatherings. Although not officially part of

[57] A. D. Le Monte, "'Alcoholics Anonymous' Co-Founder Tells of Breaking 35-Year Drunk," *Vindicator* (Youngstown, OH) reprinted in "What Others Think of Alcoholics Anonymous" (Akron, OH: Friday Forum Luncheon Club of the Akron AA Groups, n.d. [circa 1944]) in Pamphlet Box 3, file "Ohio," GSOA; *Dr. Bob and the Good Oldtimers*, 71, 96, 151.

[58] *Alcoholics Anonymous*, 225. Also see pages 264, 322.

[59] A. J. R. in Chicago, IL, "Look Not Thou Upon the Wine; It Biteth Like a Serpent," *The Grapevine* (August 1949): 26–7.

[60] Anonymous in Little Rock, AR, "Out of My League," *The Grapevine* (January 1957): 44.

[61] *Final Report: Twenty-Ninth General Service Conference of AA* (New York: Alcoholics Anonymous, 1979), 41, GSOA. *Final Report: Thirty-Fifth General Service Conference of AA* (New York: Alcoholics Anonymous, 1985), 33, GSOA.

Came to Believe 127

AA, retreats were organized throughout the middle and latter twentieth century for members. The GSO had no particular policy on such activities, although it discouraged explicit association of the AA name with such retreats, but not always successfully. Whether or not members thought, or cared, about the retreats' official status, many attended. One study in the mid-1960s found that about 15 percent of members did so.[62] Some retreats were denominational, some were broadly Christian,[63] some were (at least in theory) interfaith,[64] and a few emphasized their nondenominational spirituality.[65] Some of these appear to have emphasized family togetherness as much as spirituality.[66]

A number of alcoholic priests who had found sobriety in AA organized retreats for fellow members, whether Catholic or not. In the late 1950s and early 1960s, for instance, members in Indiana, Illinois, Michigan, and Minnesota attended regularly scheduled retreats for AA members that were held at Our Lady of Fatima Retreat House at Notre Dame, IN.[67] Every few months members in Northern California and surrounding areas could attend a priest-run retreat that consisted of "a series of spiritual conferences given by the priest retreat director, periods of prayer and meditation, quiet strolls in the verdant, tranquil surroundings of the

---

[62] Bailey and Leach, *Alcoholics Anonymous*, 29–31.

[63] There was a Matt Talbot Retreat Movement that organized "nonsectarian" retreats for alcoholics in AA. Matt Talbot was a Catholic man who (before the founding of AA) kept himself sober through extreme asceticism, self-mortification, and works of charity. Some Catholic AA members wanted him canonized as the patron saint of drinkers. The retreat movement referred even in the brochure to praying to "'The Venerable Matt Talbot, True Servant of God' to intercede for another 24 Hours of Happy Sobriety." While the group may not have advocated Roman Catholicism, it clearly could not have welcomed non-Christians. "Come Aside with Me...And Rest Awhile," [brochure] (New York: Matt Talbot Retreat Movement, Inc., n.d.), The Stepping Stones Foundation Archives, Bedford Hills, NY.

[64] In upstate New York, The Salvation Army, the local diocese, Area Council of Churches, and Alcoholics Anonymous cooperatively held a retreat that included a rabbi on the program. "Retreat for Alcoholics Slated Here Labor Day," *Schenectady Gazette* [NY], August 16, 1967, "Retreats" in Vertical Files, GSOA; "Interfaith Retreat Group," [1972], "Retreats" in Vertical Files, GSOA. However, around the same period, Ben, a nonobservant Jewish atheist struggling to find God, wrote an angry letter to the GSO after attending a California retreat that he had imagined would be interfaith turned out to be explicitly Christian. It was unclear how the retreat advertised itself. Ben I., to AA World Services, Studio City, CA, n.d. [1971], "Retreats" in Vertical Files, GSOA.

[65] See "Serenity Retreats," "Retreats" in Vertical Files, GSOA; "Monteagle AA Roundup, 1–3 May 1964," "Retreats" in Vertical Files, GSOA.

[66] "Monteagle AA Roundup, 1–3 May 1964," "Retreats" in Vertical Files, GSOA.

[67] "Home Town Slants: AA Retreats Due," *Truth* [Elkhart, IN], April 11, 1963, "Retreats" in Vertical Files, GSOA.

128 *American Protestantism in the Age of Psychology*

retreat ground and mass and benediction each day." Non-Catholics were welcome and not expected to attend mass. Those attending maintained silence throughout much of the weekend.[68]

Retreats were not the only gatherings devoted to supplementing the spiritual resources of AA. Some members organized auxiliary groups and organizations to pursue this, sometimes known as "eleventh-step groups." These groups tended to tie the program to either evangelical Protestantism or Catholicism, although some that developed by 1960 appeared to allow members to pursue more exotic forms of spirituality. One woman from Florida wrote Bill Wilson to complain about what she deemed to be "metaphysical," cult-like groups that had sprung up in the Miami area in which participants meditated communally.[69]

The two largest orthodox movements were Alcoholics Victorious (AV) and Calix. The former was founded by Dr. William Seath roughly a decade after AA was in response to what he saw as both the promise and the limitation of AA. The psychoreligious blend seemed a perfect way to rescue and redeem alcoholics, but he considered the spirituality too vague. He established AV as an adjunct group – whose principles would clarify the identity of the Higher Power as Jesus Christ. Seath at first contemplated calling it the "Thirteenth Step" but, perhaps because in AA slang the Thirteenth Step implied an illicit sexual involvement between two AA members, he settled on Alcoholics Victorious. Groups were set up in evangelical churches and rescue missions for homeless addicts, including The Salvation Army Men's Social Service Centers.[70]

At the same time as Seath founded AV, some Catholic AA members also wanted to clarify the identity of the Higher Power as Jesus, and clarify the proper ways to seek spiritual guidance and maturity as through the Roman Catholic Church. They started another adjunct group, Calix, that promoted church involvement and participation in a Catholic fellowship of sober alcoholics, through monthly breakfasts, holy hours, and retreats. Although they remained a tiny movement compared to the larger AA

---

[68] James Brown, "Members of AA Retreat from World to Seek Spiritual 'Battery Charge,'" *Sacramento Bee* [CA] (April 25, 1965), "Retreats" in Vertical Files, GSOA.

[69] Mary H., to Eve Marsh, West Hollywood, CA, February 22, 1960, Box 18, file 4.1, pp. 186–90, GSOA.

[70] Alcoholics Victorious [Internet homepage], Association of Gospel Rescue Missions, Kansas City, Missouri, www.alcoholicsvictorious.org.

Came to Believe

fellowship – 2,500 people were affiliated with the group in 1964 – they established groups in eighteen states and enjoyed a smattering of coverage from the Catholic and local press.[71]

Theist Apologetics

Since many entering the fellowship were atheists or agnostics, members felt it necessary to disabuse newcomers of secular materialist philosophies and ideas. Just as the fellowship reasoned some emotions precluded faith and others prepared one for it, more accurate ideas and perspectives led to outlooks and feelings more conducive to sobriety. Therefore apologetics were commonly printed in *The Grapevine* and included in major AA publications. They appear also to have been articulated in meetings as well as in private, informal discussions among members. This was not apologetics in the traditional sense, which argued for the validity of a one particular religious tradition. Arguments could not come either from the Bible or the witness of a specific faith community, since that would violate AA's commitment to pluralism. Nor would the GSO publish anything that made highly specific claims about divine nature. Arguments aimed only to convince materialists of the possibility of an extra-material presence that might take an interest in them.

There were three major claims or themes that surfaced repeatedly in AA apologetics. The first was the contention that belief was neither unscientific nor illogical, even though the existence of God could not be proven. Members were cautioned in the *12 & 12* against making the error of believing that "denying God is scientific." They were urged to realize that atheism was often merely a form of hidebound prejudice that was itself unscientific in its refusal to consider a theory without fair consideration and testing: "we [atheists] recoiled from meditation and prayer as obstinately as the scientist who refused to perform a certain experiment lest it prove his pet theory wrong. Of course we finally did experiment, and when unexpected results followed, we felt different; in fact we *knew* different."[72] An apology printed in *The Grapevine* in the early 1950s

---

[71] Elmer Andersen, "The Andersen Letter: The Calix Society," *Union* [Anoka, MN] (June 15, 1962), "Retreats" in Vertical Files, GSOA; "Calix: A Catholic Answer to Alcoholism," reprinted from *Catholic Digest* (September 1964), "Retreats" in Vertical Files, GSOA.

[72] *12 & 12*, 27–9, 97.

130 American Protestantism in the Age of Psychology

echoed a theme common in the popular media after World War II that scientists affirmed they found evidence for God in their work.[73]

By the latter 1960s and 1970s, postmodern versions of this argument appeared. They did not endeavor, as before, to show that empirical investigation validated faith, but that much of science was itself based on theory and best guesses about what was true.[74] Thus, an apologist thirty years later noted that scientists themselves take many things "on faith," such as the existence of subatomic particles such as quarks that have never been seen or photographed, the existence of absolute zero although it had never been reached or recreated by human machine, and the constancy and pace of the speed of light.[75]

Another common argument, somewhat at odds with the first but similarly aimed at attacking the sense that faith was an insult to one's intelligence, was the claim that belief was more a matter of the heart than the head, of personal commitment rather than ratiocination. In "Letter to an Agnostic," M. S. in Honolulu counseled those struggling with faith, especially those who dabbled in the study of philosophy and comparative religion as the writer had, to "Give the anti-God boys a rest" because God could not be proved analytically.[76] Another woman confessed that she believed "simply because I can't *not* believe," although only saints enjoyed proof of the existence of the object of their veneration.[77] One Californian even invoked Kierkegaard in asserting that faith was "a leap into the unknown."[78] A psychology professor in Delaware who had believed God to be one of the "fictions of primitive people," was helped toward faith in part by the realization that "God is a word for what is beyond understanding."[79]

[73] B. L. Z. in Des Moines, IA, "Is There a God?" *The Grapevine* (August 1951): 6–7; Hudnut-Beumler, *Looking for God*, 43. See also Clark R., ed., *As I See It* (St. Louis, MO: The Auxiliary AA Group, n.d. [circa 1948]) in Box IIA "Pamphlets Distributed by Other AA Groups," file "Missouri," GSOA.

[74] James Gilbert (*Redeeming Culture*) also found the early 1960s – particularly the 1962 publication of Kuhn's *The Structure of Scientific Revolutions* – a transitional point in the discussion of the relationship between science and religion.

[75] J. S. in Pebble Beach, CA, "Faith and the Speed of Light," *The Grapevine* (April 1979): 10–11. For a similar argument, see also G. P. W. in San Antonio, TX, "The Power Is," *The Grapevine* (January 1967): 26–31.

[76] M. S. in Honolulu, HI, "Letter to an Agnostic," *The Grapevine* (November 1960): 40–2.

[77] J. S. C. in New Hartford, NY, "Spirit of Love," *The Grapevine* (February 1968): 13–14.

[78] J. S. in Pebble Beach, CA, "Like a Frog in a Frying Pan," *The Grapevine* (January 1978): 26–9.

[79] D. N. in Newark, DE, "The Gift of Surrender," *The Grapevine* (April 1978): 11–14.

Came to Believe

Although AA's spiritual apologists denied that there was any way to analytically demonstrate the existence of God, they often insisted that the pragmatic truth of the Higher Power was incontrovertible. They meant a series of related propositions derived from both a philosophical and lay American pragmatism: Faith worked, that which was useful and "works" was true, and the fact that faith worked was evidence that it tapped into something truly extant. This allowed apologists to reassure seekers that they need not aspire to an understanding of the nature of God, for this was beyond human knowledge. Various doctrines about God's essence were debatable, but a core of faith in a personal Higher Power willing to help was true. This emphasis on knowledge of a Higher Power not through the lessons of dogma, but rather through a personal relationship with it, was far from unique to AA. Religious historians Stephen Prothero and Robert Orsi have argued that it characterized Christian belief across the twentieth century.[80]

Some who asserted this made explicit the origins of this line of thinking in philosophical pragmatism and William James. Many others simply echoed this argument, which was easy enough to understand and articulate without any reading in intellectual history. AA members who carefully read *Alcoholics Anonymous*, and this was the majority of them, were introduced to William James there. A Texan named G. P. W. compared the "moral force" exerted by God to gravity in the sense that both were forces about which humans knew little but which pervaded their lives.[81] An apologist in California insisted that belief in God was beside the point since, "The facts of what 'turning your will and your life over' to some other power does for you are incontrovertible."[82] A more ambivalent version of the pragmatic argument was articulated by a member in Pennsylvania, who struggled with the spirituality of the program, but finally decided that "it makes more sense – is more practical – to believe than not to believe."[83] Brochures targeting newcomers and members struggling with the "spiritual side" of the program expatiated in similar fashion.[84]

[80] Orsi, *Between Heaven and Earth*; Prothero, *American Jesus*.
[81] G. P. W. in San Antonio, TX, "The Power Is," *The Grapevine* (January 1967): 26–31.
[82] Anonymous in California, "Not My Weak Will But a Greater Power," *The Grapevine* (February 1968): 14–17.
[83] W. O. P. in Meadville, PA, "Comfortable with God," *The Grapevine* (August 1972): 12–14.
[84] "The Secret Behind AA Recoveries" (n.p.: n.p., n.d.) in Box II "Pamphlets Distributed by Other AA Groups," file "Colorado," GSOA; "Spiritual Milestones in Alcoholics Anonymous" (Akron, OH: Alcoholics Anonymous, n.d.) in Pamphlet Box 3, file "Ohio,"

132   *American Protestantism in the Age of Psychology*

AA members tried to convince each other not only through apologies, but also through testimony, including relaying extraordinary encounters with the divine. One atheist in California, for example, wrote the GSO to relay his experience in calling out to God to "Teach me to pray" and suddenly seeing an evil apparition flee the room (s)he was in. (S)he then felt "coming toward me from all directions... a vibrating, pulsating, magnetic current" that left the writer filled with a sense of great relief and whom (s)he had "since become happy to call God."[85] Within AA, however, the most famous such experience was that of Bill Wilson's. His was a "typical" extraordinary encounter in a hospital that led him to quit drinking and eventually to found the fellowship:

All at once I found myself crying out, "If there is a God, let Him show Himself! I am ready to do anything, anything!" Suddenly the room lit up with a great white light. I was caught up into an ecstasy which there are no words to describe.... and then it burst upon me that I was a free man. Slowly the ecstasy subsided.... All about me and through me there was a wonderful feeling of Presence, and I thought to myself, "So this is the God of the preachers!" a great peace stole over me.[86]

Although not all reports of divine manifestations were this spectacular, they almost invariably involved some combination of light; voices; overwhelming feelings of warmth, love, and peace; sudden restful sleep after anxious sleeplessness; and the rapid eradication of the compulsion to drink.

Similar to testimony of extraordinary encounters was testimony from those who had felt God had intervened to deter them from catastrophic decisions. These accounts pointed thus toward sometimes small but always profoundly significant interventions in their lives. For example, members occasionally talked about encounters that kept them from suicide. One AA dropout became so filled with despair that he headed out one wet night to a pier from which he could jump into the ocean. En route, he chanced across a priest walking in the rain who recognized him and stopped to talk. By the time the two parted way, the unfortunate had lost his determination to die, and eventually he made his way back into the fellowship and sobriety.[87]

GSOA. Copies of this last brochure with varied costs indicate that it was repeatedly printed over a long period, and other evidence shows it was being distributed in the 1980s and 1990s.

[85] "Figure of evil," in *Came to Believe...*, 16.
[86] *Alcoholics Anonymous Comes of Age*, 63.
[87] "A Rainy Night," in *Came to Believe...*, 70–2.

Came to Believe   133

Only a lucky minority, and probably a small one, enjoyed such unusual visitations, however. Their testimony was publicized because it was useful in bolstering spiritual apologetics. But it was also potentially demoralizing because so few could look forward to them. It was crucial that newcomers not be deterred by the idea that they must have had such an experience to attain sobriety, or that older members fear that their spiritual paths were stunted if they never did. These concerns were such that beginning with the second printing of *Alcoholics Anonymous* in 1945, the authors included a disclaimer in the appendix that "sudden and spectacular" upheaval was *not* necessary for the cure that the book outlines, and was not, in fact, the norm. Citing William James's research, readers were reassured that most achieved slow spiritual development as they devoted themselves to following the twelve-step program.[88]

The fellowship felt it important to affirm "ordinary" evidence of God, since many found the simple fact of their own sobriety, and their own redeemed lives that it enabled, the primary evidence of divine presence and concern in their lives. Almost invariably they had tried to cease drinking and live better before AA had prompted them to turn their lives over to a Higher Power. They had always failed (which was why they ended up in AA in the first place). Thus, this achievement had come only when they followed the program, and was thus taken as evidence. This experience repeated on a mass scale, as it was in AA, was taken as further evidence. As one member argued: "If a man believes in a moral power greater than himself, a fool may challenge him to produce a miracle. That's easy for me now. I'm a miracle. Those I meet in AA are miracles. We should all be dead."[89] Another member, not yet two months sober, acknowledged that while (s)he was far less certain about any Higher Power, "The miracle of these once-hopeless thousands in AA can't be laughed off."[90] It is likely that at meetings and in informal exchanges with older members, (s)he would have encountered assertions such as that of W. S. in Toledo, Ohio, who after over a year's membership announced: "That a loving God exists is evidenced by these facts: I have fourteen months' continuous sobriety; the promises on pages 84–85 of the Big Book are being fulfilled in my life; I have real, loving, caring friends in AA; today, I have a little peace of mind."[91] W. S. thus echoed a theme common in AA and other

[88] *Alcoholics Anonymous*, 400.
[89] J. S. in Pebble Beach, CA, "Faith and the Speed of Light," *The Grapevine* (April 1979): 10–11.
[90] L. W. B. in East Greenwich, RI, "After Step One," *The Grapevine* (April 1955): 46–7.
[91] W. S. in Toledo, OH, "The Key Is Simplicity," *The Grapevine* (April 1980): 15–17.

134 American Protestantism in the Age of Psychology

psychoreligious combinations: The search for and attainment of peace of mind through psychospiritual means had not replaced God, as critics feared, but rather stood as confirmation of divine reality and love.

Finding evidence among the ordinary required educating members to see the hand of the divine in the long-term changes in their lives and slow changes in their consciousness. This was particularly difficult because they lived in a world in which they could readily apply other systems of explanation for these changes. Thus older and more comfortably spiritual members worked to alter the paradigms of newcomers and those who struggled with the prospect of faith. Such coaching was explicit – members insisted on the truth of spiritual experiences in which there were no fantastic phenomena. G. B. in Ohio, for example, insisted that, "No lights flashed. No angels came and sang. No bells rang. Nothing spectacular happened. It was just God giving me what I could handle when I was ready for it."[92] Saying there were "no lights" and "no bells" sometimes was used as a short-hand way of dismissing the importance of the extraordinary in recognizing the vital but unspectacular work of God in their lives. One woman writing in the late 1970s even valued her slow, deepening trust and inquiry into God's will for her and a sense of love for his creation as superior to the spiritual development to a friend who had been using LSD to attain mystical insights. Although he may have had visions worth raving about, she noted, he had "applied no spiritual principles in his life."[93]

Fundamentally, this meant that opening themselves up to God gave them the strength to change their personality and emotions; to develop a sober and better self. Occasionally, this meant understanding that what appeared to be useful "coincidences" that helped a person find therapeutic help or avoid slips were really gentle divine interventions. The word "coincidence" itself is freighted with a materialist metaphysics and a theory of human life as marked by random, meaningless occurrences. AA encouraged members to reinterpret life events from one of meaningless coincidences to deliberate choices God made for them. For example, members passed along stories that defied probability: One story that made the rounds, probably by the late 1960s, told of a Chicago member with a few years of successful sobriety who, in a fit of despair over severe financial and family hardship, decided to drown his troubles in booze.

---

[92] G. B. in Columbus, OH, "A Quiet Awakening," *The Grapevine* (April 1982): 12.

[93] M. B. in Coronado, CA, "We Seek Glimpses of the Absolute," *The Grapevine* (April 1978): 2–5.

Came to Believe 135

He went to a bar and ordered a drink, but the bartender recognized the patron as a speaker at an AA meeting that he had attended and gently let him know it. Stunned by the recognition, the man left the bar, having lost his desire for a drink. Given the many thousands of bars and bartenders in Chicago, members emphasized the unlikelihood of the patron encountering someone who recognized him as an AA member. AA headquarters publicized the story in *Came to Believe*, a collection of testimonies about the process of members' search for faith published in 1973.[94] It was only one such story in a chapter devoted to challenging the belief that such events were random, rather than divine interventions, entitled "Coincidence?"

AA members testified to how such coaching transformed their way of looking at their lives. The slow triumph of a spiritual over a materialist hermeneutic was elaborated by a member who testified:

all during my early sober months, things would happen that guided me toward working on myself and away from that first drink. I just laughed them off as coincidences. But as the months went by and I could look at myself more honestly and with a more open mind, they began to look more like God doing for me what I could not do for myself.... It's been a few years now, and the coincidences are still happening – only now they have the right label: God working with and through whomever and whatever he can.[95]

"Whatever" means were often subtle and unspectacular. B. B. in San Francisco, for example, testified that he was in AA for almost two years without ever really believing in a Higher Power until one day he had a strong compulsion to drink while walking to his car after work. Feeling helpless to resist the temptation, he begged God to take away his desire immediately. Suddenly a coworker called to him for help starting his own car. By the time he finished assisting his colleague, B. B. discovered that his earlier compulsion had abated entirely. He understood this small event as an intercession on his behalf by a benevolent God, who wanted to show him that his own help would come by helping others.[96]

Most of the time, however, AA members felt this divine nurture manifested not in fortuitous occurrences but as a slow and subterranean support that was not perceived easily while it was happening. One had to reflect on changes in one's life over a span of time to perceive the pattern. Sometimes recent members could not do this for themselves. Joe, for

---

[94] *Came to Believe.*
[95] B. B. in Florida, "Coincidences Still Happen," *The Grapevine* (September 1983): 7.
[96] San Francisco, CA, "Who's Under the Hood?" *The Grapevine* (April 1986): 13–15.

136 *American Protestantism in the Age of Psychology*

example, was still a neophyte, struggling, as many did, to find the faith the program demanded. When he spoke of his sense of God's absence, older members reminded him of an experience he had relayed of how kind his family was to him at a recent reunion and of how proud and happy his elderly, beleaguered mother was to see him sober after so many years. They made him realize that such simple, poignant joys were made possible by God, although previously he had failed to perceive such seemingly ordinary events as divine interventions.[97] For other members, the process of discernment took even longer. Some testified that they followed the program for years before they recognized the work of God in their lives. One middle-aged man, who had served time in prison for his inebriety, spent at least half a decade as a member before "I understood that I really had *had* a spiritual awakening."[98]

What most of these apologies and testimonies shared was that they adduced evidence for God from the democratic, grassroots psychological experiences of alcoholics. They did not point to world events as an arena of proof. They invoked neither the Lord of History as envisioned by an old and orthodox Judeo-Christian tradition, nor the Force for Progress heralded by the liberals who emerged in the early twentieth century. This Higher Power worked not in macro-time, in historical time, but rather in micro-time, in the hours and days of unhappy individuals seeking relief. Apologists and witnesses spoke not of a being who had revealed itself at Sinai or in the person of Jesus Christ. They told each other instead of the divine fingerprints they found in strange psychic phenomena, in private, room-sized fireworks revealed not to saints but rather to the miserably drunk and hung over. They reassured each other that such traces were everywhere inside them, in relief from their own compulsions, in their own peace of mind. They had only to feel and perceive aright to find them already in their own hearts.

God as We Understood Him

Although AA members thought of themselves as belonging to a fellowship – rather than a self-help group, a therapeutic group, a movement, or an organization – and although they agreed that spirituality was a, or

[97] E. B. in Chicago, IL, "Speaking of Manifestations," *The Grapevine* (November 1946): 8.

[98] P. S. C. in Alton, IL, "No Trumpets Blew," *The Grapevine* (February 1953): 31–3.

the, key to their program, they did not share a single conception of God. Many members, and certainly the GSO, promulgated a strong ethos of the right, and even sometimes of the need, for each member to develop or choose his or her own conception. Through carefully vague and inclusive language, AA maintained its unity despite the extraordinary diversity this commitment permitted. There were two sources of diversity in understandings of God in AA. One was simply the broad pluralism of the movement, which attracted troubled drinkers from all spectrums of society in the United States. Another was the fact that members' conceptions were often in motion.

This is not to say that all AA members found faith, or that they found faith in anything remotely related to orthodox, traditional, or even mainstream understandings of God. As noted before, many newcomers entered the fellowship as atheists or simply as people who hardly thought about God and felt very distant from anything divine. A minority of members, and probably a minority that increased over the years, never changed their minds about this.

Maintaining an atheist stance was difficult given that the AA program guided members through a narrative process of psychospiritual recovery. The most important developments in this process was overcoming a rejection of or alienation from God to (re)discover a Higher Power (Steps Two and Three), to confessing one's "defects" and misdeeds to this Power and soliciting its help in rectifying them (Steps Four and Six), and eventually to embark on a lifelong journey to deepen one's "conscious contact" with this entity (Step Eleven). The steps implied a progression over time. Even though they were not always attempted in sequence, members usually talked about "going back" or "retaking" a step, implying chronology. Therefore, atheism was difficult to assert not because the paradigm made no place for it, but because its place was at the beginning. To remain an atheist was understood as rejecting or undercutting everything that normally followed submission to the Higher Power. The narrative force of this paradigm made it very difficult for committed atheist members to be heard by their fellows, who often understood them as simply stalled out in this aspect of the program.

Despite this difficulty, the fact that the population who needed and was attracted to AA held a disproportionate share of the religiously disaffected, combined with the paucity of other recovery paradigms, meant that there would always be at least some committed nonbelievers in its ranks. Atheists appear to have made up a small but vocal percentage of the fellowship in the earliest years. It was their outraged persistence that

138   *American Protestantism in the Age of Psychology*

kept the religiosity of the Big Book to a minimum and pressed for the use of "Higher Power" instead of "God."

Nevertheless, *Alcoholics Anonymous*, which includes a chapter addressed entirely to nonbelievers, assumes that lack of faith is a condition that must be transcended. In fact, it reassures readers that the "main object [of this book] is to enable you to find a Power greater than yourself, which will solve your [drinking] problem."[99] AA was not in the evangelism business for its own sake, but rather members believed that faith was integral to their therapy. Atheism was a common symptom of alcoholism. Just as they were expected to leave behind their drinking days, they were expected to move beyond their rejection of supernatural forces – abstinence and faithfulness would each synergistically bolster the other. Therefore, when it came to overcoming alcoholism, many AAs believed that atheism was therapeutically contraindicated. This was a devastating argument within the context of the fellowship, especially while the broader culture so disdained atheism, as it did in the fifteen years after World War II. Atheists were on the defensive during this period in the broader culture as well as in AA, but a few began to argue in print that their lack of a higher power had not doomed their sobriety.[100]

In the early 1960s, however, disbelievers appear to have been emboldened by a thawing of the Cold War's cultural intensity and broader culture's softening toward irreligiosity and iconoclasm. *The Grapevine* began to air atheists' demands for tolerance and their testimony that they managed to stay sober without having sought the aid of a nonhuman Higher Power. With very tentative steps in the late 1960s, and especially in the early 1970s, the magazine began to run occasional articles on how atheists could adapt the program.[101] It is noteworthy, however, that all the articles from the 1980s on this theme were the work of a single Californian. Although the magazine sometimes solicited pieces on a specified topic from talented regular contributors, it did not need to repeat authorship frequently because so many members volunteered so much

---

[99] *Alcoholics Anonymous*, 57.

[100] L. S. in Scarsdale, NY, "One AAs Answer to Dr. Taylor," *The Grapevine* (November 1953): 5; "On the Other Hand," *The Grapevine* (January 1954): 29–31.

[101] *The Grapevine* began running articles in its February 1968 issue on "approaches to AA that work for alcoholics who are 'nonbelievers.'" Nevertheless, the first batch was by writers who denied or highly qualified their disbelief. For example, one of the writers, J. S. C. in New Hartford, NY ("Spirit of Love," *The Grapevine* (February 1968): 13–14), clarified that she was agnostic only in the sense that she did not think God's existence could be proven; nevertheless, she devoutly believed.

material each month.[102] *The Grapevine* – whose name conjured the democratic structure of spontaneous mass communication[103] – prided itself on its broad grassroots, nonprofessional authorship, calling itself an "AA meeting in print." The fact that the editors seemed to turn to her repeatedly, therefore, suggests that they did not receive a great deal of material on this topic.[104]

Atheism remained problematic and controversial even into the late 1980s. One article from 1987, and the responses it sparked, illuminates simultaneously the acceptance of nonbelievers in the program as well as the difficulties they faced when confronted by many who disbelieved such disbelief or found it therapeutically dangerous. J. L., a woman in Oakland, CA, told *The Grapevine* that she rarely talked about her atheism in the fellowship because "it goes against the grain of most members and is contrary to AA literature." She wanted more tolerance and assistance in helping atheists adapt the steps.[105] Many readers wrote in to respond.[106] A couple who had struggled in vain to find God, and one who had refused to look, were grateful for her assertion that faith was not a prerequisite for sobriety. A few felt this contention was not true, and that it was not safe or fair to leave people with the impression that it was. A few somehow managed to find religious inspiration in her article, and a few denied that J. L. was really an atheist, because no one who diligently followed the spiritual program of AA could be. One letter writer had witnessed a fight that broke out in a meeting in the mid-1980s in which members were discussing Step Two (realizing that only a greater Power can save the alcoholic). The group's "religious fanatics" clashed with those who held secular or totemic interpretations of the Higher Power (e.g., a "light bulb" or the group itself). One man finally tried to reconcile the groups by noticing that "Step Two doesn't say you have to believe. It says we

---

[102] Levine, interview.

[103] "Grapevine" also probably played on alcohol production – substituting the vine that produced grapes, wine, and inebriety to the one that conveyed members' thoughts to one another, nurturing sobriety instead.

[104] *Grapevine* editor Jack M., however, noted that by 1970 "We have a continuous controversy between atheists and the believers." He felt it the magazine's duty to air this dispute. *Final Report: Twentieth General Service Conference of AA* (New York: Alcoholics Anonymous, 1970), 13, GSOA.

[105] J. L. from Oakland, CA, "Is There Room Enough in AA," *The Grapevine* (October 1987): 4–6.

[106] See the ten letters to the editor printed in response to J. L. in *The Grapevine* (April 1988).

140   *American Protestantism in the Age of Psychology*

came to believe. And God doesn't care what you call him. He knows who he is."[107]

Although for most AA members, the psychoreligious blend of AA facilitated their spiritual reconciliation and development, those determined to keep God out of their alcoholism treatment were sometimes left with only the psychological aspect of the program. This may have translated into a more selfish, less ethically oriented program. Thus, the atheist J. L. sounded like a poster child for critics of the therapeutic when she explained how she translated Steps Ten and Eleven, which commit the member to a life of continual moral introspection, honesty, and prayer to know and carry out God's will:

By proper nutrition, exercise, and regular living habits, I worked at taking care of myself physically. I looked after my emotional and mental health by attendance at AA, repeated introspection, some outside therapy, consultations with trusted AA friends, and avoidance of relationships or decisions I knew were likely to bring emotional chaos to me. The positive actions I was able to make on my own behalf in my daily life nourished the well and happy person in me and were my Steps Ten and Eleven.[108]

Other members had noted that nonbelievers tended to rely entirely on the "group therapy" of AA, although they were divided on whether this was an adequate substitution. Most, however, felt it was not, leaving one's sobriety with only precarious support.[109]

However, most AA members did not long feel comfortable with an ideological commitment to atheism. This was true despite the fact that most entered the fellowship either aggressively rejecting faith; tenuously connected to a vague, distant faith; or dogged by a mix of disbelief, hatred, and fear of an image of a God of vengeance that they had developed in youth or while drinking. Plunged into the spiritual education of AA,

---

[107] G. F. in Milford, MA, "Sparks began to fly," *The Grapevine* (April 1988): 32.

[108] J. L. in Oakland, CA, "Atheist," *The Grapevine* (January 1980): 9–10. Despite the banality and self-absorption of the translated steps, J. L. demonstrated her personal sense of responsibility toward the larger fellowship by taking on the job of helping other nonbelieving alcoholics adapt the program. It was her advice, not the model of her behavior, that urged members to focus exclusively on themselves.

[109] Bill [Wilson], to Humphry Osmond, April 17, 1961, Box 18, file 4.1, pp. 211–12, GSOA; Leo C. in Portland, OR, "On the Subject of Dependence," *The Grapevine* (January 1948): 5; Doc. in Portland, OR, "Having One Primary Purpose," *The Grapevine* (November 1950): 20; B. E. in Memphis, TN, "An Agnostic's Higher Power," *The Grapevine* (April 1973): 13–14; Gary R. in Fenton, MI, "Recovery Feels Better than 'Feeling Good,'" *The Grapevine* (August 1989): 4–5; J. S. C. in New Hartford, NY, "Spirit of Love," *The Grapevine* (February 1968): 13–14; E. S. in Manhattan, NY, "Spiritual Spectrum," *The Grapevine* (April 1980): 11–15.

the vast majority abandoned these initial positions.[110] At the very least, newcomers' rejection softened as they were warned that committed atheism compromised their sobriety and as others testified and demonstrated their own faith. A recent study (by far the most rigorous one) determined that although *all* addiction treatment reduced alcoholics' agnosticism and atheism, it is reduced *more* by "Twelve Step Facilitation" (TSF), in which patients work the first five steps under the guidance of counselors, than by secular therapies. When alcoholics were randomly assigned to one of three therapies (one spiritual and the other two secular), 43 percent of the self-identified atheists and agnostics in TSF shifted at least one category in the direction of softening their denial of God and toward spirituality and religion. In comparison, only 27 percent of the atheist and agnostic clients assigned to Cognitive Behavioral Therapy or Motivational Enhancement Therapy similarly shifted.[111] An example of this trend was R. C. in Alhambra, CA, who had long prided himself on disdaining what he considered the religious amalgam of ignorance, fear, and superstition. He was initially appalled by all the "God talk" and praying he found when he entered AA about 1950. But after a decade in the program, he found that, although he had not come to believe in God, he had progressed to agnosticism.[112]

It is likely that most also shook off any residual images of an unloving, wrathful God.[113] Part of the spiritual education of Alcoholics Anonymous was to replace such a vision with an understanding of a God who could play the role of helpful Higher Power. As one brochure made explicit,

The Jehovah of the Old Testament was a stern, wrathful God, ever ready to punish. That, however, is not God as Christ teach[es] us. The God of the New Testament is like Dad, kindly and helpful, full of compassion and ever ready to

---

[110] I drew this conclusion from textual evidence. The only methodologically and statistically rigorous study that sheds light on this question came to the same conclusion. It determined that while all addiction treatment reduces agnosticism and atheism, "Twelve-Step Facilitation Therapy," in which patients work the first five steps in rehab with the aid of counselors, reduced disbelief more than secular therapies. It also found that atheists and agnostics in AA did not always become believers, but often moved one step away from their disbelief. Tonigan et al., "Atheists, Agnostics, and Alcoholics Anonymous."

[111] Participants were asked to self-identity as one of five categories: atheist, agnostic, unsure, spiritual, and religious. Ibid., 537.

[112] R. C. in Alhambra, CA, "From Atheist to Agnostic," *The Grapevine* (April 1961): 7–8; ibid.

[113] It should not be assumed that a friendlier image of God was necessarily a more believable or engaging one. The one study that investigated this question found the *opposite*. However, it suffered sufficiently serious methodological flaws to render its conclusions highly tentative. See Posey, "Correlation between the God-Image of Alcoholics."

142 *American Protestantism in the Age of Psychology*

forgive. We should always strive to make God a companion rather than someone from whom we constantly demand gifts.[114]

This image of a friendly, loving, approachable God, who nonetheless was no Santa Claus, pervaded both the literature and guidance of AA. The effect of such an education on M. L. of Missouri, led him to testify that "I no longer imagine a God of wrath and revenge, as I did in my active alcoholic years."[115]

The process of this education was laid out poignantly by one member, whose childhood understanding of a vengeful deity led him, as an adult, to veer between distant disbelief and a tragic sense that God had wreaked vengeance upon him by killing his son in a traffic accident. When he admitted this feeling in an AA meeting, another member told him to change his view of God from a cold and punishing being to a friendly and kind one. This kind of advice slowly led him, when he began praying again, to get rid of the religious language that he had been taught, but which supported his old notions. In place of "thee," "thine," "Great and Mighty God," "have pity on me though I deserve damnation," he explained, he substituted "you" and "I didn't do as well yesterday as I had hoped. I need your strength to be the kind of person I want to be." Eventually, the author decided that the God he had imagined all his life before AA was not the real God. He began to search for the real God. He read C. S. Lewis's *A Grief Observed*, which cited a line from the New Testament (1 John 4:16): "'God is love, and anyone who lives in love lives in God, and God lives in him.'" He began to believe love to be central to God and the life of faith, as it moved through people to other people.[116] He eloquently described the slow and difficult journey to arrive at this point:

As I worked the Second and Third Steps, it proved difficult for me to reconcile my lived experience of a Power that cares enough to keep me sober every day with the God of my childhood. It took me years to sort out the confused ideas,

---

[114] "Spiritual Milestones in Alcoholics Anonymous" (Akron, OH: Alcoholics Anonymous, n.d.) in Pamphlet Box 3, file "Ohio," GSOA. Although the brochure has no publication date, it appears to have been reprinted continually over a long period, as different brochure copies in the archive range from 15¢ to 50¢. They were distributed in 1983 and 1997.

[115] M. L. in Cape Girardeau, MO, "'This I believe,'" *The Grapevine* (February 1954): 13. For a similar testimony, see C. G. in Sydney, N. S., "Fighting Fear with Forgiveness," *The Grapevine* (April 1986): 16–17. M. U. in Ft. Collins, CO, "'As I Understood Him,'" *The Grapevine* (November 1963): 40–1, reassured fellow AAs that God is "not remote, cool, given to caprice, fierce or punishing, *if you* don't believe He is."

[116] J. C. in West Henrietta, NY, "A Sometimes Painful Concoction," *The Grapevine* (July 1988): 8–13.

Came to Believe
143

the tangled attitudes, the feelings that pointed in so many bewildering directions. It has taken years to move from that agnostic prayer [said when he first asked for help], that glimmering of *possible* faith, to a stronger faith in which is nevertheless still fragile, mixing belief and unbelief in a sometimes painful concoction which, somehow, proves to be sufficient for a spiritual life.[117]

Those who had some faith inevitably testified it had been badly vitiated by their drinking. When these members entered the fellowship, they began trying to bridge the distance from God that they felt. Those who had had extraordinary religious experiences were able to draw on them as they tried to move toward God. For others it was a more gradual progress. There was, for example, a subgroup within AA of priests, many of whom affiliated in their own distinct groups. (Vocations in which revelation of alcoholism would be particularly professionally humiliating or devastating, such as priests and pilots, sometimes established their own restricted AA groups.) Father B. H. in New York, for instance, testified that his faith and religious practice was eroded badly by his descent into alcoholism but renewed in AA.[118]

Thus, the vast majority of those in AA made movement toward God. Since both their starting points and their spiritual trajectories were so different, however, they did not necessarily end up in the same places. Their visions of God differed, some were very vague and truncated; others were more elaborate and sophisticated. Some fell well inside church teachings; others ranged across American New Thought traditions that had first flourished in the nineteenth century.[119] The second step for those with no faith was often to envision God as G.O.D. – group of drunks – that is, as the AA fellowship itself. Some combination of humor, superstition, and despairing or enraged resistance to the program may have led some to fixate on a fetish, such as a coffee table or light bulb. Those with more abstract habits of mind discovered they could more readily imagine a Higher Power that was nonpersonal, a sort of First Cause, cosmic unity and force for good, or just Something Out There. During the 1960s and 1970s, members sometimes based a nonpersonal conception on Americanized versions of Buddhism or other exotic Eastern imports.[120]

---

[117] Ibid.

[118] B. H. in Staten Island, NY, "Spiritus Contra Spiritum," *The Grapevine* (May 1982): 11–13. See also Anonymous, "God Shapes a Priest," *The Grapevine* (September 1973): 20–3; D. M. in Northbrook, IL, "Let Go and Let God," *The Grapevine* (April 1979): 7–9.

[119] The history of this tradition has been best plumbed by Robert Fuller. See *Americans and the Unconscious; Mesmerism;* and *Spiritual, but Not Religious.*

[120] There was some concern about whether this was "permissible," but in general it was welcomed like any other vision. Occasionally a writer insisted that Buddhism was

144   *American Protestantism in the Age of Psychology*

AA's conceptions of God sometimes remained simple or crude, but they often developed further. Many members' nebulous ideas crystallized, becoming more personal and conventional. Most appeared to have moved at least to a sense of some personalistic Power from whom they could seek help, and whose will for their lives they might discern. Despite the enormous variety and tolerance of diversity in AA, the program created a space for a certain conception of God, and placed this conception at the center of its therapeutic mechanism. It had to be an image of God who was in some sense a person, that is, a being capable of having a will, intentions, and actions. The AA program envisioned a God who was concerned, capable, and willing to help an alcoholic get and stay sober. This God wanted to hear confession of sins (although did not judge), related to humans individually and in fellowships, responded to prayers (although in unpredictable ways), and nurtured people in their struggles to be sober, responsible, honest, and loving. This God had a plan for people and the world, unfathomable to individuals but far greater than anything they could imagine. Yet this God was not so much a distant Lord of History as a loving friend. Critics might rightly point out that this vision precluded the awesome grandeur of Karl Barth's vision of a deity of almost infinite distance or Jonathan Edwards's Lord flicking humans like spiders into the fires of hell. And yet AA's gentle discouragement of the many Platonic or exotic visions of divinity available to Americans must also be recognized.[121]

In fact, this highly personal vision of God resonated most closely with an evangelical understanding of Jesus that emerged in the nineteenth century as a loving and sympathetic friend.[122] AA took this vision of God and

---

identical to a twelve-step program. This claim had been made more frequently for the spiritual exercises of St. Ignatius earlier in the program. *Final Report: Eighteenth General Service Conference of AA* (New York: Alcoholics Anonymous, 1968), 25, GSOA; N. M. S. in Eugene, OR, "On AA and Buddhism," *The Grapevine* (March 1969): 37–8; "Spiritual Milestones in Alcoholics Anonymous" (Akron, OH: Alcoholics Anonymous, n.d.) in Pamphlet Box 3, file "Ohio," GSOA; Bill [Wilson], to John Ford, S.J., May 14, 1957, Box 30, file 18.2, pp. 170–5, GSOA; [John Ford], "Suggestions for final revision of A.A. COMES OF AGE," n.d. [1957], Box 30, file 18.3, p. 35, GSOA.

[121] Fuller, *Spiritual, but Not Religious*. Although there were few AA members who testified that their understanding of God became vaguer, such testimony was not entirely absent. Frank F. published a pamphlet of his thoughts on AA in which he noted that prior to AA, "God was only what others had taught me to believe he was. Now He is as I understand Him, credible and positive, though far less detailed" (57). See Frank F., *A Reasonably Happy Man* (Crestwood, NY: Frank F., 1971) in Pamphlet Box 4, file "Anonymous Sources/Unidentified," GSOA.

[122] Fox, *Jesus in America*; Hutchinson, *The Modernist Impulse*; Prothero, *American Jesus*.

Came to Believe 145

stripped it of much of its identity and its traditional, doctrinal, and Scriptural context. The groundwork for such a denuding was made possible because there was already a strong tradition within American Protestantism that had moved from the "sola Scriptura" of the Reformation to "solus Jesus." Nineteenth-century Protestants, by placing a personal belief in and relationship to Jesus himself at the center of their faith, had consigned Scripture and doctrine as ways of knowing about God to secondary roles. There they withered. A similar argument might be made about lay Catholics, for whom intense relationships with heavenly beings probably superseded extensive doctrinal knowledge.[123] AA's depiction of the Higher Power was probably a vision that seemed amenable to Catholic alcoholics (even if inadequate to some).

Given that evangelical Protestant understandings of Christ were the model on which the AA Higher Power was based, it was hardly surprising that Jesus *was* God as many AA members understood him. This, however, varied greatly over time, place, group, and individual. Earlier in the fellowship, during the 1950s and early 1960s, the movement as a whole was more comfortable than it would later become with the public pronouncements of those who explicitly identified the Higher Power as Jesus. Indeed, the ministers and priests who spoke at AA international conventions during the mid-century did not shy away from this identification,[124] and no protest appears in the written record. In 1960, Reverend Sam Shoemaker asserted, for instance, "The whole world, non-Christian as well as Christian, owes an unspeakable debt to Jesus Christ for revealing to us a God who is like Himself, loving, patient, forgiving, eager to help, while yet expecting us to live according to His laws." Some groups at mid-century became dominated by clergy members who saw AA as fundamentally a religious movement.[125] In later decades, explicitly Christian references at conventions could provoke protest, and few groups – regardless of the absence or presence of a religious tone – would have tolerated outsider domination.

Probably more important than time, however, was variation across regions. Ernest Kurtz – the foremost historian of AA – found in his

---

[123] Orsi, *Between Heaven and Earth*.

[124] Conference talks by Father Edward Dowling and Reverend Sam Shoemaker are reprinted in Sam Shoemaker, "The Spiritual Part of AA," *The Grapevine* (November 1960): 9–15; *Alcoholics Anonymous Comes of Age*.

[125] *Final Report: Second General Service Conference of AA* (New York: Alcoholics Anonymous, 1952), 13, GSOA.

146   *American Protestantism in the Age of Psychology*

research that during the latter half of the twentieth century, the movement was much more spiritually focused and explicit about its ties to Christianity throughout much of central and western Florida, the coastal Carolinas, large areas around Houston and Galveston, most of Arizona, the better part of Southern California, most of Ohio east of Akron, and parts of metropolitan midwest cities including Chicago, Detroit, and Cleveland.[126] This was dubbed "Akron-style AA" from AA's founding in Akron and from the fact that the movement that radiated from this city was more closely aligned to evangelical Protestantism than the movement that spun off from the New York City pioneers.

Of course, there was also variation on a group and individual level. Over the course of the century, AA groups proliferated and diversified.[127] A common saying in AA circles was that all one needed to start a new AA group was a grievance and a coffee pot. Thus, in religiously and spiritually diverse areas, it was easy to form groups catering to various strands within the AA population. Of course, even within groups, there was diversity of belief about the Higher Power. Evidence for such diversity tended to emerge when it caused friction. A woman in Pittsburgh, for instance, wrote to Bill Wilson to complain that

There are quite a number of people who, in their leads [when speaking at an AA meeting], tell of their renewed faith, or even new founded faith, and these people have been extremely criticized for being churchy, religious, etc. I would not be sober today if my faith in God and the power of Jesus Christ had not been renewed.[128]

Throughout the history of AA there is evidence of those who *did not* identify the Power as Christ complaining about those who did, and vice versa. Paradoxically both groups seem to have felt in the minority – and perhaps it was the few Christians in largely non-Christian groups and the non-Christian minorities among Christian majorities who were most moved to protest.[129]

---

[126] For this theme and history, see Kurtz, *Not-God*, 62, 102, 301–2.

[127] Johnson, "Alcoholics Anonymous in the 1980s: Variations on a Theme."

[128] Eleanor Dierst, to Bill W[ilson], Pittsburgh, PA, February 2, 1966, Box 18, file 4.1, pp. 273–4, GSOA.

[129] Anonymous in Worcester, MA, "I'm Confused," *The Grapevine* (April 1954): 45–6; Ben I. to AA World Services, Studio City, CA, n.d. [1971], "Retreats" in Vertical Files, GSOA; John M. in Lexington, KY, "The Kingdom Within," *The Grapevine* (May 1989): 21–3. Similar debate apparently emerged over questions about whether groups of explicit non-Christians (e.g., Buddhists, Moslems) who prayed out of their own traditions could be said to constitute AA meetings; see *Final Report: Eighteenth*

Came to Believe 147

One thing that is clear, however, is that many AA members disliked explicit references to Christ. This seemed to have been not always a rejection of Jesus himself, but because he was an emblem of larger Christian traditions – complete with doctrine, "church-ianity," and a heavy panoply of social and psychological associations – that some members disliked, and against which others had rebelled. It is likely that the ease with which the Higher Power could be mapped onto Jesus (who was, after all, the archetypal Power) generated particular anxiety. In some AA crowds, idiosyncratic mappings (e.g., light bulbs, Nature) were probably more easily tolerated precisely because they were offered as one individual's vision, stripped of any dogmatic or institutional obligations. They could also be understood as way stations on the spiritual journey of members embarked on a quest for sobriety and improved "conscious contact." Christ entailed Christianity, which no one understood as an interim form of faith. For this reason, publications and public statements of the New York offices of the GSO or *Grapevine*, out of a concern that AA unity might be threatened by religious disputes, tended to filter out tradition-specific "God talk."[130]

Local offices representing "confederations"[131] of regional AA groups – because they addressed smaller and more homogenous constituencies – could invoke Jesus more freely than the New York-based, nationally oriented GSO or *Grapevine*. It is likely that the unusually cosmopolitan outlook of New Yorkers and the national orientation of the offices and their publications discouraged explicit Christian references. It was significant for the movement that New York, and not Akron, became the center of the movement. This was a contingent development, however, based largely on the fact that it was the unemployed Bill Wilson, and not the practicing Dr. Bob Smith, who was able to devote himself full time to the fellowship. When *Alcoholics Anonymous* was published, it directed correspondence to Wilson in New York. Thus, this group soon emerged as a kind of national center merely because it was with them that

---

General Service Conference of AA (New York: Alcoholics Anonymous, 1968), 25, GSOA.

[130] Santon, interview.

[131] AA groups need neither to register nor obey dictates of these offices – known as intergroup offices. Connections and contributions to support such offices are voluntary. They serve to connect various groups and refer potential members. The main coercive force they appear to have is that they often publish listings to local groups, and so they can insist that a representative observe a meeting to ensure its conformity with AA traditions before agreeing to list it.

148　　*American Protestantism in the Age of Psychology*

many fledgling groups corresponded, forcing the New Yorkers to address questions and grievances nationally and thus help determine the tone and policies of the group.

Local groups could invoke Christ without worrying about opposition, however.[132] Thus, a 1946 issue of the *Weekly Bulletin* of the Top o' Texas Group of AA discussed the failure of humanity to respond adequately to the message of Jesus and his example through his crucifixion.[133] A more limited claim was made by the editor of the *San Francisco Secretary's News Letter* in 1976 when, in his Christmas edition, he shared with readers the fact that "I can believe in and revere the Christ whose birthday this is, the God as I understand Him, who made mine a sober life at last."[134]

Disagreement between those who identified the Higher Power as Jesus and those who did not should not obscure the fact that anonymous alcoholics disagreed about his nature just as did the larger mid-century Protestant community. Understandings of Jesus ranged from more orthodox ideas of Christ as divine savior to those that verged on denying his divinity but elevating him to a man of extraordinary moral courage and wisdom. This reverence for Christ, alongside a doubt or denial of his divinity, was consistent with much Protestant practice,[135] some of which maintained a belief in a supernatural deity but attributed to God all the attributes of an evangelical Protestant vision of Jesus Christ. This was one common belief among AA members. But precisely because Jesus was, in the words of religious historian Stephen Prothero, a "national icon," differing interpretations among members could be downplayed by a sense of shared reverence. For example, perfect ambiguity was achieved by a man in California in the mid-1950s. He posed to fellow members a series of rhetorical questions that seem designed to unite those who might answer them in very different ways:

Did Christ live? Did He perform the miracles that are accredited to Him? And die on the Cross with the primary objective of having that sacrifice of His so

---

[132] For example, see *Central Bulletin*, published by the Central Bulletin Foundation, Inc., in Cleveland, OH, Newsletters, Box III, GSOA; *The Brighter Side*, newsletter of Alcoholics Anonymous in Waterloo, IA, Newsletters, Box III, GSOA; and *Here's How* published by Alcoholics Anonymous in Chicago, IL, Local Newsletters, Box III, GSOA.

[133] *Weekly Bulletin*, Top o' Texas Group, Alcoholics Anonymous (2 November 1946), Newsletters, Box II, GSOA.

[134] "Dear Santa Claus," *San Francisco Secretary's News Letter*, December 1976, Local Newsletter Files, San Francisco, CA, GSOA.

[135] Prothero, *American Jesus*.

Came to Believe

emblazoned on the minds of men in the centuries to come that His philosophy of life might be studied for the benefit of humanity?[136]

Came to Believe

On the simplest level, the therapy offered by AA nurtured the moral and civic lives of its members. It taught them that to feel better, foster their own well-being, and improve their lives, they had to evaluate themselves with greater honesty than they had previously. They had to own up to their faults. They had to make amends as best they could. It did not merely admonish them; it showed them how to do it. Of course, members' ethical achievement was not always great. But they usually became better people than they had been. AA also taught them that their individual salvation from their problems could be found only through the mutual support of others like themselves. Selfishness and isolation would not cure them. Their hope lay in democratic, therapeutic fellowship. Atheist and agnostic members who never came to think of the Higher Power in anything beyond sociological terms took their own moral and civic transformations as the "spiritual awakening" recommended by AA.

Many members went beyond this, however. Their new spirituality hovered closer to the essence of the word. They awakened, or more commonly reawakened, to a sense of the spirit of God.[137] They became more receptive to faith in a divine presence and more attuned to it through prayer and AA fellowship. Continually throughout the history of the fellowship, members spoke of this transformation to one another, wrote articles to *The Grapevine* about it, and described it in letters to Bill Wilson and the GSO. They were circulated in the magazine, reprinted in brochures, and collected in a 1973 book entitled *Came to Believe* that was aimed at those in the program who struggled to find faith. A

---

[136] Bill Mc. in Monterey, CA, "Were You There, Charlie?" *The Grapevine* (May 1954): 3–5.

[137] For most of AA's existence there were few studies on this question, and even fewer methodologically rigorous ones, so textual sources necessarily form the bulk of the historical evidence. Five studies subjected to a meta-analysis in the early 1990s were found to demonstrate "Weak, yet consistently positive, relationships...between AA involvement and having a more active religious life" (60). The authors called for more and better studies on the subject. Emrick, "Alcoholics Anonymous," 60–1. Recently a few researchers have begun to respond with careful scientific studies, which have all upheld and further clarified the spiritual and religious effects of AA participation; see Tonigan et al., "Atheists, Agnostics, and Alcoholics Anonymous"; Worth et al., "Longitudinal Perspective of Changes in Religiosity."

150 *American Protestantism in the Age of Psychology*

member in the service stationed in the South Pacific during World War II, for example, sent a letter to *The Grapevine* editors explaining that he previously "had never given consideration to spiritual thought.... [But] through the Program... a 'Higher Power' has... reached into corners of my life far apart from the problem which led me to A.A."[138] Years later, a member in Texas testified about moving from atheism to a "newfound belief in God," which was "not a complete religious philosophy": "My God lacks many of the sophistications He exhibits among the organized faithful, but I do learn something new about Him every day. Perhaps the time will come when I'll walk through the doors of the First Something-or-Other Church and find Him standing before the altar."[139] A decade after that a cynical atheist in Philadelphia joined the program and over the course of the ensuing eighteen months experienced not only sobriety but also occasional "violent swings toward faith" without entirely making that "quantum leap." Nevertheless, R. E. had discovered that "without a doubt" prayer worked, and this fact had proven to him that "an unseen realm does exist" and that his sobriety was "a reflection of the good attributes of some higher power" rather than of "any moral virtue or strength of will" on his own part.[140]

Of course, not all of this effect was due entirely to AA. Certainly, sobering up after years of alcoholism – regardless of the therapy used – was likely to improve all aspects of a person's functioning, including their spiritual lives. Many adults also become more faithful as they age. And yet the two rigorous studies that investigated these variables found that they did *not* explain the long-term changes in spirituality that active AA members experienced.[141]

Even granted that AA *did* promote spiritual growth as part of its therapy for alcoholism, one might reasonably wonder if it had done so at the expense of traditional religious forms and groups. Whether or not this possibility is cause for concern or celebration depends on the valuation of spirituality vis-à-vis religion. Some scholars have recently mounted defenses of spirituality and both of their arguments resonate with the experience of AA. Religious scholar Robert Fuller holds that it is better than the atheism or religious apathy that would otherwise characterize a

---

[138] Y. G. [letter to the editor], *The Grapevine* (August 1944): 5.
[139] D. B. in Texas, "First Steps Out of Agnosticism," *The Grapevine* (April 1968): 9–10.
[140] R. E. in Philadelphia, PA, "Prayer," *The Grapevine* (January 1980): 7–8.
[141] Tonigan et al., "Atheists, Agnostics, and Alcoholics Anonymous"; Worth et al., "Longitudinal Perspective of Changes in Religiosity."

Came to Believe

large segment of Americans. This was certainly true of many AA members. One explained that he spent six futile years "trying to find God in church" but had not done so until he joined AA.[142] Even if the spirituality AA failed to revitalize this member's church participation, it had revitalized his faith. Meanwhile, Robert Wuthnow defends spirituality by arguing that intrinsically it is neither good nor bad, but rather is capable of being either, depending on the seriousness and self-discipline with which it is developed.[143] By this yardstick, AA must be commended. It coached members through the disciplines of regular prayer and meditation, spiritual reading including the Bible, and behaving toward others in line with their spiritual beliefs.

Those who denigrate spirituality are often concerned most with religion's democratic and civic functions. They point out the functions that Tocqueville observed religion fulfilling in the United States: binding Americans together despite the centrifugal forces scattering them wide and far, and gently lifting their earthbound gaze toward more noble and heavenly horizons. To the extent that spirituality – that is, a concern with the relationship between the individual and ultimate unseen realities – *replaced* organized religion, it therefore weakened civil society. A statement recorded by two researchers in the 1980s would alarm any Tocquevillian today: "'Since I've been in this program I've gained tremendously in spirituality. I don't go to church anymore. God speaks to me through AA.'"[144]

Whether religion and spirituality were complementary or antithetical was an issue that AA members did not agree upon. Their disagreements about the relationship and the persuasiveness of any particular argument followed the patterns in the broader culture. In the middle third of the twentieth century, they tended to be seen as complementary. But attacks on churches as institutions in the 1960s raised spirituality to prominence as the truer, more vivid faith freed from moral trivia, ossified dogma and ritual, and bureaucracy. This latter critique resonated with some AA members, who had been disappointed personally by the failures of their youthful faith to keep them from descending into alcoholism. The personal transformation made possible by the organization's psychoreligious blend charged its spirituality with intensity and honesty. Traditional faith

---

[142] T. H. in Albuquerque, NM, "A Gift Unexpected," *The Grapevine* (December 1976): 21–3.

[143] Fuller, *Spiritual, but Not Religious;* Wuthnow, *After Heaven.*

[144] Rudy and Greil, "Is Alcoholics Anonymous a Religious Organization?" 47.

152   *American Protestantism in the Age of Psychology*

and church life could seem inert in comparison. This was suggested by John in Kentucky who devoted more of his time to AA than to his church, which he had sometimes attended drunk, because it had never helped him get or stay sober.[145] Neither of these views ever became hegemonic in AA, however. Rather they constituted two sides of a quiet, ongoing disagreement, or agreement to disagree, within the fellowship.

AA emphasized spirituality as a solution to the problem of religion and civil society in a diverse nation. Its spirituality functioned to protect it from the divisiveness that religious disagreement could arouse in a private voluntary organization recruiting from across the demographic spectrum of a heterogeneous nation. It helped to emphasize Americans' shared religiosity while sidestepping potential institutional, doctrinal, and social tensions. It embodied the vision articulated by President Dwight Eisenhower who, along with "many Americans," was derided as "a very fervent believer in a very vague religion."[146] This common-denominator faith may have been problematic theologically, but civically it was brilliant.

Not only did spirituality protect AA from religion, but it also protected religion from AA. Spirituality enabled the group to become a vibrant ecumenical organization that protected the denominational commitments of its members, particularly of members from the minority faiths, most especially Catholicism. Thus, the most devout atheists teamed up with the most devout believers, especially Catholics, to ensure that AA did *not* set itself up as an alternative Protestant church. Its origins in a Protestant revival movement highlighted such concerns. Thus, its spirituality must ultimately be understood to have bolstered civil society by helping one of the largest nonchurch civil organizations to maintain its coherence and unity for the larger half of a century, and by allowing it to bring together citizens from diverse backgrounds.[147]

In the end, there is very little evidence that the spirituality of AA substituted for its members' traditional religious ties and beliefs. While it did seem to nurture a small but solid minority of members with long-lasting contempt for organized religion, it seems unlikely that much of this group would have pursued actively a religious affiliation. "Fred Murphy," for

[145] John M. in Lexington, KY, "The Kingdom Within," *The Grapevine* (May 1989): 21–3.
[146] William Lee Miller quoted in Marty, *Modern American Religion*, vol. 3, 303.
[147] One big limit to diversity was the disproportionate scarcity in AA of African Americans, relative to their proportion of the population. It is not known, however, what proportion of alcoholics they constituted. White, *Slaying the Dragon*, 161.

Came to Believe 153

instance, a junior-high-school dropout and alcoholic from age 15 who had spent years in jail and panhandling on the streets, eventually had found not only sobriety in AA but also a social club and "church."[148] Without AA, Fred might have joined a congregation. But he might well have not, remaining in his middle age as socially and spiritually disconnected and dysfunctional as he had been in his younger adult years. Although there has been almost no research on this question, doctoral student Kim Bloomfield found in the 1980s that AA membership modestly *reduced* antireligious hostility and involvement in "New Age" spirituality among homosexuals while modestly increasing their traditional religious observance.[149] Although Bloomfield's large sample was not a scientific one, all the textual evidence and other surveys conducted point to the fact that the trend she observed was true for AA members more broadly throughout the history of the group.[150]

Ultimately, the psychoreligious blend of AA helped pave the way for many members to turn, or return, to traditional forms of faith and church life. Members not only moderated antireligious hostilities, but they increased their traditional religious practices such as prayer, meditation, church attendance, and Bible reading.[151] The program spurred many to seek out clerical help who had not sought it out while drinking.[152] One study in the mid-1960s found that although only a generous quarter of newcomers with less than six months' sobriety in AA attended worship services regularly, the longer they stayed with the program, the more they began going to church. Over half of "old-timers" with at least five years' sobriety in the program went routinely. A generous quarter of such long-term members attended retreats, leading the authors of the study to conclude that "increased sobriety is often accompanied not only by spiritual development within the AA program, but by a return to former religious affiliation or by membership in a new religious group."[153]

---

[148] Vaillant, *Natural History of Alcoholism*, 201–2.

[149] Bloomfield, "Community in Recovery."

[150] Her findings are in accord with the decline in atheism and agnosticism found by Tonigan et al., "Atheists, Agnostics, and Alcoholics Anonymous."

[151] Worth et al., "Longitudinal Perspective of Changes in Religiosity."

[152] John Norris, "Analysis of the 1977 Survey of the Membership of A.A.," paper presented to the 32nd International Congress on Alcoholism and Drug Dependence, Warsaw, Poland, September 3, 1978, Figure 8A, in file "Survey 1977," in Box "AA Surveys, 1958–1978, Box I," GSOA.

[153] Bailey and Leach, *Alcoholics Anonymous*, 39.

154   *American Protestantism in the Age of Psychology*

It is not surprising then to find that AA was sometimes understood by ministers[154] and members alike as a God-ordained instrument for bringing an alienated flock back to faith. Numerous clergy during the middle decades of the twentieth century looked to it longingly as a model for their own flocks, whose commitments at times seemed tenuous in comparison.[155] Reverend Samuel Shoemaker, for example, concluded in 1955 that although AA had originally been influenced by the church, it was then time to reverse the process.[156] AA members – some of whom had seen AA as designed by the Creator or as "Christianity in action"[157] – echoed this understanding in a motif that intensified in the final third of the century. As we saw in the case of clinical pastoral education pioneer Anton Boisen, a few AA members even came to see their compulsion, their mental illness, as a divine malady. They thanked God for it. Doug, in Florida, put it most bluntly when he said that discovering his "higher power" had "been worth every bit of the hell I had to go through to get

[154] William J. Smith, S.J., "A Jesuit Applauds AA" (reprinted from *Crown Heights Comment*, Brooklyn, NY, 1951) in Pamphlet Box 4, file "Religion and Alcoholics Anonymous," GSOA.

[155] Samuel M. Shoemaker, "What the Church Has to Learn from Alcoholics Anonymous," (Pittsburgh, PA: Calvary Episcopal Church, 1955) in Pamphlet Box 4, file "Religion and Alcoholics Anonymous," GSOA; Samuel M. Shoemaker, "The Twelve Steps of AA: What They Can Mean to the Rest of Us," reprint (New York: *The Evangel*, n.d. [circa 1963]) in Pamphlet Box 4, file "Religion and Alcoholics Anonymous," GSOA; Dilworth Lupton, "Mr. X and Alcoholics Anonymous" (Cleveland, OH: Channing Press, The First Unitarian Church, n.d.) in Pamphlet Box 4, file "Religion and Alcoholics Anonymous," GSOA; J. E. Doherty, C. S. S. R., "Alcoholics Anonymous" (Liguori, MO: Liguorian Pamphlet Office, Redemptorist Father, 1954; reprinted from *The Liguorian*) in Pamphlet Box 4, file "Religion and Alcoholics Anonymous," GSOA; John A. Redhead, Jr., "Religion and AA," sermon preached May 19, 1957 at First Presbyterian Church in Greensboro, NC (Greensboro, NC: Greensboro Citizens Committee on Alcoholism, n.d. [probably 1957]) in Pamphlet Box 4, file "Religion and Alcoholics Anonymous," GSOA; Duncan E. Littlefair, "Alcoholics Anonymous," [sermon] (Grand Rapids, MI: Fountain Street Baptist Church, 1945) in Pamphlet Box 4, file "Religion and Alcoholics Anonymous," GSOA.

[156] Samuel Shoemaker, "The Spiritual Angle of AA," *The Grapevine* (October 1955): 2–7; Samuel M. Shoemaker, "What the Church Has to Learn from Alcoholics Anonymous" (Pittsburgh, PA: Calvary Episcopal Church, 1955) in Pamphlet Box 4, file "Religion and Alcoholics Anonymous," GSOA.

[157] H. T. in Dallas, TX, "What Price Sobriety," *The Grapevine* (January 1954): 23; John T., "AA: God's Instrument" (Chicago: Alcoholics Anonymous [Chicago], n.d. [circa 1955]) in Box IIA "Pamphlets Distributed by Other AA Groups," file "Illinois," GSOA; J. S. in Pebble Beach, CA, "Like a Frog in a Frying Pan," *The Grapevine* (January 1978): 26–9; 12 &12, 129; G. A. T., "Carrollisms" (Shakopee, MN: n.p., n.d. [circa 1972]) in Box IIA "Pamphlets Distributed by Other AA Groups," file "Minnesota," GSOA; Clyde G., "My Quiet Time" (Salt Lake City: Utah Alcoholism Foundation, n.d.) in Pamphlet Box 4, file "Miscellaneous," GSOA.

Came to Believe
155

there."[158] For in the search of AA for an effective therapy, they had found the fellowship of AA, and in AA, they had found faith.[159]

Conclusion

AA did contribute to the postwar therapeutic ethos in America – that is, it did help spread therapeutic ideas and practices beyond disciplinary boundaries. It taught members about psychology and encouraged them to adopt the psychopathological identity of "alcoholic." It turned groups of inebriates into therapists. It helped convince the public that medicine should lay claim to a realm of human behavior previously understood as vice or character weakness.

However, the effects of all this were not at all what the literature about the therapeutic has found. AA showed members that turning inward was necessary only so long as it served to cultivate the honesty necessary for moral self-improvement. Members were to look inward long enough to illuminate how they had ill fit into the world around them and what they needed to do to change that. The solution to their inner problems was to be found in aligning themselves with two external sources of power, healing, and virtue: the fellowship and a Higher Power, often conceived as God. The model of selfhood AA promoted, by harnessing individual happiness and self-determination with transcendent and communal relationships, seems particularly well-suited to the cultural needs of a liberal democracy.

In the previous chapter, I argued that in AA – contrary to the literature on the therapeutic – community and therapy were not competitors but rather were mutually constitutive of one another. Similarly, in this chapter I hoped to show that the relationship between psychological and spiritual perspectives were not what has been alleged. In AA, the therapy *was* the spiritual education, just as spiritual growth was a way to resolve members' mental problems. Furthermore, the fellowship helped the religiously indifferent and disenchanted by adducing evidence for God's presence and

---

[158] Doug S. in St. Augustine, FL, "An Agnostic's Spiritual Awakening," *The Grapevine* (October 1990): 19–21.

[159] C. J. R., Manhattan, NY, "The Joy that Walks Ten Feet Tall," *The Grapevine* (November 1969): 30–2; P. H., "Alcoholism – Divine Malady?" *The Grapevine* (May 1968): 14–16; Oliver R. Whitley, "Life with Alcoholics Anonymous: The Methodist Class Meeting as a Paradigm," *JSA* 38, no. 5 (1977): 839; K. G. in Potts Camp, MS, "Me and God," *The Grapevine* (August 1974): 2–6; R. A. in Fallon, NV, "Glowing from the Inside Out," *The Grapevine* (April 1986): 11–12.

benevolence from their own democratic, grassroots psychological experiences. AA increased members' participation in activities such as praying, reading spiritual literature, consulting clergy, engaging apologetic arguments for God, and attending retreats and church services. Thus, as in clinical pastoral education and other psychospiritual programs, psychological well-being in AA did not usually *substitute* for spiritual truth – as the literature on the therapeutic ethos contends – rather, it *confirmed* it.

Although not a church or formal institution of faith, AA epitomizes Tocqueville's vision of the civil society building role of religion in a democratic republic. It did it in inauspicious times. Despite the burgeoning of civil society in the postwar United States,[160] American society was rapidly turning problems such as addiction over to the care of professionals.[161] None of the professional solutions to alcoholism would have fostered faith, social trust, or self-governance. But AA fought successfully to keep management of the problem largely within the hands of citizens, while fruitfully collaborating with medical professionals. Over the sixty-five years since the end of the Great Depression, members built democratic, independent, tolerant, and inclusive nationwide and international fellowships.

AA's efficacy in fostering the spiritual engagement and civic connections of its membership depended on its autonomy. Unlike the chaplains and CPE students whose ministries were profoundly shaped by the secular and often public institutions in which they conducted them, AA was free from all such pressures. Nevertheless, because it was also independent of organized religion, and because it was so democratic and decentralized, it was very susceptible to wider currents in the culture. As the larger society become more comfortable and familiar with therapy, so did AA members. This invariably was imported and integrated into AA. As more Americans came to be or to accept atheists, this too was invariably imported and integrated into AA. When participation in conventional, organized religion was the wisdom of the day – as it was in the twenty-five years after World War II – this shaped the understanding of AA members, who often saw it as a pathway to (or back to) faith. As ensuing generations came to value disorganized spirituality over organized religion, this too had its effects on the interpretation of the program. Contemporary

---

[160] Putnam, *Bowling Alone*, 48–64, appendix III.
[161] The post-World War II burgeoning of expert society and its sociopolitical entanglements are examined by Balogh, *Chain Reaction*. Lasch indicts and laments this development as one of the major sources of a therapeutic ethos in *The Culture of Narcissism*.

sociological research comparing AA in different countries reveals that the program is not necessarily religious in many other nations into which it has been imported. It tends to reflect the religiosity of the host society. As I argued in the introduction, the relationship of faith to psychology was not philosophically predetermined but rather culturally shaped.

Americans would not have embraced psychotherapeutic perspectives unless they figured out ways of accommodating them to their egalitarianism, their pluralism, and their religiosity. This accommodation undoubtedly propelled the spread of a therapeutic ethos in American culture. It also brought some of the nation's most alienated citizens into new communities and helped return them to the bosoms of their families, friends, and churches.

PART THREE

THERAPY AS EVANGELISM IN THE SALVATION ARMY

Introduction

The Salvation Army has tried to convert homeless men since the early years of the twentieth century. This mission was gradually transformed into a rehabilitation program in the wake of World War II. It was housed in institutions that, for many decades, bore the name Men's Social Service Centers (MSSCs).[1] The army's ability to cast as therapeutic its evangelism of the indigent depended on the psychoreligious efforts of other people of faith. It relied in part on the mid-century convergences described in the previous two case histories – those that were forged between pastoral guidance and therapeutic counseling, between Christian fellowship and group therapy. The centers drew on lay Christians and clergy to help counsel the men they served, whom they called their beneficiaries. MSSCs hosted groups of Alcoholics Anonymous (or more religiously orthodox imitators) as the antiaddiction component of their program. Although the army used others' efforts, it also contributed its own innovations about what constituted therapy and who could administer it. It was among the pioneers of the American Protestant evangelical community to recognize the potential of psychoreligious syntheses.[2]

[1] These institutions were originally known as Industrial Homes. Their name was changed to Men's Social Service Centers (MSSCs) in the 1920s, and then again in the late 1970s to Adult Rehabilitation Centers (in part to indicate the presence of a small minority of women). I generally refer to them as MSSCs because that was their name during my main period of investigation.
[2] It should be noted that the timing of American evangelicals' engagement with therapeutic perspectives as relayed in the historical and sociological literature is wrong. It expanded significantly but did not begin in the 1970s with the writing of Ruth Carter

159

160   *American Protestantism in the Age of Psychology*

This therapeutic reorientation in no way enervated the evangelical efficacy of this mission. In fact, the psychoreligious blend that the army forged in the postwar period paved the way for greater salvific success. It enhanced the army's ability to build community among isolated men and to help set them on a path toward greater social responsibility. Many beneficiaries became rehabilitated Christian converts; that is, they became "new creatures in Christ" (2 Cor. 5:17). The psychospiritual program Salvationists built in the decades after World War II transformed the centers from an organizational backwater that boasted few conversions into the most religiously successful branch of the army's social service ministries.

> Stapleton. Relying on cultural history in this case misleads. All of my cases show evangelical groups getting involved institutionally in psychoreligious efforts decades earlier: The Southern Baptist seminaries started CPE in the 1950s; Alcoholics Victorious and other more religious AA emulations began as early as the late 1940s; the army recast evangelism as rehabilitation in the 1940s and 1950s. These institutions' efforts were the pioneers among evangelicals.

6

Freud Is Not a Suitable Psychologist

The Salvation Army began in 1865 as a British Protestant evangelical ministry to the urban poor run by the itinerant minister William Booth and his wife, Catherine.[3] Drawing on the military motifs with which some Christians had begun to promote a muscular Christianity, the Booths cast every aspect of their own movement in martial metaphors.[4] The army "opened fire" on the United States in 1880. Their American ministry made early use of informal social service help as a tool of evangelism. The help was practical, not therapeutic. When a few Depression-era Salvationist clergy (called "officers") began suggesting to their peers that they begin raiding psychology's toolbox, too, they faced great resistance. Opponents held that sin, not pathology, was the root of humankind's troubles.

Nevertheless, the psychological pioneers in the United States eventually won out after World War II. This was due to the fact that their proposals

---

[3] The Booths drew on the ideas and techniques of several religious traditions from their own upbringings and the larger cultural milieu of Victorian England: Methodism, Wesleyan revivalism, Quakerism, and the Holiness movement. They emphasized salvation above all else and viewed their efforts as part of the work of bringing on the millennium that would precede the return of Jesus. Green, "William Booth's Theology of Redemption"; Murdoch, *Origins of the Salvation Army*; Walker, *Pulling the Devil's Kingdom Down*, 22. See these latter two works for recent scholarship on the army in Britain. Coutts, *The Salvationists*, is one of the most useful introductions written by a Salvationist. Also see Coutts, *The History of The Salvation Army*; Sandall, *The History of The Salvation Army*. Although secular historians have long neglected the American branch of the army, scholars outside the organization have begun to explore its development in the late nineteenth and early twentieth centuries. See Spence, *The Salvation Army Farm Colonies*; Taiz, *Hallelujah Lads and Lasses*; Winston, *Red-hot and Righteous*. An excellent denominational history that also covers the twentieth century is McKinley, *Marching to Glory*, 2nd ed.

[4] Winston, *Red-hot and Righteous*, 83.

162   *American Protestantism in the Age of Psychology*

enabled the army to protect itself from the intrusions of an increasingly regulatory federal government. The opponents' fears were not realized, however. The army's independence permitted it – like Alcoholics Anonymous (AA) – to mix a psychoreligious formula uncontaminated by the secularizing atmosphere of public institutions. Furthermore, the fact that it was a church with a strong tradition of hierarchical authority and spiritual leadership meant that it was not as vulnerable to broader cultural currents as AA. Even when brewing psychoreligious admixtures, it reached for many traditional Protestant components.

These components originated in the army's late-nineteenth-century outreach to homeless men. In the 1890s, the army began providing them with cheap meals and places to sleep. Men who had no money at all were asked to perform some work in exchange for their room and board, such as salvaging used goods or cutting and bundling firewood, which were sold cheaply to poor families. These arrangements were institutionalized in the early twentieth century in the men's Industrial Homes. By the 1920s the homes, which began to be called Men's Social Service Centers (MSSCs), had even become modestly successful salvage businesses.[5] In such places men could eat, sleep, and work in a Christian environment sheltered from the temptations of drink and debauchery.

Nevertheless, men did not often stay long in these homes, and they do not appear to have been fruitful environments for securing religious conversions. Before World War II, these institutions met men's most basic human needs. But they took neither a strongly evangelical nor a therapeutic approach. After the war, however, they began to be reorganized as psychospiritual rehabilitation programs for the emotionally troubled.

"Service to Man": Religious Therapy for the Psychosocially Impaired Sinner

The therapeutic turn in centers enabled them simultaneously and synergistically to intensify their efforts both at earthly rehabilitation and otherworldly salvation. The sections that follow show exactly how they did this by detailing the six psycho-spiritual therapies that Salvationists crafted for those under their care. The army utilized what was known as a multitherapeutic approach to treating men. This allowed it to retain elements of the program from the pre–World War II period – work, religious services, and residence in an army institution – by recasting each

[5] McKinley, *Marching to Glory*, 1st ed., 161.

Freud Is Not a Suitable Psychologist   163

of them into a new rehabilitative mold. Each old component became a distinct therapy. In addition, the MSSCs added new ones. Even Salvationists who resisted the centers' therapeutic turn in the immediate postwar period would have been pleased with the outcomes of such activities. As I demonstrate in the chapter's final section, as programs became increasingly psychoreligiously oriented, more and more beneficiaries felt their souls stirred.

Farsighted officers in the Men's Social Service Departments (MSSDs), inspired by larger trends in the philanthropic universe, began to rethink their mission.[6] (The army in the United States was carved into four territories – east, central, south, and west – each of which had its own MSSD that oversaw centers in its region.) Ambitious officers took advantage of the crisis in the centers wreaked by World War II – when mass mobilization of men, minimal unemployment, and resource shortages both obviated and crippled the MSSCs.[7] They pushed through a series of deep reforms in their philosophy, strategies, and goals between 1944 and 1948. Their compelling justification for doing so was the intermittent but increasing pressure the federal government was bringing to bear on the MSSCs for perceived violations of the 1938 Fair Labor Standards Act, which set a national minimum wage.[8] This threat strengthened the hand of a few individual center administrators who had by the late 1930s and early 1940s begun introducing such innovations as casework services and AA meetings. It was these administrators and their Salvationist allies, sped along by pressure from the Labor Department, that led the rest of the centers down the same road in the quarter century that followed.

The reform became known as the "Service-to-Man program." The goal of this new program was the rehabilitation of psychologically damaged indigent men. These unfortunates had ceased to be able to function in

---

[6] Other private philanthropic organizations in the 1930s had begun redefining their missions in light of the massive increase in state welfare intervention. Many were beginning to disentangle themselves from economic relief to the poor to focus on offering professional social work services to the troubled; see Morris, *The Limits of Voluntarism*. Ambitious officers began to reform the MSSCs in the hopes of comparing favorably to some of the army's other, more modern, social services, such as its prison and women's outreach; see McKinley, *Somebody's Brother*, 119–20; McKinley, *Marching to Glory,* 2nd ed., 180; Hofman, "Relating the Salvation Army Program on Alcoholism to the Community."

[7] McKinley, *Somebody's Brother*, 115.

[8] The army continually denied that its centers qualified for inclusion under the new act since they were charitable and not commercial enterprises. But the Labor Department cast a jaundiced eye on the notion that the MSSCs were simply a Christian charity, setting the stage for a protracted battle; see McKinley, *Somebody's Brother*, 112–14, 20, 41–3, 62–5, 96–9, 208–9.

164 *American Protestantism in the Age of Psychology*

society – any society. They were usually homeless and lacked ties to family or community. Many drank to excess. They did not form a community among themselves, living lives of loneliness and boredom and fear. A few such people were able to open their hearts to Jesus, but most could not. Few of the small group who could were able to grow in their faith or live a Christian life while they remained unemployed and homeless. In 1947, before New York's Bowery corps had adequate facilities to house and help men, the corps officers wrote in frustration to their supervisors to tell of their precious converts wandering the streets aimlessly and alone, waiting all day for the evening worship service.[9] Rehabilitation in all facets of such men's lives was necessary for their spiritual rebirth. The entire program was to be restructured along therapeutic lines.[10]

Service-to-Man became official policy in 1948, but implementation took another dozen or more years. Inadequate resources and the resistance of those who feared the changes would vitiate the centers' religious character slowed the reforms. Programmatic elements appeared piecemeal and represent a trend more than a sudden accomplishment.

The ability to evangelize through a therapeutic milieu depended ultimately on the commanding officer (CO) of each center. Few if any of these officers were professional psychologists or psychiatrists, although some were trained as social workers. For most of the history of the MSSCs, relatively few administrators even had extensive university or professional education. And yet, like so many other Americans in this period, they did not doubt that they could master enough of a psychological perspective to offer therapy. Although COs were clergy, they were closer to the AA pioneers than chaplains in their disdain for highly trained psychotherapists. For they, too, believed such social scientists misconstrued fundamental aspects of human nature and cosmology. This kind of sentiment was aptly expressed in the 1950s by one Salvationist who reflected on his summer school course at Yale on the sociology and psychology of addiction: "Sociologists are a funny lot of people. They seem to believe nothing, hope for nothing, yet require much education to become that way. We never met such confused people."[11] Thus, COs believed that they could

---

[9] Bowery Corps Officers, "Report on Present Program and Proposals" (New York: Salvation Army, 1947).

[10] "The 'Service-to-Man' Program"; Agnew, "The Casework Process"; Baggs, "Answering the Challenge"; Baldwin, "Answering the Challenge"; Guldenschuh, "Aiding Alcoholics"; Hofman, "Answering the Challenge"; Hofman, "Serving the Client"; *The Salvation Army Social Service for Men*.

[11] Bodine, "The 1959 Yale Summer School on Alcohol," 19.

Freud Is Not a Suitable Psychologist 165

draw on the strengths of what psychological professionals knew while augmenting it with the healing and salvific insights of Christianity.

The ability to blend these worldviews began for many aspiring officers in the postwar period at one of the nation's four Schools for Officer Training (SFOT), the Salvationist seminaries. Before 1960, the program lasted only an academic year, but this was then doubled and the intervening summer dedicated to supervised fieldwork.[12] The curriculum consisted primarily of courses in theology, scripture, and ministry.[13] Officers learned the major beliefs of evangelical Protestantism in the twentieth-century United States. Salvationists believed firmly in the transcendent divinity of a triune God. A personal relationship with this God was possible through Jesus Christ, the source of earthly and eternal life. After conversion, believers could deepen their faith through obtaining a second blessing of grace that freed them from conscious sin. Heaven awaited the righteous, and hell the wicked.[14] With this as their metaphysical backdrop, and rigorous training in Scripture, homiletics, and pastoral care, SFOT cadets were sent out each summer as interns to minister to believers and non-believers in the army's churches ("corps") and its many institutions.

But they were not sent out armed only with Christian tools. They were trained in the concepts and techniques of psychology through standard courses in social work, sociology, pastoral counseling, Christian education, and psychology. During the 1960s, the Western SFOT, in Rancho Palos Verdes, CA, may have offered the fullest complement of psychology coursework: a six-course series comprising Introduction to Psychology, Understanding Group Behavior, Developmental Psychology,

---

[12] J. R. Baittinger, Jr., "History of the Training Program," New York: Salvation Army Archives and Research Center, 1976, "SFOT-History (East)" Vertical File, Salvation Army Archives (SAA); "School for Officers Training Curriculum," [pamphlet] New York: Salvation Army east, n.d., "SFOT-History (East)" Vertical File, SAA.

[13] Information on curricula is taken from the SFOT vertical files, SAA. A report in 1968 determined that SFOT curriculum spent 64 percent of course hours on theology and scripture and pastoral care, 13 percent for music, 12 percent on social work and psychology, 6 percent for humanities, and 5 percent for business administration. See Booz Allen & Hamilton Inc., "The Salvation Army in the United States: General Survey of Administration and Operations" (New York: Booz Allen & Hamilton Inc., 1968), Exhibit XI.

[14] See www.salvationarmy.org for the Salvationist eleven-point creed. Salvationist theology is treated by Booth, *In Darkest England*; Coutts, *The Salvationists*; Green, "William Booth's Theology of Redemption"; McKinley, *Marching to Glory*, 2nd ed; Murdoch, *Origins of the Salvation Army*; Taiz, *Hallelujah Lads and Lasses*; Waldron, *Creed and Deed*; Walker, *Pulling the Devil's Kingdom Down*; Winston, *Red-Hot and Righteous*.

166   *American Protestantism in the Age of Psychology*

Psychology of Religion, Counseling, and Leadership in Christian Education.[15] Around the same period, the southern SFOT, located in Atlanta,
GA, offered fewer such classes: two quarters of developmental psychology and a quarter of pastoral counseling.[16] There does not seem to have
been a clear pattern to the development of SFOT curricula. For instance,
by the 1980s, the western SFOT had trimmed its psychology offerings[17]
but the southern SFOT had begun to mandate an extensive program in
pastoral care and counseling.[18]

After graduation the majority of officers served as ministers in Salvationist corps, but those who entered SFOT with more education, or
obtained it after being commissioned, were likely to be assigned to social
work positions such as leading MSSCs. Neither college nor SFOT were the
only training MSSD officers received, however. There were many other
ways that they learned about trends in psychology, applied sociology, and
social work. They took university coursework and attended continuing
education classes that the army itself offered.[19] They maintained memberships in national health and welfare organizations, attended workshops,
and read the growing library of works on psychologically informed pastoral care.[20] The army made sure that new ideas were disseminated and

[15] *Cadet Handbook, 1979–1980* (Atlanta, GA: Salvation Army southern territory, 1979),
20–7, 95–113, "Southern Territory SFOT" Vertical File, SAA.
[16] *Cadet's Manual, 1965* (Atlanta, GA: Salvation Army southern territory, 1965), 23–30,
"Southern Territory SFOT" Vertical File, SAA.
[17] Cadet David Birks, "School for Officers' Training – A Hundred Years in the West"
(Rancho Palos Verdes, CA: Salvation Army western territory, n.d. [1980]), pp. 14–16,
"SFOT-West" Vertical File, SAA.
[18] *Curriculum Statement, 1986–1987* (Atlanta, GA: Salvation Army southern territory,
1986), pp. 11–33, "Southern Territory SFOT" Vertical File, SAA.
[19] See, for example, Capt. Martin L. Cox, Newark, NJ, to Lt. Col. E. A. Marshall, January
20, 1958, Acc. 78–24, SAA; Lt. Col. E. A. Marshall, New York, NY, to Brig. Paul Kaiser,
January 23, 1958, Acc. 78–24, SAA; Lt. Col. William H. Roberts, Chicago, IL, to Mrs.
Col. Lloyd Robb, August 1, 1979, "SFOT-Central" Vertical File, SAA; Lt. Col. Victor
Danielson, Indianapolis, IN, September 8, 1982, Re: Cycle Seminar "The Officer as a
Social Worker," "SFOT-Central" Vertical File, SAA; Robb, interview.
[20] For professional affiliation, see McKinley, *Somebody's Brother*, 200. For seminars, see
Baldwin, "National Commission on Alcoholism"; Barber, "Group Work"; Barber, "The
Program at Work"; Bodine, "The 1959 Yale Summer School on Alcohol"; Duplain, "The
Use of Professional Workers"; Foote, "Theory and Practice"; "Group I–Counselling";
"Group II–Alcoholism"; Guldenschuh, "Aiding Alcoholics"; Malpass, "Techniques of
Counseling; Mina Russell, "Building a Healthy Personality"; Telfer, "Pasadena Alco-
holics Anonymous"; Tobin, "Group Therapy."
For an example of the kind of pastoral literature they were reading, see Clinebell,
Understanding and Counseling the Alcoholic. This well-known book evaluated a variety
of religiously based alcohol treatments, including that of the army. This book was

Freud Is Not a Suitable Psychologist 167

implemented through networks of officer correspondence, newsletters, and the regular rounds of centers made by regional MSSD supervisors.[21]

A vivid depiction of the impression such education made was reported by an officer who attended a 1959 summer session of the cutting-edge Yale School for Alcohol Studies.[22] Despite his and other Salvationists' initial resistance to the secular assumptions of the School, he came to appreciate a new set of concepts for thinking about misbehavior:

> After listening to the lectures over the weeks, one began to realize that alcohol is not such a simple problem as we may sometimes think. Behind it, are deep-seated sociological, psychical and psychological problems.... Indeed, a whole new vocabulary [e.g., "motivation"] impinged itself on [my] mind while listening. In listening to these lectures...the student certainly would obtain a better grasp of the psychological background of the mental conflicts that assail the human mind.[23]

Thus when COs in MSSCs contemplated the men whom they had committed themselves to helping, they were armed with the lessons of Scripture and faith as well as with the ideas and techniques of modern social science. Salvationists saw the men before them as sick sinners or men who had sinned in their sickness. They were far from God and far from society. They needed regeneration in all senses of that word. Their chaotic lives could be ordered by the therapeutic discipline of regular work, which also served to redeem their wasted gift of years. The army

promoted among social service officers as early as 1958 and still is today; see Major Kenneth Anderson, "The Salvation Army and Alcohol: A Billion Dollar Tragedy," in *Salvation Army Sessions, National Council of Social Work 1958*, Chicago, IL (New York: Salvation Army, n.d.): 31–6; Cheydleur, interview.

[21] My sense of typical office correspondence derives from my opportunity to review all fourteen boxes of the correspondence of Frank Guldenschuh, MSSD secretary for the east from 1959 to 1965 (Acc. 78–24), as it was being processed by the SAA archivists during the fall of 2002. The SAA also maintains a collection of newsletters. For dissemination of new findings, see, for example, *News of the Moment*, newsletter of the MSSD east, Salvation Army Newsletter Collection, SAA. For a sample of inspection evaluations and correspondence, see, for example, Lt. Col. J. O. Dowdell, *Inspection Report for Utica, NY*, MSSD eastern territory (New York: Salvation Army, 1944); Brig. Richard Baggs, Boston, MA, to Lt. Col. Ernest Marshall, November 7, 1957, Re: Providence Inspection, Acc. 78–24, SAA; Sr. Maj. George Hulihan, "Regional Inspection – Atlantic City Men's Social Service Center," March 23, 1956, Acc. 78–24, SAA.

[22] The Yale School, which a number of MSSD leaders attended, was a major source of ideas for army programming. See "The 'Service-to-Man' Program," 116–23; Pisani, "Milieu Therapy"; Robb, "The Yale Summer School of Alcohol Studies"; "Schedule of Lectures" (New Haven, CT: Summer School of Alcohol Studies, Laboratory of Applied Physiology, Yale University, 1946).

[23] Bodine, "The 1959 Yale Summer School on Alcohol," 19–20.

168 *American Protestantism in the Age of Psychology*

could offer them the fellowship of group therapy and the group therapy of fellowship. COs encouraged beneficiaries to probe their past and psyches in order to disclose their great pain and guilt. They encouraged their men to seek ultimate catharsis and healing for these burdens in their acceptance of the loving atonement of Jesus' death.

Spiritual Rehabilitation

The centers had emerged out of the army's earliest efforts to convert isolated and unemployed men, and they remained throughout the twentieth century fundamentally an evangelical mission to the homeless. As one CO explained to beneficiaries, "The programs of this center are just tools that we have to aid us in our rehabilitation but Christ is and will be the head of this Center and I, as His servant, will service Him and the men and women to the best of my ability."[24] As the army's traditional evangelical efforts to convert the unsaved and to build their church began to stagnate in the postwar period, the importance of MSSCs blossomed. Both the eastern and central territories had begun to decline at mid-century, and the number of corps nationally shrank steadily after 1950. Membership increased, but not nearly as fast as the overall American population.[25] Thus by 1959 one officer spoke of the centers as "a precious opportunity. At least we have sinners before us, the Corps and Church find it hard to get outsiders in. The very people that in early days were Army converts are in our hands."[26] One corps officer even said he wanted to transfer to the MSSD because he was tired of going out after people and wanted a captive audience![27]

The distinction between church and mission is important to understanding the army's esteem of the MSSCs. They were never strong recruitment instruments for swelling the ranks of the army.[28] But, more

---

[24] Capt. Richard R. Kuhl, open letter to ARC beneficiaries, *The Erie Street Bugle*, newsletter of Jersey City ARC, NJ, 1978, ARC Newsletter Collection, SAA. The department was geared toward the needs of homeless men, who accounted for the majority of assistance seekers from the MSSCs throughout much of their history. Nevertheless, administrators began admitting enough women to prompt a 1977 name change from Men's Social Service Centers to Adult Rehabilitation Centers. The proportion of women in this program always remained small.

[25] McKinley, *Marching to Glory*, 1st ed., 216–17.

[26] Allen, "Teaching Mission," 40.

[27] William Chamberlain, "Cooperating to Build a Better Salvation Army" (paper presented at the MSSC, Asbury Park, NJ, 1959), 18–19.

[28] A survey of Salvationists in the late 1970s found that nearly half of the respondents (45.1%) had become involved in a corps because of previous family involvement, whereas another 18.7% joined because a friend encouraged them. Very few (5.3%) became

Freud Is Not a Suitable Psychologist

important, they were effective in building the ranks of God. For the army to appreciate its own missionary efficacy via the centers, however, it had first to expand its vision of how one recruited for Jesus.

Protestant missions that reached out to alcoholics tended to be – like the army – strongly evangelical, and through much of the century they probably reflected a long-standing anti-Catholicism in American Protestantism. But center clientele generally reflected their region's religious demographics,[29] and American cities were home to many Catholics, especially in the east and midwest, in the first half of the century. This heterogeneity stymied the centers as ambitious officers at the end of World War II tried to reform them and turn them into effective soul-catching centers. In 1945, one even lamented:

In this area more than fifty per-cent of our clients are Roman Catholics. They like Protestant food, clothing, social and medical services, recreation, and even money, but I am afraid at times a great deal of damage is done to our spiritual program. I, with you, bewail the lack of real conversions that come as a result of our services to these men.[30]

Fortunately, the army was able to make a virtue of necessity. It never seriously considered turning away Catholic alcoholics. Conversion, after all, was the whole point of their mission and excluding Catholics would have been bad business sense for the centers, which depended on a steady supply of labor. Furthermore, the army, unlike other conservative Protestant denominations, had found it in its best interest to forge institutional

---

members because of their initial involvement in a social service program. The actual percentage of social service recruits may be higher since only 35% of those surveyed responded, and they may well have been disproportionately from the more educated and affluent spectrum of Salvationists, exactly those most likely to come from Salvationist families and least likely to have been recruited through a social service. The survey also did not break down recruitment channels for those who were first-generation Salvationists. Nevertheless, the institutions clearly did not account for the bulk of church membership. International Marketing Group Inc., "The Second Hundred Years," appendix, p. 29.

[29] "Monthly Case Load Analysis: Philadelphia Men's Social Service Center," July 1961, Acc. 78–24, SAA; "Monthly Case Load Analysis: Philadelphia Men's Social Service Center," August 1962, Acc. 78–24, SAA; "Monthly Case Load Analysis: Philadelphia Men's Social Service Center," September 1962, Acc. 78–24, SAA; Dexter, "Aspiration Level in Relation to the Homeless Man"; Katz, *Alcoholic Rehabilitation Project*; Katz, "The Salvation Army Men's Social Service Center, II. Results,"; Leparte, "Rehabilitation of the Homeless Man"; Lukens and Scott, "Some Characteristics of Two Hundred Transient Men"; "Service To Man Program Review" [for Manhattan] (1976) in "New York ARC" Vertical File, SAA; *MSSD Handbook, 1960;* Mrs. Brigadier Margaret Troutt, "Men's Social Service in the United States," in *The Salvation Army Yearbook* (London: The Salvation Army, International Headquarters, 1967).

[30] Guldenschuh, "Aiding Alcoholics."

American Protestantism in the Age of Psychology

ties of friendship to other major faith groups. It could hardly have wanted to antagonize its relationships to Catholics and Jews, with whom it shared fundraising efforts and some interests vis-à-vis the government.

Finally, more than other evangelical denominations, the army was receptive to mid-century currents in mainline Protestantism. World War II and the early Cold War were important periods for the displacement of old religious hostilities and bigotries at the center of American cultural life.[31] On the eve of World War II, mainline American Protestants had vigorously protested the appointment of a U.S. representative to the Vatican. But the sense of shared enterprise during the war eroded old religious and ethnic distinctions among European Americans. And the differences between Catholics, Protestants, and Jews in this country paled when set against the shared threat of godless communism abroad in the decade following the Allied victory. Between the early 1930s and the early 1950s, the Supreme Court went from defining the United States as a "Christian" nation to a "religious" one. In 1954, the United States redefined itself officially as a "Nation, Under God."[32] By 1960, sufficient numbers of Protestants felt comfortable electing a Catholic president to bring John F. Kennedy to power.[33]

Thus the centers had both internal and external pressures to figure out a way to evangelize Protestant and Catholic beneficiaries alike. They learned to deal with it theologically as well as programmatically. Theologically, they came to see their mission as reuniting beneficiaries in personal relationships with Jesus Christ, evidenced by sober, ethical living and ties to Christian communities. This goal could be embraced by both Catholics and Protestants.[34] Programatically, they reached out to Catholic beneficiaries by inviting priests to give talks[35] and decorating the stark Salvationist chapels with crosses and decorations to evoke Catholic

---

[31] On an international level, the army was conflicted about ecumenicalism. It participated in the World Council of Churches (WCC), but this generated an ongoing controversy within the organization. Some Salvationists felt that WCC was too inclusive, and in the 1950s, the army temporarily withdrew from its central committee. Coutts, *The Salvationists*, 32.

[32] Marty, *Under God, Indivisible*, 296.

[33] Ibid.

[34] Other faith groups would have challenged this ecumenicalism more deeply, but it was not a problem for most of the century. Jews rarely applied to the centers for help. In recent decades, however, Adult Rehabilitation Centers have begun to treat African American Muslims, many of whom have been converted in prison. They are often hostile to Christianity and pose a challenge to centers. White, interview.

[35] *Brockton Barometer*, February 1978, ARC Newsletter Collection, SAA.

churches.[36] By the last decades of the century, the centers cooperated with a variety of local churches to send vans to pick up men who preferred other denominations' services on Sunday mornings.[37] Although the army would have liked clients to worship with it, of course, that mattered less than that they worshiped. Thus, the centers in the postwar period became ecumenical missions.

Even with this accommodation, the army could not simply set up its mission to the homeless any way it liked if it hoped to be successful. It wanted to appeal to a certain kind of person in a very intimate and powerful way. The men to whom the centers reached out came and went of their own free will. Therefore the MSSD had to take their clients into account when designing their program. There were other attributes of their clients in addition to creedal diversity with which the army had to contend. For starters, most of the men entering centers at mid-century had had previous experience with missions. Many had reluctantly attended services or feigned conversion to obtain food and shelter from missionaries. This sort of interaction, officers worried, fostered "cynicism and even hatred for all organized religion" among the very men they were trying to convert.[38] The army wanted to break down this "wall of indifference" toward God and to avoid being conned by "nose divers," men who simulated a religious response for the material benefits and attention they would receive.[39] These goals required time, a steady and honest relationship between missionary and alcoholic, and the promise that material aid would not be predicated on spiritual growth. MSSDs cautioned that this did not mean center staff should dampen their religious zeal, but rather they were urged to implement "an adroit, careful, thoughtful and intelligent *organization* of that very spiritual zeal."[40]

Few if any of the beneficiaries retained ties to church and faith when they entered the MSSCs. In 1946, an investigator noted that nearly all "spoke of their religion in the past tense."[41] Nevertheless, few men refused

[36] "The 'Service-to-Man' Program," 112–13.

[37] White, interview.

[38] "The 'Service-to-Man' Program," 105. The 1960 MSSD Handbook (7:9:2–3) warns officers that they not antagonize or alienate beneficiaries with overly aggressive evangelizing. It was more effective to develop a relationship of trust before pressing spiritual claims on a man.

[39] The problem of nose-diving for missionaries emerges repeatedly in the literature. For a vivid description of it, see Clinebell, *Understanding and Counseling the Alcoholic*, 80, 86.

[40] "The 'Service-to-Man' Program," 105.

[41] Straus, "Alcohol and the Homeless Man," 385.

American Protestantism in the Age of Psychology

to identify with any religion at all and most still held conventional ideas about God.[42] But this was not an image of divinity that attracted them or prompted them to reform their lives. The MSSD explained that "homeless addicted men tend to imagine God as a punishing and rejecting deity whom their guilt and fear make them want to shun."[43]

This situation meant that few beneficiaries were primarily interested in being evangelized. Men who entered programs in the Bay area of California in the early 1960s, for instance, were not overwhelmingly interested either in religion or even in treatment.[44] Like beneficiaries in centers across the country, many sought merely to rest up, eat a lot, and get a new set of clothes.[45] Many or even most clients, however, were probably indifferent or even hostile.[46] This created difficulty for the army because even a client who was truly spiritually inclined had to put up with the "persecution" of fellow beneficiaries in the form of "very profane and uncomplimentary remarks... [implying that] the man is professing salvation to gain favor or special privileges from the staff, or that he is working the old confidence game for his own gain."[47] Nevertheless, these obstacles of indifference, hostility, and harassment were by no means overwhelming. The army learned to expect and work around them because they knew that forcing beneficiaries to "walk the Christian walk,"[48] willingly or not, would nurture faith in a significant minority of them. As one man confessed in 1981 while reflecting on his treatment at the Chicago Adult Rehabilitation Center:

In the beginning, I resented attending chapel. It seemed that the songs were childish as well as the service. It took some time before I realized that the staff

---

[42] Katz, for instance, found that beneficiaries in the early 1960s in San Francisco had conventional religious beliefs, *Alcoholic Rehabilitation Project*, 41.

[43] *MSSD Handbook, 1960*, 7:9:3.

[44] Katz, *Alcoholic Rehabilitation Project*; Katz, "The Salvation Army Men's Social Service Center, II. Results." Major Marilyn White, who spent fourteen years as ARC administrator in the Washington and Baltimore areas, found that many clients, especially African American clients, prefer army services to other rehab programs because they desire religious rejuvenation as part of their recovery efforts.

[45] A lack of beneficiary interest in rehabilitation is another common finding; see Dexter, "Aspiration Level in Relation to the Homeless Man"; Katz, *Alcoholic Rehabilitation Project*; Leparte, "Rehabilitation of the Homeless Man," 56–8; Lukens and Scott, "Some Characteristics of Two Hundred Transient Men."

[46] Leparte, "Rehabilitation of the Homeless Man," 59.

[47] Capt. Walter Guldenschuh, "Spiritual Counseling in the Men's Social Service Center," Rochester, NY, 1960, Acc. 78–24, SAA.

[48] The phrase was used in an explanation of Central Territory's mandatory religious activities by McPherson; interview.

was deadly serious because alcoholism is deadly serious. And the songs were good for me because God *is* Good![49]

The most basic tools of spiritual rehabilitation were traditional religious activities. Service-to-Man required at least two worship services weekly and brief communal daily devotions, often fifteen minutes in the morning when the men gathered together to pray before work. But new religious programming was added into the late 1950s and afterward. In the immediate postwar years in Columbus, OH, for instance, the MSSC offered only Sunday morning services. But within a decade, it had added prayer services on Friday nights, morning devotions daily, Bible study, a fellowship group for converts, and an in-house AA.[50] In Minnesota in the late 1960s, beneficiaries attended Sunday services, Bible classes, converts' club meetings, morning devotions, and a chaplain's class, where they discussed how they had come to find themselves in need of the center. Biannual spiritual retreats were offered to men who had shown concern for their souls.[51]

Fostering community was an important activity for both spiritual and psychosocial development. To achieve this, the centers set up fellowships that allowed men to gather with likeminded religious seekers. These fellowships made ample room for dealing with scriptural, theological, and personal issues alike. Sometimes these groups were limited to converts, but other times they embraced the entire beneficiary community. At the Los Angeles center in 1959, all clients were enrolled in the Fellowship Club, which had numerous committees that organized activities such as entertainment, alcohol education, recreation, and hospital visitation of hospitalized center residents.[52] In the early 1960s, the Buffalo center ran a Henry F. Milans Club. These clubs were named after a rehabilitated alcoholic Salvationist. The Buffalo staff had an AA group as well and did not want the club to be redundant, so they shaped it as a tool to promote Salvationism as well as fellowship and leadership among the men.[53] Every new client was required to attend four meetings, after which they

---

[49] Len W. to Moses A., March 9, 1981, attached to "Chicago Central Adult Rehabilitation Center" Writing Contest Entry 38, manuscript, in MSSD central territory Vertical File, SAA.

[50] Lawrence Castagna, "Brief: Columbus, Ohio, Men's Social Service Center" (1958), Acc. 78–24, SAA.

[51] Troutt, "Men's Social Service in the United States."

[52] Johnson, "Fellowship Clubs."

[53] Brigadier Clarence Simmons, Buffalo, NY, to Col. Frank Guldenschuh, October 23, 1962. Acc. 78–24, SAA.

174 American Protestantism in the Age of Psychology

received a certificate. Members visited hospitalized beneficiaries, participated in a weekly fellowship hour, planned center entertainment, conducted Sunday evening vespers services, and educated center residents about the work of the army.[54]

Two other forums allowed the army to blend an evangelical appeal with rehabilitation. Sometimes it staged revival retreats and camp meetings. Centers made vans available to transport interested residents to local events, but these mass meetings were probably not very effective in reaching MSSC clients.[55] Better results were probably obtained from targeted retreats where revivalists adapted their message specifically to center beneficiaries. Such a specialized retreat in 1959, for instance, led to seventeen of the nineteen guests either coming forward for salvation, consecration, or special prayer requests.[56]

A less intense but more ubiquitous forum for psychospiritual exhortation were newsletters. Many large centers published newsletters of significant length and quality. Although few were preserved, those that remain demonstrate in their very layout the way centers constantly juxtaposed evangelical and therapeutic appeals. For example, the two main features of the newsletter of the Los Angeles center in the early 1960s were a short sermon and an article about the physiology and psychology of alcoholism. One issue ran a testimonial entitled "My Rehabilitation." It told the story of an educated CPA named William who, after divorcing his wife, began drinking heavily and was eventually fired from his job and rendered homeless. Eventually, he was admitted to the Los Angeles center, where he stayed away from alcohol by reading and became active in the Men's Fellowship Club. He came to realize the extensive emotional, physical, and spiritual damage alcoholism had caused him. William advised new program members to "follow the program to its fullest extent" and to "put your trust in God and let him help you."[57]

The spiritual program of center beneficiaries was effective in the most important way possible: It encouraged the religious growth of beneficiaries, as will be demonstrated in detail in the final section. But is also

---

[54] Brigadier Clarence Simmons, Buffalo, NY, to Col. Frank Guldenschuh, November 27, 1962. Acc. 78–24, SAA.

[55] See, for example, Harry Ashby, "Report of Spiritual Campaign Jan. 8–14 Inclusive," Buffalo, NY, MSSC (1962). Acc. 78–24, SAA.

[56] Harold Watson, "Report: Retreat, Sept. 12–13 1959, Star Lake Camp, Hempstead and Mt. Vernon Centers" (paper presented at the MSSC, Asbury Park, NJ, 1959).

[57] The Broadcaster, newsletter of the Los Angeles MSSC, MSSC Newsletter Collection, SAA.

worked in another way: It contributed to the rehabilitation of beneficiaries. The army officers were always quick to point this out based on their own experience. When outsiders evaluated their work, they agreed. One study at the San Francisco center in the early 1960s tried to assess the factors that determined beneficiaries' chances at rehabilitation. The study found that religion stood out as a major factor, leading the researcher to conclude, "When a religious conversion is sincerely experienced rehabilitation sometimes seems to flow almost 'automatically.'"[58]

Work Therapy

In his famous book *The Culture of Narcissism*, Christopher Lasch laments the therapeutically driven decline of the Protestant work ethic. He contrasted it with a contemporary emphasis on the ability to gain others' admiration and cooperation in place of work and deferred gratification.[59] Had he turned his gaze from the relatively elite precincts that furnish much of the evidence for his book to the run-down neighborhoods that hosted MSSCs, he might have been pleased. Work had been the bedrock of army assistance to indigent men since the turn of the century. The Industrial Homes had primarily been places where such men could receive shelter and food in exchange for productive labor, the fruit of which went to pay for their care (as well as to help other poor people). This aspect of army help for needy men never changed over the twentieth century: Beneficiaries always had to bear, at least in part, the cost of their own care. Inculcating a work ethic, both to enable beneficiaries to be useful to the larger society and to develop themselves, was a key goal of Salvationist therapy.

Furthermore, financial self-reliance was imperative for the MSSCs so they did not have to accept outside monies. Other army programs, such as the Harbor Light Centers, which were transformed in the 1950s from the old Bowery corps that ministered to skid-row alcoholics, could not rely on their own businesses to fund them. At mid-century, they survived by soliciting funds and donations from charitable Americans, demanding that residents with jobs pay bed rent and meal charges, and selling army magazines.[60] But by the 1980s, Harbor Light Centers found it

---

[58] Katz, "The Salvation Army Men's Social Service Center, II. Results," 645.

[59] This distinction is articulated at greater length in Susman, "'Personality' and the Making of Twentieth-Century Culture."

[60] *The Salvation Army Manual for Harbor Light Centers; The Salvation Army Manual for Harbor Light Centers*, 2nd ed.

176   *American Protestantism in the Age of Psychology*

necessary to solicit public funds, which interfered with their evangelical mission.[61] They could no longer require or strongly encourage attendance at religious activities. Men who wanted to participate had to sign wavers affirming that they did so of their own free will.[62]

This fate did not befall the MSSCs, however. Each center was also a salvage business that collected donated materials of all kinds (e.g., furniture, clothing), refurbished them, and then resold them at low cost to the poor in thrift stores. This independence meant that the army could run its centers without public interference, although it also meant that funds were limited. Centers faced the normal pressures of small businesses, including competition from other salvage companies and nonprofits that also rely on refurbishing donations, such as Goodwill Industries.[63] It also meant that centers were not all equally wealthy. Big centers in urban areas with large caseloads had higher revenue than smaller centers in more rural or suburban environments. As a result, big centers – such as those in Chicago, Cleveland, Los Angeles, Rochester, and New York City – could often afford to offer a more varied program, implement new therapies sooner, and more easily hire the services of professionals. Although funding variations meant that some centers lagged far behind others in the program elements discussed in this chapter, it should be noted that the bigger centers also accounted for a larger share of the people who received army rehabilitation.

Work therapy was the single largest therapeutic component of the center because the beneficiaries spent roughly 40 hours a week engaged in it. They assisted truck drivers who went to collect and solicit donated materials. They sorted donated materials and helped clean and refurbish them for sale. They helped out in army stores. They were assigned responsibilities to help maintain the centers, such as working in the kitchen or at the canteen. Beneficiaries who demonstrated good progress toward recovery and wanted to stay in the centers could aspire to becoming an army

---

[61] White, interview.

[62] Ibid.

[63] For evidence of concern about competition curbing center revenue, see Brig. Bissell, "Farewell Brief for Erie [PA] Men's Social Service Center," Acc. 78–24, SAA; Laune, "A Survey of The Men's Social Service Center," 15; McPherson, interview. The army sometimes cooperated with other nonprofits that relied on donations; see, for example, "Inter Agency Meeting," [minutes], May 6, 1963, Dayton, OH, Acc. 78–24, SAA; Brig. Clarence Simmons, Buffalo, NY, to Col. Frank Guldenschuh, May 28, 1963. Acc. 78–24, SAA.

Freud Is Not a Suitable Psychologist 177

employee and working as a truck driver, watchman, foreman, deskman, houseman, or even a counselor.

The transformation of work into work therapy was strategic, but it was not cynical. The army rechristened the name of the task due to the Labor Department pressure described earlier, but this did not change the way the organization believed the activity functioned. It had always believed work was good for people, for *all* people. Drawing on an old Protestant work ethic and eschewal of idleness as pernicious,[64] Salvationists themselves worked very hard, often donating large amounts of their earnings and leisure time to civic, church, and philanthropic activities.[65] Officers worked extremely hard, and COs probably endured seven-day work weeks routinely. Two extremely dedicated officers at the Bowery corps in New York served for years with hardly a day off much less vacation, until their doctors finally appealed directly to their supervisors out of fear for their deteriorating health.[66]

The army believed that work would benefit its clients far beyond any money they might earn. It was a therapy tailored for the kind of individuals assisted by the centers. Beneficiaries' low social functioning in all realms of their lives extended to the inability to get or hold down a job. It constituted a grave disability for most beneficiaries. This was due partly to irresponsibility, inebriation, and irascibility, but it was also a function of limited schooling and job skills.[67]

---

[64] For a richly detailed discussion of the origins of the Protestant work ethic in the United States, see Innes, *Creating the Commonwealth*.

[65] For a breakdown of hours and earnings donated by Salvationists in 1980, see International Marketing Group Inc., "The Second Hundred Years," appendix, p. 30. In *Marching to Glory*, 2nd ed., McKinley talks about the unusually high level of demands put on Salvationists as a curb to further growth (p. 283).

[66] The history of the fascinating and almost heroic story of two women officers who ran the Bowery Corps in New York from 1945–1960 can be recounted from the materials in Record Group 4.5, SAA. For medical concerns about their health, see William W. Field, New York, NY, to Col. Harold Smith, July 15, 1957, RG 4.5, Box 208/1, SAA.

[67] Troutt, "Men's Social Service in the United States." Low academic achievement is also noted in "Monthly Case Load Analysis: Philadelphia Men's Social Service Center," July 1961, Acc. 78–24, SAA; "Monthly Case Load Analysis: Philadelphia Men's Social Service Center," August 1962, Acc. 78–24, SAA; "Monthly Case Load Analysis: Philadelphia Men's Social Service Center," September 1962, Acc. 78–24, SAA; "Service To Man Program Review" [for Manhattan] (1976) in "New York ARC" Vertical File, SAA; Dexter, "Aspiration Level in Relation to the Homeless Man"; Judge, "Alcoholism Treatment at The Salvation Army," 464; Leparte, "Rehabilitation of the Homeless Man"; Lukens and Scott, "Some Characteristics of Two Hundred Transient Men"; McKinley, "'A Lodging Place for Men – and More!'"; Straus, "Alcohol and the Homeless Man."

178 *American Protestantism in the Age of Psychology*

Work therapy was a tutor in reliability and cooperation. The men generally responded well to it. Some, of course, did not perceive the work as a therapy, and complained about the small size of gratuities they received.[68] But others took pride in it.[69] And all enjoyed earning cash, which gave them a small measure of much-treasured independence.[70] Outside investigators were also impressed with the work therapy and viewed it as a legitimate component of the army program, the efficacy of which had been demonstrated by research.[71] Nor was work as therapy unique to the army. Vocational therapy was already a well-publicized and researched notion in psychological and psychiatric circles in the 1940s. The field expanded throughout the rest of the twentieth century, and the use of vocational rehabilitation for alcoholics became a topic of investigation during the early 1960s.[72]

Milieu Therapy

One of the most basic therapies that MSSCs offered beneficiaries after the Service-to-Man reforms was that of a rehabilitative milieu. The idea of milieu therapy was first articulated in wake of World War II. In the postwar explosion of interest in, study of, and demand for psychotherapy, the idea of what constituted therapy itself expanded. Along with the democratization of *who* could practice therapy, there was a democratization of what practices could be considered to constitute therapy. Perhaps sensitized by a new widespread awareness of totalitarianism, practitioners began to look at the total environment in which patients were treated. They began to perceive that recovery depended not only on what happened for the few hours each week that a patient spent with a doctor, but on everything that happened to that patient for his or her other hundred

[68] Dexter, "Aspiration Level in Relation to the Homeless Man," 48–50.

[69] A poignant example of this was clear in a letter written in 1981 by a grateful rehabilitated alcoholic to a staff member at the Chicago MSSC, "The work program was just the therapy I needed." Len W., to Moses A., Chicago, IL, March 9, 1981, appended to "Chicago Central Adult Rehabilitation Center," Writing Contest Entry 38, manuscript, in MSSD central territory Vertical File, SAA.

[70] Leparte, "Rehabilitation of the Homeless Man," 69–70.

[71] Moos et al., "Evaluation of a Salvation Army Alcoholism Treatment Program," 1273; Dexter, "Aspiration Level in Relation to the Homeless Man"; Katz, *Alcoholic Rehabilitation Project*; Laune, "A Survey of The Men's Social Service Center," 16.

[72] In the mid-1960s, articles began appearing in peer-reviewed journals about alcoholics and vocational rehabilitation, articles on "vocational therapy" had begun as early as the mid-1930s, and more than six dozen articles discussed vocational rehabilitation between 1940 and 1950. The number increased 160% in the next decade. See PsychWeb, published by Ovid Technologies, Inc. © 2000–2002, at http://gateway1.ovid.com.

Freud Is Not a Suitable Psychologist 179

or so waking hours. The physical environment, other patients, other staff, and other activities could all contribute to whether or not a mentally ill person got well. The idea caught on rapidly in the 1950s.[73] An important book, *Ego and Milieu* (1962) by J. Cumming and E. Cumming, defined milieu therapy as "a scientific manipulation of the environment aimed at producing changes in the personality of a patient."[74] The approach attempts to impress on the patient both his individual value and his responsibility to peers.[75]

Milieu was one of the therapies that that the MSSCs were most easily able to offer because of the ease with which the idea of a wholesome Christian environment – sheltered from temptation, close to religious reminders, and under the guidance of Christian leaders – could be transformed into the idea of a rehabilitative milieu. The army's first order of business in developing a feasible claim to offer such treatment was to transform the crude accommodations of the pre–Word War II era into a humane and homey environment. The décor of the centers was domesticated, for instance, as officers replaced long mess tables with smaller, linoleum-topped tables.[76] They also tried to make available a lounge area furnished with such items as pool tables, television sets, magazines, and a canteen stocked with sweets and cigarettes. At a 1959 meeting of eastern center administrators, officers agreed that the canteen had "usefulness as a distinct therapy" when they had time to work behind the counter because they discovered that "it was an excellent time to get to know the men better, as well as to be in a position to listen when a fellow wanted to talk."[77]

Beneficiaries were very private and easy to antagonize. Those who wished to assist them had to see the entire day as an extended potential therapeutic hour and patiently and sensitively "await opportunities for counseling."[78] Officers and counselors frequently commented on how

---

[73] PsychWeb's database lists eight articles on "milieu therapy" or "therapeutic community" between 1940–1950. This number increased ninefold during the 1950s. Thousands of articles have been written since then. PsychWeb, published by Ovid Technologies, Inc. © 2000–2002, at http://gateway1.ovid.com.

[74] Cited in Pisani, "Milieu Therapy and the Multi-Treatment Approach," 257.

[75] Ibid., 258.

[76] McKinley, *Somebody's Brother*, 130.

[77] Sr. Maj. Paul Harvey, Syracuse, NY, to Lt. Col. Frank Guldenschuh, February 6, 1959, Re: Regional Meeting Minutes, Acc. 78–24, SAA.

[78] Sr. Maj. Ronald Irwin, "Summary of Findings of The Salvation Army Men's Social Department, Regional Conference," Philadelphia, PA, March 13, 1956, Acc. 78–24, SAA.

180   *American Protestantism in the Age of Psychology*

much more likely residents were to open up about their problems during informal conversations conducted while sharing a truck ride or standing in a hallway than during formal counseling sessions.[79]

Recreational activities fostered interaction, friendships, and a sense of community among the men. Such benefits, officers knew, were therapeutically essential since poor socialization, loneliness, distrust, and alienation afflicted their beneficiaries and caused many of their other problems. Clients were rarely romantically attached when they entered the program, and seemed to be far less likely than the larger population to have ever been married.[80] Few enjoyed contacts with any immediate family members at the time of admission. Such connections would have been difficult given that, beginning in the 1960s, an increasing number of beneficiaries were violent, antisocial, and deeply cynical. The extent of their alienation was apparent when a graduate student interviewed twenty beneficiaries in an MSSC in Providence, RI, in 1967. He discovered that all of them believed that even the smallest gestures of friendship to their peers left them vulnerable to being robbed, conned, or humiliated. Only a few – in the hope that at least some people were not so predatory – had the courage to reach out to others.[81] A large minority in many centers were veterans,[82] and some had been profoundly scarred by wartime duty. More than 70 percent of clients in the San Francisco center in the early 1960s had been in jail (many possibly for charges related to public drunkenness).

The instability and frustrations in beneficiaries' personal lives heightened the importance of a nurturing and socializing environment. Centers

[79] A manager in Atlantic City, NJ, reported that he "found that men talk a great deal more to him about their problems while in the process of playing a game than through the procedure of the scheduled interview." This was such a routine occurrence that some centers, such as Newark MSSC, required that staff fill out a form describing the content of such informal discussions so that they could be added to a beneficiary's official record. Sr. Maj. George Hulihan, "Regional Inspection – Atlantic City Men's Social Service Center," March 23, 1956, Acc. 78–24, SAA; Brig. Ronald Irwin, Newark, NJ, to Lt. Col. Frank Guldenschuh, December 5, 1960, Acc. 78–24, SAA.

[80] Only a handful of homeless addicts have romantic ties when they enter a MSSC, and all investigators note the disproportionately high percentage of such men who had never married at all. For example, see Dexter, "Aspiration Level in Relation to the Homeless Man"; Judge, "Alcoholism Treatment at The Salvation Army," 464; Lukens and Scott, "Some Characteristics of Two Hundred Transient Men"; Straus, "Alcohol and the Homeless Man"; Troutt, "Men's Social Service in the United States."

[81] Leparte, "Rehabilitation of the Homeless Man," 76–8.

[82] Lukens and Scott, "Some Characteristics of Two Hundred Transient Men"; McKinley, "A Lodging Place for Men-and More," 25–6.

Freud Is Not a Suitable Psychologist

began to provide games and recreation in the evenings and on weekends. In the early 1950s, a typical center may have offered one activity each evening; for example, an AA meeting, a Bible class, an occasional movie or a performance by an army band.[83] Increasingly in the 1960s and 1970s, large centers typically offered a panoply of evening and weekend group activities. By 1980, the Adult Rehabilitation Center in Rochester, NY, hosted a Christian Fellowship Group; a variety of AA meetings, alcoholism lectures, and other twelve-step groups; a Family Problem Group; a basic education class; and opportunities to participate in choir, bingo, bowling, and ceramics.[84] During the late 1970s, at the center in Columbus, OH, beneficiaries could participate in a wide range of group activities, including a newly formed consciousness-raising group for women, which offered "a supportive, non-judgmental environment" in which "members can talk with other women, share common experiences and develop insights into oneself and others."[85]

As with work, the transformation of a wholesome Christian environment into a therapeutic milieu was not a cynical maneuver by the army. The organization had always believed that the men in its care were better off in such environments than in the degraded and temptation-ridden streets from which they had come. Furthermore, they made the changes necessary to upgrade the industrial environment and minimal program of the pre–Service-to-Man days into a rehabilitative milieu. This was one of the first changes that the centers implemented after the reforms of the late 1940s. That they had succeeded is evident in the seriousness with which their efforts were taken by professional psychologists and psychiatrists. When in the early 1960s the San Francisco MSSC – the center with the most sophisticated psychotherapy offerings at that time – was evaluated to assess the therapeutic efficacy of various program components, the investigator, Laurence Katz, singled out "therapeutic milieu" as a treatment on its own. Katz bundled environment and the work program together, asserting that the therapeutic milieu comprised the structure of the program, beneficiaries' relationships with the institution and army staff, opportunity for productive work, and opportunity for

---

[83] For example, see issues from the early 1950s of *The Discoverer*, Columbus, OH, MSSC Newsletter Collection, SAA.

[84] *Center Tidings*, January 1980, Rochester, NY, ARC Newsletter collection, SAA.

[85] *Adult Rehabilitation Center*, Columbus, OH, March 1978; *Adult Rehabilitation Center*, Columbus, OH, April 1978; *Adult Rehabilitation Center*, Columbus, OH, July 1978; *Adult Rehabilitation Center*, Columbus, OH, November 1978. All newsletters in ARC Newsletter Collection, SAA.

182 *American Protestantism in the Age of Psychology*

reconstitution and spiritual regeneration.[86] And the milieu aided recovery. Half of those who stayed at least one month reduced drinking and improved work patterns. Other articles on army rehabilitation that appeared in major peer-reviewed psychiatric and addiction journals also mentioned therapeutic milieu or therapeutic community as a significant aspect of the army program.[87]

Counseling and Case Work

With the Service-to-Man program, the MSSCs adopted the goal of providing personalized treatment for each beneficiary. This focused casework would help each member overcome his particular problems, develop his individuality, and feel an important part of the center.[88] To oversee this, the MSSDs reconstituted the existing role of "personnel worker," a job with origins in the Industrial Home era. Personnel workers had oriented and managed the workers and dealt with their problems to the extent that they impaired the productivity of the center. Personnel workers, after the reforms, became "personnel counselors," or – to even more thoroughly eradicate vestiges of the old production-oriented mindset – simply "counselors."[89] Counselors served as unprofessional center social workers.[90]

---

[86] Katz, *Alcoholic Rehabilitation Project*, 78–9.

[87] Bromet et al., "The Social Climate of Alcoholism Treatment Programs"; Judge, "Alcoholism Treatment at The Salvation Army." Bromet et al. agreed not to identify the army program they evaluated, but a close review of their work and knowledge of army services suggests that it was probably a Harbor Light Center and not an MSSC. Nevertheless, Harbor Light Centers and MSSCs were very similar in their program structure and the authors explicitly treated the therapeutic offerings at the center they investigated as paradigmatic of army alcohol rehabilitation. For a review of the investigation, see Moos et al., *Alcoholism Treatment*.

[88] Major A. E. Agnew, *Officers' Councils, Salvation Army, Men's Social Service Department-east* (Atlantic City, NJ: 1954), SAA. Captain A. Ernest Agnew, who was a professional social worker, began to actively promote case work in the eastern centers. A few other like-minded COs such as Major Richard E. Baggs in Philadelphia, PA, Adjutant Peter Hofman in Cleveland, OH, Major Frank Guldenschuh in New York, NY, and Major Herbert Sparks in Pittsburgh, PA, began instituting casework in their centers by the late 1930s and early 1940s, drawing on their own social work training and/or the use of hired professionals. McKinley, *Somebody's Brother*, 120–1. For the invention of and broader move toward casework in the nonprofit sector, see Morris, *The Limits of Voluntarism*.

[89] Agnew, "The Casework Process in the Men's Social Service Center."

[90] *MSSD Handbook, 1960,* 5:7:2.

Freud Is Not a Suitable Psychologist   183

The way the army saw the role of center counselor was very broad and even somewhat vague, spanning the range between social worker, pastoral counselor, and therapist.[91] Not all counselors could master all tasks. And the presence of other professional staff – such as trained psychotherapists or chaplains – affected job descriptions in individual centers. Generally, however, counselors were responsible for at least some of a wide gamut of tasks, including conducting intake interviews, orienting new beneficiaries, drafting individualized rehabilitation plans, religious counseling, therapy, organizing group activities, and helping to secure additional services for the center and individual men.

The capaciousness of the counselors' role eased psychoreligious blending. For example, a CO at the MSSC in Newark, NJ, reported in 1960 that the center took great pains to ensure that a staff member, usually the chaplain, counseled all incoming men so as

> to get acquainted with the man and gain his confidence. To learn his desires, his hopes, ambitions and needs; and how best the Men's Social Center can help him. Paramount above all other considerations would be the salvation of his soul.[92]

Centers hired as counselors people from a variety of different backgrounds: rehabilitated alcoholics, ministers, sympathetic Christians, and professional or student social workers, psychotherapists, and pastoral counselors. Early versions of the MSSD handbook emphasized the importance of a counselor's spiritual qualifications, demonstrated by having had a "dynamic religious experience." A shift in emphasis occurred between the 1948 and 1960 editions and the one revised in 1987, since the more recent handbook put far greater priority on adequate training than matters of the soul.[93] This trend in ideas about qualifications is not, however,

---

[91] The army was aware of this vagueness. In 1963 there was a discussion of the broad and variable way it used the term "counseling." Participants talked about it in terms of helping a person develop a clearer sense of himself; developing a relationship of support and acceptance; confronting the individual with the reality of his situation; guiding him toward broader perspectives; and helping him to become capable of making good decisions. The group also discussed the issue of how to balance evangelism during counseling with respect for the client's personality and his right to make his own decision. See "Group I–Counseling."

[92] Brig. Ronald Irwin, Newark, NJ, to Lt. Col. Frank Guldenschuh, January 4, 1961, Acc. 78–24, SAA.

[93] *MSSD Handbook*, 1960, 5:7:2; *The Salvation Army Men's Social Service Handbook of Standards, Principles and Policies*, ed. Commissioners' Conference (The Salvation Army, 1987), 64; *The Salvation Army Social Service for Men*, 38.

American Protestantism in the Age of Psychology

paralleled by other evidence of counselors' day-to-day duties, which suggests no decline in counselors' spiritual responsibilities over the fifty-year postwar period. In fact, it sometimes points to even greater integration into the religious program.[94] It is possible that with the expansion of postwar higher education generally, pastoral counseling training, and the efficacy of the center's evangelism of beneficiaries, centers were increasingly able to hire counselors who were both better trained and more deeply committed to the army's evangelical mission.

During the 1950s, the early period of implementing the Service-to-Man reforms, centers struggled to meet the new guidelines with old staff. Most acquired at least part-time counselors during this period, but they were not always competent to perform all the duties desired from a counselor. For instance, in 1957, the MSSC in Poughkeepsie, NY, Charlie M., the personnel counselor, was "well liked by the men" and highly regarded by the CO because "He does a good job of interviewing and keeping the records up to date. [But] He is not strong as a spiritual counselor, (not many counselors are), so [the C.O. has] acted as a Chaplain to overcome this deficit."[95] Meanwhile, Paul F., who worked in the mid-1950s for the Trenton, NJ, MSSC as personnel worker was competent with records but "doesn't seem to have the personality for counseling, as his personality seems to keep the men at a distance and he never gains their confidence."[96]

Charlie M. and Paul F. may have been rehabilitated alcoholics themselves. COs often recruited from the ranks of successful beneficiaries or center employees. The best men from these ranks were those who had a natural talent for counseling and who had had a "dynamic religious experience." One successful example was Cleo Z., who was the counselor for the Cincinnati MSSC in the mid-1950s. Although Cleo's beginnings were inauspicious – he had been repeatedly thrown out of the center for drunkenness – he had finally experienced a spiritual conversion and remained sober for five months. At that point, he was promoted from beneficiary to employee and hired as counselor. He impressed the Service-to-Man inspector as "earnest, hard working, and intelligent." His face bore the

---

[94] The source of most of the written historical evidence about counselors are the SAA MSSD/ARC newsletter collection; files from the office of Frank Guldenschuh from the east, covering the mid-1950s through the early 1960s; and published statements in handbooks and minutes from officers' meetings.

[95] Capt. Raymond E. Howell, "Farewell Brief for Poughkeepsie [NY] Men's Social Service Center," (1957), Acc. 78–24, SAA.

[96] Sr. Maj. George Hulihan, "Farewell Brief for Trenton [NJ] Men's Social Service Center," (1955), Acc. 78–24, SAA.

Freud Is Not a Suitable Psychologist

marks of years of dissipation, making him look far older than his 53 years, and he was missing many of his front teeth. "In spite of all this, however," the inspector Sr. Major A. E. Agnew reported, "he appears kindly and tolerant – the kind of person that a man could easily confide in." Cleo worked longer hours than necessary at his job, explaining that "he felt that he was compelled to make up as well as possible for the many years that he had wasted as an alcoholic."[97]

Another rehabilitated beneficiary, Howard W., who worked for the center in Erie, PA, in the early 1960s, did not seem to have had such promising religious qualifications but did bring greater training to his counseling job. He was a parolee who had studied psychology and other related subjects with the goal of making a career for himself as a counselor. He had filled in for Erie's regular counselor when she went on vacation and had done such a good job that his superiors were trying to help him land a permanent position at another center.[98]

Some officers emphasized the importance of using believers – either ministers or lay people – as counselors. In one of the New York centers in the mid-1950s, a devout Christian who had been a music teacher in the public school system became a counselor out of a desire for a more fulfilling job. He performed regular intake and interviewing with the men and, if the conversation turned to spiritual matters, handed out copies of the New Testament.[99] The activities of the counselors at the Adult Rehabilitation Center in Kenmore, NY (near Buffalo), in the late 1970s demonstrated a seamless psychoreligious integration. Each issue of the Kenmore newsletter featured a notice from the counselors that was invariably evangelical. In addition to holding personal conferences with beneficiaries, Kenmore counselors led group therapy and helped organize various outings and activities, such as art classes or excursions to softball games. It was thus natural for them to remind center residents that, "The struggle for personal growth is always a combination of many things, both large and small.... The counseling staff is here to help you assess and achieve your personal goals."[100] It was thus *also* natural to remind them frequently to think of what God had done for them and

---

[97] Sr. Maj. A. E. Agnew, "Report of Visit to Cincinnati Men's Social Service Center," November 27, 1954, Acc. 78–24, SAA.

[98] Brig. Charles Bissell, "Farewell Brief for Erie [PA] Men's Social Service Center" (1963), Acc. 78–24, SAA.

[99] Sr. Maj. A. E. Agnew, "Report on Visit to Park Avenue Men's Social Service Center," n.d. (between 1953–1956), Acc. 78–24, SAA.

[100] *Buffalo Billboard*, September 1980, Kenmore, NY, ARC Newsletter Collection, SAA.

186   *American Protestantism in the Age of Psychology*

wanted of them. Blending psychological and theological concerns, they enticed men toward greater health and salvation with comments such as, "Commitment to God's will eliminates conflicts within ourselves."[101]

Salvationist or other Protestant ministers also made good counselors, and such people were increasingly able to offer pastoral counseling that blended social work, psychology, and spiritual advice. In the late 1950s, the Scranton, PA, center hired the officer of the local corps as a part-time counselor since the center could not afford to hire a full-time counselor.[102] In Brockton, MA, Reverend Owen Thompson worked as counselor from the late 1960s to late 1970s.[103] In addition to counseling the men, he led chapel services[104] and held daily devotions.[105] Sometimes, people with social work or counseling backgrounds – or students in the process of getting training – worked as counselors. These employees brought greater knowledge of psychological concepts and techniques than the others. However, they were not necessarily unsympathetic to the religious goals of the army. In the late 1950s, the Wilmington, DE, center offered the job of counselor to a retired YMCA secretary who was a college graduate, a member of the National Association of Social Work, and an active Christian.[106] Another counselor who easily blended increasingly sophisticated psychological knowledge and techniques with religious goals was Raymond Selke, a thoughtful and talented Christian counselor for the MSSC in Rochester, NY, in the 1950s and 1960s. While working for the army, he was also taking psychology coursework at the University of Rochester[107] and learning to implement a variety of psychological and social work techniques at Rochester, including psychological testing of new beneficiaries,[108] developing individualized case plans for each client, and creatively experimenting with leading a variety of group therapies and types of AA meetings. Selke reported to his superiors that "The most ideal group seems to function best with about 12 people," and then, invoking the gathering of Jesus' first apostles, asked rhetorically, "I wonder why the number 12? I wonder."[109]

---

[101] *Buffalo Billboard*, April 1982, Kenmore, NY, ARC Newsletter Collection, SAA.
[102] "Minutes," Regional Meeting of Salvation Army MSSD, Pennsylvania and Southern New Jersey, November 19, 1957, Acc. 78–24, SAA.
[103] *Brockton Barometer*, February 1979, ARC Newsletter Collection, SAA.
[104] *Brockton Barometer*, February 1978, ARC Newsletter Collection, SAA.
[105] *Brockton Barometer*, April 1981, ARC Newsletter Collection, SAA.
[106] Maj. G. Newton McClements, Wilmington, DE, to Col. Frank Guldenschuh, August 12, 1959, Acc. 78–24, SAA.
[107] Raymond Selke, "Changes in Self-Concepts of Homeless Men," Acc. 78–24, SAA.
[108] Ibid.
[109] Selke, *Group Therapy*.

Freud Is Not a Suitable Psychologist 187

Because center counselors boasted a wide range of backgrounds and preparation for their work in the army, on-the-job and continuing training was necessary to ensure that everyone could perform to at least a minimum standard. The army offered a variety of training opportunities to those who counseled. Officers after 1960, of course, received training in pastoral counseling while at the School for Officer Training. The army also offered continuing education courses in pastoral counseling to help officers learn how to conduct pastoral counseling in social work settings and use it as a tool of evangelism and church building.[110] By the early 1980s, such seminars – usually lead by a Christian psychologist – were frequent.[111] Officers also heard lectures and participated in discussions on counseling in conferences and retreats.[112]

Counselors with little background besides on-the-job training also got additional preparation. Occasionally, counselors were students in social work, psychology, or pastoral counseling who took classes while working for the army. As noted earlier, Selke had attended the University of Rochester. Other opportunities were also available. Counselors were sometimes sent with officers to the Yale School for Alcohol Studies.[113] In the late 1950s, and perhaps later, divisions (each of the four territories is subdivided into divisions) tried to host special institutes for counselor training. An example of the agenda remains from an institute held in 1958 in the New England division. Attendees learned about the broader work of the army, the MSSD, and the Service-to-Man program; discussed casework; and tried to get to know themselves better by interrogating their own psychological motivations for taking the job as counselor.[114] Counselors were urged to read books on psychology and counseling and to

---

[110] For example, the CO of Altoona, PA, Brig. Milton Kippax, attended in 1960 an all-day seminar for ministers, social workers, and Christian education workers on counseling and psychology by Dr. Clyde Narramore, Christian psychologist. Brig. Milton Kippax, Altoona, PA, to Lt. Col. Frank Guldenschuh, July 15, 1961, Acc 78–24, SAA.

[111] "Tentative Schedule – Regional Seminars – 1982," "Counseling" Vertical File, SAA; "Principles of Referral," "Counseling" Vertical File, SAA; "Officer-Counselor Program Orientation Seminar," October 26, 1984, Salvation Army southern territory, Atlanta, GA, "Counseling" Vertical File, SAA; Maj. Birgitta Nilson, Chicago, IL, to Officer Counselors, October 11, 1984, "Counseling" Vertical File, SAA; "Comments Made by Officer Counselors at 1983 Survey," "Counseling" Vertical File, SAA; "Minutes," Officer-Counselor Seminar, October 26, 1984, Salvation Army southern territory, "Counseling" Vertical File, SAA.

[112] Lyell Rader, "Immediate Release, 6/25/62, The War Cry" (Syracuse, NY: Salvation Army, 1962), Acc. 78–24, SAA; Malpass, "Techniques of Counseling."

[113] Sr. Maj. James Simonson, Portland, ME, to Lt. Col. Frank Guldenschuh, March 31, 1959, Re: Counselor, Acc. 78–24, SAA.

[114] "Minutes of the Counselor's Institute, Springfield, MA, 1958," pp. 2–4, Acc. 78–24, SAA.

188 *American Protestantism in the Age of Psychology*

take a psychological perspective in their interactions with clients, delving into their background to help formulate rehabilitation plans.[115] Such institutes were popular and deemed helpful by counselors, but the money was not always in the budget to host them.[116] In-house training was also available in some centers. For example, in the late 1960s, in Minneapolis, MN, a staff psychologist trained counselors.[117]

The implementation of counseling as a central program component did not occur at a uniform pace throughout the centers. During the 1950s, there was pressure on all centers to ensure that they offered counseling even if most could not afford to offer professional casework. Over the decade, more and more centers instituted counseling, although they sometimes struggled to find, retain, and train the right person for the job. By 1957, for instance, a review of counselors in six metropolitan New York centers revealed one excellent incumbent (who had "a rich religious experience" and "a real passion for the souls of men"), three dedicated counselors who had too much work or too little training to adequately maintain records, one CO who did the counseling himself, and one vacancy.[118] Two years later, inspections showed that eight of the ten centers in the region had counselors.[119] By 1964, every MSSC in the nation reported that it offered spiritual counseling.[120] By then, a significant minority also offered professional social work counseling as well: Although none in the east and only one-tenth in the west did, one-fifth of all southern centers and almost one-third of all western centers did.[121]

The western centers were a window on the future. Centers increasingly obtained the services of full-time, trained counselors and placed their roles at the heart of the rehabilitation program. By the 1987 revision of the

[115] Ibid., 6.
[116] Sr. Maj. Paul Harvey, Syracuse, NY, to Lt. Col. Frank Guldenschuh, January 29, 1959, RE: Counselors' Institutes, Acc. 78–24, SAA; "Minutes," Regional Meeting of Salvation Army MSSD, Pennsylvania and Southern New Jersey, November 19, 1957, Acc. 78–24, SAA; "Minutes," Salvation Army MSSD Regional Meeting, Metropolitan New York, February 27, 1958, Acc. 78–24, SAA; Lt. Col. Frank Guldenschuh, New York, NY, to Brig. Richard Baggs, September 30, 1959, Acc. 78–24, SAA.
[117] Troutt, "Men's Social Service in the United States."
[118] Brig. Frank Guldenshcuh, New York, NY, to Lt. Col. Ernest Marshall, November–December 1957, inspection reports to centers in Metropolitan, NY, Acc. 78–24, SAA.
[119] Brig. Harold Watson, Hempstead, NY, to Lt. Col. Frank Guldenschuh, April 23, 1959, Re: center counselors, Acc. 78–24, SAA.
[120] Katz, "The Salvation Army Men's Social Service Center, I. Program."
[121] Ibid.

MSSC department handbook, the army instructed that whereas work therapy is "a major ingredient" in rehabilitation:

Individual counseling is the key to the center's entire rehabilitation program, beginning at intake and continuing at least monthly throughout the beneficiary's stay. It is usually done by the counselor, supplemented by the administrator, chaplain, and other staff persons. It may be informal sessions or casual.... [as well as] formal counseling [which] is used as therapy, to review progress, and to revise and update the rehabilitation program.[122]

The therapeutic trajectory of such a directive is clear. Nevertheless, this emphasis on counseling – freighted as it was with therapeutic goals, techniques, and language – in no way enervated the centers' spiritual success. In fact, as will be discussed in greater detail in the final section, the centers achieved their all-time highest rates of religious response on the part of beneficiaries in the late 1980s.

Anti-Addiction Therapy

The religious rehabilitation offered in army MSSCs was developed to awaken spiritually and meet the needs of a very specific group of Americans. At the most basic level, the centers tended to attract homeless men, most of whom drank heavily. For perhaps two of every three men who sought army assistance, alcohol was an acid that ate away at their former social and support networks, although for the rest it was their consolation after such webs had worn away for other reasons.[123] New acids and new consolations emerged in the 1960s.[124] As late as 1975, the Manhattan program reported no drug addicts in its large center,[125] but the proportion of users increased afterward.[126]

AA met many needs for the centers. The Service-to-Man focus on rehabilitation demanded that they offer more than work or milieu therapy, neither of which were particularly geared toward alcoholism. To many

---

[122] *MSSD Handbook,* 1987, 90–1.
[123] Straus, "Alcohol and the Homeless Man," 394.
[124] McKinley, "A Lodging Place for Men-and More," 25–6.
[125] "Service To Man Program Review" [for Manhattan] (1976) in "New York ARC" Vertical File, SAA.
[126] This assessment is suggested by the fact that the army began to open detoxification units for drug users; conversations with Social Service leaders; and contemporary conversion/rehab narratives. See in "Contemporary Conversion Narratives," Central Territory ARC Command, Des Plaines, IL (2002), SAA; Cheydleur, interview; Norris, interview; White, interview.

190   *American Protestantism in the Age of Psychology*

reformers, AA was the perfect adjunct. By the mid-1940s, it bore the imprimatur of the nation's leading secular and religious experts. It cost little more than the price of doughnuts and coffee, so all centers could afford to implement it. It was enormously flexible, allowing the army to tailor its psychoreligious messages to the larger mission of the centers. It helped answer the vexing evangelical problem that Catholics posed to centers. And, finally, it formed a natural bridge from the insulated world of the center to the larger community – the one therapy that beneficiaries could continue once they had left the shelter of the center.

Individual army officers began forging ties to AA as soon as it was formed. But in the 1940s and early 1950s, the MSSD did not, as a whole, instantly recognize what a good fit AA could be for it. Pioneers of AA–army cooperation, especially Peter Hofman, aggressively pushed for wider organization ties and highlighted the expansion of resources it would provide MSSCs.[127] Hofman's message resonated with what external experts were saying, too. Throughout the 1940s and 1950s, the Yale School for Alcohol Studies – representing the most prominent and cutting edge research in addiction – avidly promoted AA as the nation's most effective and practical rehabilitation program.[128] Pastoral psychologist Howard Clinebell, in his influential 1956 book, *Counseling the Alcoholic Through Religion and Psychology*, called AA "our greatest resource."[129]

Despite the high esteem AA enjoyed among some secular and religious authorities both inside and outside the MSSD, the relationship between it and the army faced many initial obstacles and setbacks. For starters, the nature of alcohol and alcoholism was still a controversial topic in the late 1940s within the army. This was not surprising given that a majority of Americans still thought persistent inebriation was vice or sin.[130] Among the evangelical community, such ideas were even stronger. One rescue mission leader from the Bowery at this time even reasoned that it might be better for a man to stay drunk if he was going to hell anyway.[131] So it is no surprise that at a conference in 1948, there was lively debate over whether the army should affiliate with groups that did not promote abstinence for everyone, whether a disease model of chronic drunkenness

---

[127] Hofman found allies among other Service-to-Man reformers, especially A. E. Agnew. "The 'Service-to-Man' Program"; Hofman, "Serving the Client"; McKinley, *Somebody's Brother*, 121.
[128] Bodine, "The 1959 Yale Summer School on Alcohol"; Foote, "Theory and Practice"; Robb, "The Yale Summer School of Alcohol Studies."
[129] Clinebell, *Understanding and Counseling the Alcoholic*, 110–44.
[130] Petigny, "The Permissve Turn," 70.
[131] Clinebell, *Understanding and Counseling the Alcoholic*, 89.

Freud Is Not a Suitable Psychologist 191

could be integrated with the concept of sin, and whether evangelical exhortation was really the best way to reach drunkards.[132]

Even social service officers interested in adapting AA as a resource for their clients were full of apprehension. In addition to the normal difficulties encountered by collaboration between two very different kinds of organizations – mutual ignorance, rivalry, and distrust[133] – there were serious concerns about whether taking advantage of the resources of AA was not a kind of Faustian bargain for the centers.[134] In 1947, Anita Robb, the first social service officer to receive professional training and a student of the Yale School, surveyed the increasing use of AA in MSSCs with ambivalence. The organizations, she noted, had distinct goals: sobriety versus salvation.[135] Her conversations with AA representatives at the Yale School had not inspired confidence: some had considered AA as their religion, some had discounted the spiritual aspects of their program, and a few even questioned God's existence.[136] With a mixture of hope and anxiety, she wondered, "Are we, through the use of AAs in our institutions, substituting their group therapy for a real change of heart and a life free through grace? I do not know – in some cases perhaps the AAs form the fellowship."[137]

As early as 1945, it was clear that Robb and the MSSC officers had something to fear besides fear itself from AA. For instance, wartime cooperation between AA and the New York MSSCs and Bowery corps soon came to an abrupt halt. As one of the officers involved in the termination explained to MSSD headquarters:

Because some representatives of Alcoholics Anonymous failed to credit God with their transformations and even cursed while speaking in the Salvation Army auditorium, it was the consensus of the Men's Social Officers and the Corps

---

[132] See *Salvation Army Sessions, National Conference of Social Work* (Atlantic City, NJ: National Research Bureau, Salvation Army, 1948).

[133] Another problem that cropped up sometimes was beneficiaries' lack of receptivity to AA. Often, AA groups were successful, but sometimes they were not. The fragmentary evidence on this gives no clues as to why. Making AA attendance mandatory, as MSSCs later did, obviated high levels of client enthusiasm. See Brig. Horace Clifford, "Brief: Utica [NY] Men's Social Service Center," (1960), Acc. 78–24, SAA; Brig. Paul Harvey, Philadelphia, PA, to Col. Frank Guldenschuh, October 5, 1962, Acc. 78–24, SAA; Col. Frank Guldenschuh, New York, NY, to Brig. Paul Harvey, December 12, 1962, Acc. 78–24, SAA; Barber, "The Program at Work."

[134] "The 'Service-to-Man' Program"; Barber, "The Program at Work"; Johnstone, "Alcoholics Anonymous Groups"; Hofman, interview; Olive McKeown to Col. Claude E. Bates, New York, NY, January 18, 1946. R.G. 4.5, Box 207/14, SAA.

[135] Robb, "The Yale Summer School of Alcohol Studies," 63.

[136] Ibid.

[137] Ibid.

192   *American Protestantism in the Age of Psychology*

Officer that The Salvation Army divorce itself from the Alcoholics Anonymous program.... [138]

The divorce nevertheless left the officers at a loss. They were eager to create a program of their own that would "compare with and even surpass the efforts made by other organizations – a program that will be recognized and appreciated from a religious as well as an up-to-date social and medical science standpoint."[139] But the MSSD supervisors found divorce a cop-out, not a solution to the difficulties in army–AA cooperation. They answered:

We cannot drop [AA]. We must evolve something to retain the skills acquired [and] those obvious values in the A. A. system – giving it all a more basic religious and spiritual emphasis: leading the men to a Person – in this case THE Person.[140]

While the MSSCs were forging greater ties with AA during the 1940s and 1950s, they were also experimenting with more religious alternatives to it. Some hosted Henry F. Milans Clubs or Fellowship Clubs instead of AA chapters.[141] Other centers – such as those in Kansas City, MO; Providence, RI; Poughkeepsie, NY – tried to host an army program based on nine steps.[142] The steps were modified from those in AA to make them more religious in language, concept, and tone. For example, the second step prompted the alcoholic not to turn to a Higher Power in order to be restored to sanity but rather to "acknowledge that only God, his Creator, can recreate him as a decent man." The third step urged him to turn over

---

[138] Frank Guldenschuh, New York, to Bertram Rodda, January 30, 1946, R.G. 4.5, Box 207/14, SAA. Problems leading to the termination of SA-AA cooperation persisted in places at least until 1960. For example, see Brig. Paul Harvey, Rochester, NY, to Robert Soule, October 20, 1960, Acc. 78–24, SAA.

[139] Ibid.

[140] Ibid.

[141] For example, see: Brig. Paul Harvey, Philadelphia, PA, to Col. Frank Guldenschuh, October 5, 1962, Acc. 78–24, SAA; Col. Frank Guldenschuh, New York, NY, to Brig. Paul Harvey, December 12, 1962, Acc. 78–24, SAA; Brig. Paul Harvey, Philadelphia, PA, to Col. Frank Guldenschuh, December 17, 1962, Acc. 78–24, SAA; Barber, "The Program At Work."

[142] Brig. Richard Baggs, Boston, MA, to Lt. Col. Ernest Marshall, November 7, 1957, Re: Providence Inspection, Acc. 78–24, SAA; "Minutes," Regional Meeting of Salvation Army MSSD, Metropolitan New York, November 21, 1957, Acc. 78–24, SAA; McKinley, *Somebody's Brother*, 154. By 1960, Poughkeepsie had begun hosting an AA chapter, although no evidence clarifies the change; perhaps their in-house group had fizzled. See Maj. E. William Worthy, Poughkeepsie, NY, to Lt. Col. Frank Guldenschuh, March 17, 1960, Acc. 78–24, SAA.

Freud Is Not a Suitable Psychologist 193

his will and life not to "God as we understand Him" but rather to "God through Jesus Christ."[143]

Another alternative to AA was Alcoholics Victorious (AV). This program was founded in 1948 at rescue mission of the Chicago Christian Industrial League. It was an explicit emendation of AA, deriving its scriptural rationale from 2 Corinthians: "If any man be in Christ, he is a new creature; old things are passed away; behold, all things are become new" (5:17). Unlike the ecumenical spirituality of AA, AV's theology was evangelical Protestant.[144] It never achieved the massive popularity of AA, but did continue to attract Americans throughout the second half of the century. MSSCs became one of the major institutions that hosted AV chapters.[145] They began in-house AV groups as early as the 1970s and have continued to use them in addition to or instead of AA up to the present.[146]

Despite the problems with the army–AA collaboration and the attempts to find a effective substitute, the MSSCs did increasingly add AA to their program between the mid-1940s, when big centers such as those in New York, Cleveland, Pittsburgh, and Philadelphia began hosting groups, and the early 1960s, when even a small center such as the one in Worcester, MA, did.[147] Over two dozen centers in the east began cooperating with AA in this period.[148] By 1964, over half of centers nationwide ran AA groups, ranging from one-third in the southern territory to almost two-thirds in the east.[149] AA cooperation was probably greater than these numbers suggest, because some centers sent their men

---

[143] Clinebell, *Understanding and Counseling the Alcoholic*, 88–9.

[144] Ibid., 75.

[145] For a brief history and current information, see Alcoholics Victorious [Internet homepage], Association of Gospel Rescue Missions, Kansas City, MO, www.alcoholics victorious.org.

[146] *Adult Rehabilitation Center*, Columbus, OH, November 1978, ARC Newsletter Collection, SAA; McPherson, interview.

[147] Maj. Edwy C. Hinkle, New York, NY, to Lt. Col. Frank Guldenschuh, September 18, 1959, Acc. 78–24, SAA; "Eighteenth Anniversary Dinner of the Cedar Group of Alcoholics Anonymous and the Men's Social Service Center of The Salvation Army" [pamphlet] (Cleveland, OH: Salvation Army, 1962), Acc. 78–24, SAA; "Minutes," Regional Meeting of Salvation Army MSSD, Pennsylvania and Southern New Jersey, November 19, 1957, Acc. 78–24, SAA; Brig. Gustav Johnson, "Brief for Worcester [MA] Men's Social Service Center," (1963), Acc. 78–24, SAA; McKinley, *Somebody's Brother*, 111.

[148] I tabulated this number by keeping a count of all files from Frank Guldenschuh's office (Acc. 78–24, SAA) that mentioned when a center began or already had running an AA group.

[149] Katz, "The Salvation Army Men's Social Service Center, I. Program," 327.

194   *American Protestantism in the Age of Psychology*

to AA meetings in the local community instead of forming their own chapter.[150] AA became increasingly common over the ensuing decades. By the late 1970s, the MSSD in the east suggested that AA attendance be mandatory for all alcoholics.[151] By the end of the century, AA or AV was mandated for all beneficiaries in their first month at southern centers and mandatory for all beneficiaries in the midwest.[152]

The central virtue of and reason for the thorough adoption of AA and similar self-help programs[153] in the MSSC was its psychoreligious flexibility.[154] The flexibility derived in part from the highly decentralized structure of AA, which allowed for a variety of interpretations of the steps and the way members gather to work through them. For instance, centers that wanted to use AA meetings as a type of, or substitution for, group psychotherapy held meetings that focused on participant discussion.[155] The eastern territory, which in the 1960s hosted many more AA groups but many fewer group therapy sessions than other territories, may have used the program this way.[156] Other kinds of meetings focused on members' testimonies, and this type could echo the kind of witness that converts gave at religious meetings. In 1960 the MSSD recommended collaboration with AA partly because many AA speakers could be counted on to "testify to the power of God in effecting their rehabilitation and developing a victorious Christian experience."[157] Peter Hofman, in trying to share the benefits of AA as a forum for Christian witness, told his colleagues in 1947, "[W]here [our Center] counted our converts by one's and two's in the past, we now began to count them by ten's and twenty's."[158] An even more definite way to ensure that the AA message was integrated

---

[150] See, for example, Sr. Maj. George Hulihan, "Service to Man Report," Scranton, PA, April 7, 1959, Acc. 78–24, SAA.

[151] Capt. Joseph Robinson, "Suggested Case Plans for Clients," in *Men's Social Program Helps* (New York: MSSD east, Salvation Army, March 1978): 55–61, Acc. 78–24, SAA.

[152] McPherson, interview; Norris, interview.

[153] In the central territory, for example, beneficiaries for whom alcoholism is not their primary problem attend Narcotics Anonymous, Chemical Anonymous, or Fellowship Anonymous rather than AA. Some central centers host Alcoholics Victorious groups instead of AA. See McPherson, interview; Adult Rehabilitation Command–central territory, *ARC Program* (Des Plaines, IL: Salvation Army, 2002).

[154] White, interview.

[155] Raymond Selke ran both group therapy sessions and discussion-oriented AA meetings at the Rochester MSSC; see Selke, *Group Therapy.*

[156] Katz, "The Salvation Army Men's Social Service Center, I. Program."

[157] *MSSD Handbook, 1960,* 9:9:6–7.

[158] Hofman, "Serving the Client," 46.

Freud Is Not a Suitable Psychologist

into the Salvationist one was to have "classroom AA," in which participants carefully worked through each step under the guidance of a center staff person.[159] By the latter third of the twentieth century, big centers most likely hosted a variety of different AA meetings.[160]

Open meetings gave officers the opportunity to monitor the proceedings, which was important since officers were concerned about AA speakers downplaying God's place in transforming their lives. Officers sometimes used their presence at open meetings to convey Salvationist messages in AA discussions, but other times stayed mute.[161] An even better system of monitoring and influencing discussions was hit upon by the Pasadena, CA, center in 1959. The Pasadena officers "felt it was necessary to give some type of direction away from risqué stories, and bad language" so they enlisted another officer – himself a rehabilitated alcoholic – to become a member to "help put a quietus on anything that would be rude or vulgar."[162] The Pasadena commanding officer also attended several open meetings, speaking up when he thought something detrimental to the rest of the MSSC program happened.[163] The temptation to hold only open meetings was so great that officers had to be warned away from it.[164] Many centers, such as the one in Pittsburgh, PA, may have held both closed and open sessions.[165]

The army wanted beneficiaries ultimately to see AA as a path to Jesus. In the late 1970s, readers of the Columbus, OH, MSSC were assured that "[Y]ou don't have to be saved in order for God to help you with your drinking problem. Thousands upon thousands of A.A. members have found their way to Christ and Salvation after finding they could trust God for help with their disease of alcoholism."[166] A publication

---

[159] Norris, interview.

[160] For example, Rochester MSSC by the late 1970s, hosted a variety of AA meetings, including a special one for women only; see *Center Tidings*, January 1980, Rochester, NY, ARC Newsletter Collection, SAA; *Center Tidings* 5(1), Rochester, NY, ARC Newsletter Collection, SAA; *Center Tidings* 5(5), Rochester, NY, ARC Newsletter Collection, SAA.

[161] Compare, for example, Capt. Lloyd Smith, "Farewell Brief for McKeesport [PA] Men's Social Service Center" (1958), Acc. 78–24, SAA; Fred Ladlow, "Farewell Brief for Wilkes-Barre [PA] Men's Social Service Center" (1958), Acc. 78–24, SAA.

[162] Telfer, "Pasadena Alcoholics Anonymous," 36.

[163] Ibid., 38.

[164] Johnstone, "Alcoholics Anonymous Groups."

[165] Sr. Maj. William Charron, "Farewell Brief for Pittsburgh [PA] Men's Social Service Center" (1958), Acc. 78–24, SAA. See also Brig. J. Douglass Seaver, "Farewell Brief for Schenectady [NY] Men's Social Service Center" (1963), Acc. 78–24, SAA.

[166] *Adult Rehabilitation Center*, Columbus, OH, July 1978, ARC Newsletter Collection, SAA.

196   *American Protestantism in the Age of Psychology*

sent out to centers in the east around the same time helped officers to translate between AA and army beliefs by matching each step with a verse of Scripture, usually from the New Testament. For example, just as Step Seven prompted alcoholics humbly to ask God to remove all their shortcomings, the apostle John had reminded Christians, "If we confess our sins, He is faithful and just to forgive us our sins and to cleanse us from all unrighteousness" (1 John 1:9).[167]

The other really valuable flexibility provided by incorporating AA was the assistance it provided in reaching Catholics.[168] Its utility in providing a channel of spiritual rehabilitation for non-Protestants was one of its selling points in the MSSD from the very beginning. Peter Hofman told the story of Joseph G., a Catholic truck driver, who sought rehabilitation from an MSSC after conferring with a priest over whether the Church approved of AA. Joseph rededicated himself to Jesus and became active in army and AA work.[169] AA was also a natural forum in which centers with high concentrations of Catholic beneficiaries could include priests. In the late 1950s, the church did not allow priests to participate in Protestant worship services, but it did allow them to speak and pray at AA meetings. The Buffalo center, located in the nation's second largest diocese, made use of this to try and reconnect Catholic beneficiaries with their church.[170]

Psychotherapy

In 1977 Salvationist John Coutts wrote, "Thoughtful Salvationists have . . . been touched by the psychological revolution in their worship as well as in their faith."[171] Army officers were among the cutting edge of evangelical acceptance and use of psychological ideas and techniques, and they introduced them to the people under their care. In the early Service-to-Man period, centers could offer psychotherapy only insofar as

---

[167] Capt. Wesley Johnson, "The Twelve Steps of A.A. and Their Biblical Comparisons," in *Men's Social Program Helps* (New York: MSSD east, Salvation Army, June 1979): 55–6, Acc. 78–24, SAA.

[168] Barber, "The Program at Work"; Hofman, "Relating the Salvation Army Program on Alcoholism to the Community"; Telfer, "Pasadena Alcoholics Anonymous."

[169] Hofman, "Serving the Client," 52–3.

[170] Sr. Maj. Clarence Simmons, Dayton, OH, to Lt. Col. Frank Guldenschuh, June 9, 1959, Acc. 78–24, SAA; Brigadier Clarence Simmons, Buffalo, NY, to Col. Frank Guldenschuh, April 2, 1963. Acc. 78–24, SAA; Brigadier Clarence Simmons, Buffalo, NY, to Lt. Col. John Phillips, October 16, 1963. Acc. 78–24, SAA.

[171] Coutts, *The Salvationists*, 79–80.

Freud Is Not a Suitable Psychologist

they offered "group work," programs that fostered community among the men, such as AA and other social activities.[172] Although group work remained an integral part of center programming throughout the rest of the postwar period,[173] it also matured into a full-blown commitment to group therapy and professional psychotherapeutic services in the mid- to late 1950s.[174] As usual, implementation of the new goal depended largely on financial resources.

It took roughly two decades for the goal of the army to provide psychotherapeutic assistance to *all* MSSC beneficiaries to be realized.[175] The MSSD east – which lagged behind the others in terms of its psychotherapeutic offerings but for which the most evidence is available – witnessed the first spurt in therapeutic services in the early 1960s. Between 1959 and 1962, services began at large centers in Erie, PA; New York, NY; Philadelphia, PA; Syracuse, NY; Wilmington, DE; Dayton, OH; and Boston, MA, as well as some smaller MSSCs, such as at McKeesport, PA.[176] By 1964,

---

[172] *Manual for Men's Fellowship League* (New York: Salvation Army, eastern territory, 1957), BB. 2541, SAA; Brigadier Clarence Simmons, Buffalo, NY, to Col. Frank Guldenschuh, November 27, 1962. Acc. 78–24, SAA; Lauren, Columbus, OH, to Ray, October 30, 1980, RG 20.109, folder 124/10, SAA; Barber, "Group Work"; Johnson, "Fellowship Clubs"; *MSSD Handbook, 1960*; Sheehy, "The Triumph of Group Therapeutics"; Col. H. R. Smith, "Impact of the Group on the Individual and the Relationship of the Group Program to the Individual Program" (Youngstown, OH: MSSD east, Regional Directors, 1954).

[173] For innovative group work in the early 1970s to foster community and leadership, see Judge, "Alcoholism Treatment at The Salvation Army."

[174] One inside observer of the Men's Social Service Department located the addition of psychotherapeutic services to the Service-to-Man reforms between 1954 and 1963. The earliest evidence for group therapy in the eastern territory – which lagged behind the others but for which SAA has the most materials – is the late 1950s. John Phillips to Paul Carlson, August 8, 1963, ARC Vertical File, SAA.

[175] The army provided such services to homeless addicts through other means as well, particularly the Harbor Light Centers, which in the 1960s and 1970s used increasingly sophisticated therapeutic techniques. This may have been facilitated by the receipt of United Way and public funds. McKinley, *Marching to Glory*, 2nd ed., 271.

[176] Capt. Raymond Howell, "Farewell Brief for Erie [PA] Men's Social Service Center" (1961) Acc, 78–24, SAA; Brig. Charles Bissell, "Farewell Brief for Erie Men's Social Service Center" (1963), Acc. 78–24, SAA; "Schedule for the Week," *The New York (No. One) Times*, newsletter for the New York MSSC, March 22, 1963, Acc. 78–24, SAA; Maj. E. William Worthy, "Farewell Brief for McKeesport [PA] Men's Social Service Center" (1961), Acc. 78–24, SAA; Wilmington Men's Social Service Center, *Introduction and Information* [pamphlet] (Wilmington, DE: Salvation Army, n.d.), Acc 78–24, SAA; Sr. Maj. Clarence Simmons, Dayton, OH, to Col. Frank Guldenschuh, June 10, 1960, Acc. 78–24, SAA; Dr. John Davis, "Summary of Progress – October 14, 1959–June 1, 1960" (Dayton, OH: Dayton Men's Social Service Center, Salvation

198   *American Protestantism in the Age of Psychology*

29 percent of centers in the United States offered group psychotherapy, and 13 percent offered it to individuals. The central and especially the western territories were at the forefront of these trends: 32 percent of western centers offered psychotherapy to groups, and 28 percent offered it to individuals.[177] A review of program schedules available at army archives suggest that, by the mid- to late 1970s, group therapy was routine. Even the eastern MSSD, which had lagged behind its counterparts in the mid-1960s, recommended mandatory group therapy or AA for all beneficiaries by the late 1970s.[178] By the mid-1980s, all centers had professional therapeutic services available to clients.[179]

For most MSSC beneficiaries, therapy meant group therapy. (Individual psychotherapy tended to be reserved for clients who were unusually disturbed.) This had the benefit of being cheaper, but it also helped beneficiaries with one of their major problems: poor socialization. Further, the patient–therapist dyad existed in isolation from the rest of the program[180] and had no obvious relationship to Christian communities. Meanwhile, it was easier to link group therapy to other center activities, especially to attempts to nurture fellowships among the men. MSSC staff fostered this convergence between group and fellowship. It structured both their own understanding of the value of therapy and the activities they arranged for beneficiaries.

Those army officers who were eager to introduce this new program component into their centers had a couple of ways in which they could understand its salvific potential. First, they thought that it might help heal beneficiaries, and healthier men would be riper for spiritual awakening. Major George Duplain, CO of the most therapeutically cutting-edge program in the country in the early 1960s, argued that, "If [the beneficiary] understands himself, he may become more amenable to the Gospel of

---

Army, 1961), Acc. 78–24, SAA; Maj. Norman Noble, Boston, MA, to Lt. Col. Frank Guldenschuh, March 14, 1962, Acc. 78–24, SAA; Gilbert, "The Salvation Army Men's Service Center"; Brig. George Hulihan, "Center Brief, Philadelphia Men's Social Service Center," Acc. 78–24, SAA .

[177] Katz, "The Salvation Army Men's Social Service Center, I. Program."

[178] Capt. Joseph Robinson, "Suggested Case Plans for Clients," in *Men's Social Program Helps* (New York: MSSD east, Salvation Army, March 1978): 55–61, Acc. 78–24, SAA.

[179] McKinley, "A Lodging Place for Men-and More," 26.

[180] Capt. Raymond Howell, who initiated psychotherapy during his tenures at Erie, PA, and then Syracuse, NY, strongly advocated integrated group therapy over private sessions. See Capt. Raymond Howell, Syracuse, NY, to Lt. Col. Frank Guldenschuh, April 13, 1962, Acc. 78–24, SAA; Capt. Raymond Howell, Syracuse, NY, to Lt. Col. Frank Guldenschuh, April 25, 1962, Acc. 78–24, SAA.

Jesus Christ."[181] This argument was echoed in the 1960 MSSD handbook, which reassured wary COs:

Group therapy and group psychotherapy both have demonstrated, among other benefits, a surprising increase in religious receptiveness. The man who has gained new understanding of his own problems is frequently the more ready to accept spiritual values as means of solving those problems.[182]

A second way for MSSC staff to understand the religious meaning of psychotherapy was to extend to it the same understanding Salvationists had of other nurturing activities. It was a fulfillment of Christian duty to care for the most needy. Every Salvationist knows that Jesus affirmed, "Inasmuch as ye did it unto one of these my brethren, even these least, ye did it unto me" (Matthew 25:40). As such, therapy was also an instance and embodiment of Christian love. Raymond Selke, a Christian counselor who led many group therapies at Rochester, NY, in the late 1950s and early 1960s, ended a report on his work by exclaiming, "What an opportunity to understand by His example what it really means to 'help' those who are lost."[183]

MSSC officers knew, however, that the real proof was in the pudding. The way services were offered, conducted, and integrated into the rest of the program would be important factors in determining whether or not they interfered with or promoted the army's other goals. Officers kept a close watch on the therapy conducted in their centers and, within funding and institutional constraints, did what they could to ensure a good fit.

One of the most important issues was finding the right person to conduct the sessions. Cost, as always, was a factor. Sometimes therapists donated their services,[184] but usually centers had to pay for them. The army records are replete with the correspondence of frustrated COs trying to acquire professional psychotherapy services for their centers only to

---

[181] Duplain, "The Use of Professional Workers," 49.
[182] *MSSD Handbook, 1960,* 9:9:11.
[183] Selke, *Group Therapy.*
[184] For example, in 1961 a civilian or soldier who worked for another division of the army offered his services gratis to the McKeesport, PA, and Pittsburgh, PA, centers; see: Maj. E. William Worthy, McKeesport, PA, to Lt. Col. Frank Guldenschuh, January 25, 1961, Acc. 78–24, SAA; Brig. Lawrence Castagna, Pittsburgh, PA, to Col. Frank Guldenschuh, March 26, 1963, Acc. 78–24, SAA; Col. Frank Guldenschuh, New York, NY, to Brig. Lawrence Castagna, March 28, 1963, Acc. 78–24, SAA; Col. Frank Guldenschuh, New York, NY, to Brig. Lawrence Castagna, May 8, 1963, Acc. 78–24, SAA; Brig. Lawrence Castagna, Pittsburgh, PA, to Col. Frank Guldenschuh, May 13, 1963, Acc. 78–24, SAA; Col. Frank Guldenschuh, New York, NY, to Brig. Lawrence Castagna, May 16, 1963, Acc. 78–24, SAA.

200 American Protestantism in the Age of Psychology

run into insurmountable financial difficulties that forced the centers to forgo, either temporarily or for long periods, the availability of such services.[185] Students were one solution, since their services were free or very cheap, and centers occasionally hired graduate students in social work, psychology and psychiatry, and pastoral counseling.[186] Another cheap option was to use lay therapists, often recruited from the ranks of rehabilitated men. In 1970, the Chicago MSSC began training lay alcohol therapists to run alcoholism-oriented sessions for beneficiaries.[187] Such leaders would have been limited in the kind of groups they were able to run, but in addition to being cheap, some were probably converts and thus could set a Christian tone for the meetings.

Besides being expensive, professional therapists did not necessarily have a Christian perspective. High-ranking officers warned that such personnel could cause problems for the army's ultimate goals. One CO who had begun to offer group therapy at his center in Los Angeles commented:

Sigmund Freud would not necessarily be a suitable psychologist for our men. We want only those people who can believe in and support our entire program. A psychologist who does not acknowledge man's relationship to God, or live according to our precepts, would not be able to achieve the goals we are seeking.[188]

The ideal way to blend professional skill with religious message was to employ a pastoral counselor. A number of western centers were able to do this. By the late 1950s, the San Francisco center had on its staff Reverend William Lindsay-Stewart, a Presbyterian minister and clinical psychologist who offered group and individual therapy as well as conducting Bible lessons and spiritual counseling.[189] At Lytton, a rural center not far from the Bay area, Lindsay-Stewart collaborated with a number of secular professionals in leading intensive group therapy retreats for selected beneficiaries. The army framed the experience for their men by ensuring that the last session of each clinic was a Salvationist one.

---

[185] See, for example, Brig. George Hulihan, "Center Brief, Philadelphia Men's Social Service Center," Acc. 78–24, SAA ; Laune, "A Survey of The Men's Social Service Center," 5.

[186] For example, centers in San Diego, San Francisco, Cleveland, and Dayton all obtained or tried to obtain student therapists in the late 1950s and 1960s; see Brig. William Charron, Cleveland, OH, to Lt. Col. Frank Guldenschuh, January 9, 1961, Acc. 78–24, SAA; Sr. Maj. Clarence Simmons, Dayton, OH, to Col. Frank Guldenschuh, June 10, 1960, Acc. 78–24, SAA; Katz, *Alcoholic Rehabilitation Project*; Woods, "Group Therapy."

[187] Maj. William Hasney, "'509' Program for the Alcoholic (1967–1974)," Chicago, IL: MSSD, 1975, BB 4784, SAA.

[188] Woods, "Group Therapy," 24.

[189] Katz, *Alcoholic Rehabilitation Project*; "Salvation Army Gives Dignity Back to Alcoholics," *California Alcoholism Review and Treatment Digest* 2, no. 1 (1959).

Freud Is Not a Suitable Psychologist

Lt. Colonel Peter Hofman ran this session by leading the retreat participants in a psychoreligious discussion aimed at guiding

the thinking of the men into the [spiritual] channels desired.... Having disturbed
the troubled waters, having raised many a question that doesn't have an obvious
answer, the men need the outstretched Hand of Christ's Love, Hope and Faith to
hold on to.[190]

Fortunately for the army, during the 1950s and 1960s, they had more
and more access to clinically trained pastors.[191] By the late 1960s, the Los
Angeles MSSC had begun using the services of the psychology faculty at
the local Fuller Theological Seminary and was trying to become a major
training facility for their graduate school. This fruitful cooperation had
allowed LA to become "a full fledged diagnostic and treatment center
specializing in personality and character disorders such as homosexuality,
passive dependent personality, alcoholism and general psychoneurotic
problems." But religion was not eclipsed: since "interns [at the Center]
are trained in theology as well as psychology, they are able to deal with
spiritual as well as psychological problems."[192]

The internal workings – both secular and religious – of these group
sessions are mostly lost to historians. A few reports do remain, however,
to give us some sense of what MSSC beneficiaries did "in group." The evidence suggests they were private people, not given to introspection, and
full of anger and pain that many would have rather not confronted.[193]
Group leaders were often forced to guide the group more than an introspective population would have required. Organizing therapy sessions as
film discussions seemed a particularly effective way to prompt men to
talk about a problem in a sustained way. Additionally, beyond emotional
anguish, these men had very basic problems functioning. Thus, centers
sometimes offered groups targeted at specific problems, such as domestic
discord, addiction, and job retention.[194]

A fascinating and rare glimpse into the kinds of issues that beneficiaries
raised was described in a therapist's report from the early 1960s. Group
members joined together to complain about the fact that the army did

---

[190] Tobin, "Group Therapy," 30.

[191] Holifield, *History of Pastoral Care.*

[192] William Pickering, clinical director of the Salvation Amy MSSC, Los Angeles, CA, "The
Clinical Application of the Gospel," September 7, 1968 *War Cry* (USA edition), 12–13.

[193] Leparte, for instance, found in 1967 that the goal of most beneficiaries was to have a
"pleasant stay" at the centers. See "Rehabilitation of the Homeless Man."

[194] William J. Gilbert, "The Salvation Army Men's Service Center: Evaluation of the Film-
Discussion Meetings, July 9 to September 11, 1963," Acc. 78–24, SAA; Selke, *Group
Therapy*; Woods, "Group Therapy," 25–6.

202   *American Protestantism in the Age of Psychology*

not subsidize their outings to the bowling alley on Saturday afternoons. The men asserted that the army should do this to prevent them from drinking. When the group leader, a psychiatric social worker, pointed out that they could afford to pay for their bowling with the gratuities they earned, some admitted that "they were trying to 'con the Sally' into keeping them from drinking by supporting their bowling." The group leader then reminded the men that refraining from drinking was their responsibility and choice.[195] Occasional insight into their own shortcomings was apparent in another group from the early 1960s when members raised the topic of unemployment. The doctor reported that when he asked whether the men themselves had anything to do with their dismal job prospects, "one of the group members stood up very stoutly and said that he felt that it did and surprisingly enough most of the other group members agreed with him although they didn't take the time or the bother to move into this at all during the session."[196]

Groups could evolve, however, as the core of long-term members were subtly coached in the lessons of group theory. The same group that neglected to discuss the factors impairing their ability to find and retain work eventually began to talk about the "factors underlying all behavior." One garrulous group member had so donned the psychotherapeutic perspective that he tried to push another man into analyzing his feelings for his father. This prompted an angry exchange as the would-be analysand resisted what he felt was an insult to his paternity. As the group progressed further, the men began to talk about their relationships to each other and each one's impressions of the others.[197]

The leaders in these examples apparently did not try to bring out the religious implications of problems raised in group discussions. Religiously oriented leaders sometimes did. For instance, Peter Hofman was sure to bring them out when he led the concluding group session at weekend-long therapy retreats at Lytton Home in California. Participants at Lytton not only were guided in obtaining a

better understanding of themselves and the motivation behind their behavior patterns. They learned about personality disorders and defects of character, guilt complexes and many other things about themselves. But best of all they learned how guilt feelings can be eliminated when God forgives, and behavior patterns

---

[195] Gilbert, "The Salvation Army Men's Service Center."

[196] Dr. F. J. Pizzat, Collection of Group Therapy Reports for Erie MSSC, October 1959–February 1960, Acc. 78–24, SAA.

[197] Ibid.

and even personalities can be changed when a complete surrender of life is made to the will of God.[198]

Centers also hosted religious therapy groups that made explicit spiritual themes part of their goal. In the late 1970s, at the MSSC in Columbus, OH, for instance, beneficiaries could participate in a wide range of therapeutically oriented group activities, including "Living Successfully Thru Spiritual Growth" and "Living Successfully Thru God's Work."[199] The success they could achieve was expressed by Shawn, who entered the Milwaukee center in the summer of 2001. There he participated in "Spiritual Journey," which combined a twelve-step recovery program with building a personal relationship with God. Shawn found this to be the most beneficial part of the program, explaining, "Through the course of my Spiritual Journey, I have begun to learn not only who I am, but also who I am in the Lord Jesus Christ."[200]

Conclusion

In the three decades following World War II, the army remade its half-century old mission to homeless men. Eager to keep abreast of cutting-edge philanthropic trends and threatened with far-reaching federal interference, it transformed the components of its traditional evangelism: work, religious services, residence in an army institution, and wholesome entertainment. These became work therapy, spiritual rehabilitation, and milieu therapy. To these it added casework and counseling, AA, and psychotherapy. Each of these activities attempted simultaneously to develop maturity and spirituality. The MSSCs were able to do this by deliberately fusing Christian fellowship and group therapy, pastoral counseling and therapeutic counseling, and the Protestant work ethic and work therapy. In their psychospiritual program, the centers added their own creative conflations to the innovations of the CPE movement and AA. These convergences gave Salvationists new rationales for delving into beneficiaries' troubled hearts and minds. And they offered Salvationists new methods to help poor, lonely men make connections.

[198] Hofman, "Keynotes," 6.
[199] *Adult Rehabilitation Center*, Columbus, OH, March 1978; *Adult Rehabilitation Center*, Columbus, OH, April 1978; *Adult Rehabilitation Center*, Columbus, OH, July 1978; *Adult Rehabilitation Center*, Columbus, OH, November 1978. All newsletters in ARC Newsletter Collection, SAA.
[200] "Contemporary Conversion Narratives," Central Territory ARC Command, Desplaines, IL (2002), SAA.

204   *American Protestantism in the Age of Psychology*

Despite its massive and innovative social service wing, the army always remained at heart a doctrinally orthodox, evangelical Protestant church. It pursued sacred goals through secular means. Center officers could scarcely have justified their decades of hard work and innovation if they compromised the salvation of the men whose souls were under their care. Did they?

7

New Creatures in Christ

By the time Shawn testified that "I have begun to learn not only who I am, but also who I am in the Lord Jesus Christ,"[1] Men's Social Service Centers (MSSCs) had more than fifty years of experience interweaving psychosocial activities with spiritual ones. Shawn responded just as center officers hoped he would. They strove to replicate Shawn's twined personal maturation and religious development with all their beneficiaries. How successful were they? Was their evangelical mission compromised as they increased the therapeutic content of their programs over the decades following World War II? No. In fact, during the second half of the twentieth century the centers were increasingly successful evangelically. Therapeutic content did not vitiate this success; it paved the way for it.

The Ministry of the Men's Social Service Department, 1945–1990

Beginning with the Service-to-Man reforms after World War II and continuing today, a growing number of beneficiaries experienced spiritual growth during their treatment at MSSCs. Each year, The Salvation Army tallies as "seekers" the number of people who claimed conversion or sanctification or holiness (levels of spiritual development that build on conversion). The annual combined seeker rate for the hundred or so centers operated between 1940 and 1990 varied from year to year, but it demonstrated an unmistakable upward trajectory. During the 1940s, the

---

[1] "Contemporary Conversion Narratives," Central Territory ARC Command, Desplaines, IL (2002), SAA.

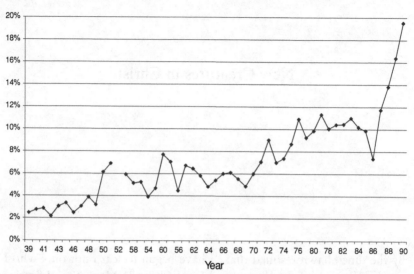

CHART 7.1. Men's Social Service Department (MSSD) Seeker Rate, 1939–1990 (# seekers/# beneficiaries served)

percentage of men converted as a proportion of all clients admitted to the centers hovered between 2 and 4 percent, with a slight upward trend. Beginning with the consolidation of the Service-to-Man reforms in the 1950s, and with the increasingly widespread proliferation of therapeutic techniques in the centers between 1960 and 1990, the rate zigzagged upward from 4 to 19.5 percent (Chart 7.1).

One way to place this increase in context is to compare it to the evangelical success of other army efforts. The Men's Social Service Department (MSSD) is the only army activity that demonstrated steady overall growth in absolute numbers (Chart 7.2). Furthermore, it accounted for an increasing proportion of the army's total annual tally of seekers (Chart 7.3). The vast majority of these seekers came from corps activities, and many represent responses from already active churchgoers. This is no surprise. What is surprising is that the MSSCs (renamed Adult Rehabilitation Centers) became the second most fruitful ministry in the last third of the century, surpassed only by purely evangelical activities.[2]

Why did the seeker rate in MSSCs ascend so dramatically in the second half of the twentieth century? There are potential explanations that

---

[2] McKinley, *Marching to Glory*, 2nd ed., 281.

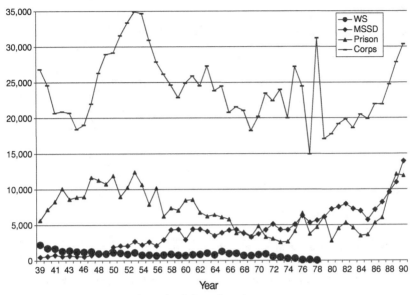

CHART 7.2. Number of Adult Seekers by Program, 1939–1990

have nothing to do with therapy. Perhaps beneficiaries felt rising pressure to respond religiously or became more manipulative. This seems unlikely given the increasing ecumenicalism and willingness of the centers to consider sobriety and independence valuable goals in their own rights. Another reason might be some larger trend in the culture that swelled church roles. But no larger trajectory entirely matches that of the centers,[3] and this would not explain why the centers benefited from a positive trend whereas other Salvationist ministries did not. A third counter-explanation would be that the Service-to-Man program increased the number and variety of standard religious activities, such as worship services and Bible classes. This probably helped raise the seeker rate, but does not explain why the rates continued to climb in the final third of the century, decades after the expansion of religious activities was implemented.

---

[3] Finke and Stark find church roles inching up steadily since the 1920s but no sudden sharp increase. Roof and Fuller find a *decrease* in church memberships, especially among baby boomers. Finke and Stark, *Churching of America*; Fuller, *Spiritual, but Not Religious*; Roof, *A Generation of Seekers*.

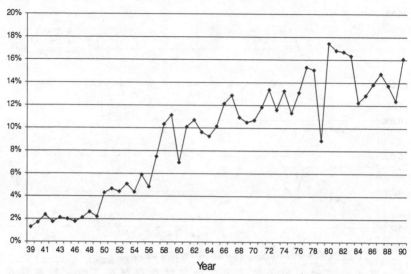

CHART 7.3. MSSD Seekers as Percentage of Total Adult Seekers for Year, 1939–1990

The most plausible nontherapeutic explanation for the rise in seeker rate is demographic. Although the army does not keep racial statistics, textual and oral evidence makes clear that during the second half of the twentieth century, and especially in the last third, more and more African Americans were admitted to MSSCs. The changed racial profile of center residents probably did buoy the seeker rate. Major Marilyn White, who oversaw Adult Rehabilitation Centers in the 1980s and 1990s, found that black beneficiaries were more interested in spiritual rejuvenation than were white ones. Furthermore, racial change also meant a religious change, since more blacks and fewer whites also meant more Protestants and fewer Catholics. Nevertheless, it seems unlikely that this totally accounts for the increase. After all, the Salvationist ministries to women and prisoners also reached out at the same time to more and more African Americans, and their seeker rates stagnated and declined.[4]

---

[4] The Women's Social Service Department – which had focused on single mothers – declined, and was even terminated in the east, due to abortions, increased public medical services, and the increasing acceptability of unwed motherhood. See McKinley, *Marching to Glory*, 2nd ed., 269–70. WSSD served African American women in integrated and semi-integrated facilities as early as the 1940s, and their proportions may well have increased both because of higher than white rates of single motherhood and the army's increasing commitment to racial fairness. There is no evidence that these women swelled

New Creatures in Christ

209

A stronger refutation of such a claim can be made by comparing MSSDs to correctional services. They are a good comparison because both departments ran for the entire period between 1939 and 1990, and the demographic profiles of their beneficiaries are similar: troubled, unattached men, often substance abusers, with relatively low levels of education and job skills. Increasing proportions of inmates were African American.[5] Researcher Lawrence Katz argued in the early 1960s that center and prison populations were similar in many respects.[6]

The army's prison activities can therefore serve as a sort of crude control, since they do not appear to have undergone the psychotherapeutic orientation to nearly the same degree that centers did. While the army did provide pastoral counseling and some psychological services to prisoners,[7] it did not control prisons and so was not responsible for prisoners' secular rehabilitation. Corrections usually focused instead on sending evangelical visitors to spend time with or correspond with prisoners, teach them about the Bible, counsel them, hold chapel services for them, and try to connect them to their families in small ways, such as helping inmates choose Christmas gifts for their children.[8] As the centers

the seeker roles before the late 1970s, which began to decline by the mid-1960s. For early integrationist efforts, see Kimball, "Experiences in Lessening Racial Tensions"; Wrieden, *Social Work in The Salvation Army.*

[5] Cahalan, *Historical Corrections Statistics*: 65, 91.

[6] Katz, "The Salvation Army Men's Social Service Center, II. Results," 638.

[7] *Salvation Army Definitive Statement of Services and Activities* (New York: Commissioners' Conference, Salvation Army, 1957), BB 2686, SAA; "In and Out" [brochure] n.d., "Correctional Services" Vertical File, SAA; "Beyond the Walls – the Correctional Services of The Salvation Army" (California: Salvation Army – Western Territory, [1962]) "Correctional Services" Vertical File, SAA; "Commitment: The Salvation Army Correctional Services," [pamphlet] (San Francisco: Salvation Army – Western Territory, n.d. [probably 1975–1981]), "Correctional Services" Vertical File, SAA, "They Can Be Helped" [pamphlet] (New York: Salvation Army, Greater New York Region, n.d. [probably 1980s]), "Correctional Services" Vertical File, SAA; J. Stanley Sheppard, *The Prison Work of the Salvation Army* (New York: National Research Bureau, Salvation Army, 1948), 39.

[8] *Salvation Army Definitive Statement of Services and Activities* (New York: Commissioners' Conference, Salvation Army, 1960), BB 870, SAA; "Volunteers in Corrections," from *Proceedings of American Correctional Association,* 103rd Congress of Corrections, Seattle, WA, 1973: 307–13, "Correctional Services" Vertical File, SAA.; *Sixty Years of Serving The Offender: 40th Annual National Report of The Salvation Army Prison Bureau, 1946–1947* (New York: Salvation Army, [1948]). "Correctional Services" Vertical File, SAA; Capt. Charles Williams, "History of The Salvation Army Correctional Program in the Eastern Territory," Report for the Historical Commission Meetings, January 17, 1975, "Correctional Services" Vertical File, SAA; M. Patrick

210   *American Protestantism in the Age of Psychology*

were fast becoming the jewel in the army's postwar crown, correctional services was losing its luster, despite the fact that it stepped up prison-based evangelical activities in the 1970s and 1980s.[9]

To compare the two departments, it is important to note that far more prisoners were reached annually between 1940 and 1980 than men were ever admitted to centers. This remained true despite the fact that the number of prisoners helped stayed roughly steady over the period, yet the numbers of social service beneficiaries grew. For instance, in 1953 (the first year comparable statistics are available for the two programs), more than 132,000 inmates were visited or paroled to the army, compared to the more than 39,000 men admitted to service centers. In 1990, about a quarter-million prisoners were visited or assigned to army supervision, whereas about 53,000 men entered centers. Nevertheless, between 1953 and 1990, centers became more effective at evangelizing their men whereas army prison services became less so. This was true both in terms of percentage of converts per man served and even in absolute numbers (Chart 7.4).

On the eve of World War II, prison work was fertile ground for reaping souls whereas the soil of men's social service proved hardscrabble. The relative fecundity of the two departments reversed in the period under study. Between 1940 and 1945, prison activities netted ten to twenty times the number of converts as MSSD did. Between 1975 and 1980, however, MSSD either caught up or surpassed corrections in absolute numbers. Comparing the two trajectories strongly suggests that a therapeutic milieu was not hostile to the cultivation of religious experience and, in fact, abetted it.

To understand why the centers became such effective sites of evangelizing requires considering the implications of the increasingly therapeutic reorientation of the MSSD beginning with the Service-to-Man reforms. Before the reforms, many men did not stay long at the centers. Besides the need for an adequate labor force, there was no rationale for it. Centers also served as shelters for transient men, renting them beds for cash or labor. The little evidence that exists suggests that hotels and transient

---

McCabe, "The Salvation Army Partnerships with the U.S. Department of Justice," *The IARCA Journal on Community Corrections* (August 1993): 27–9, "Correctional Services" Vertical File, SAA; Bollwahn, interview; McKinley, *Marching to Glory, 2nd ed.*, 305–6.

[9] Charles Williams, "Future of Correctional Services from Historical Perspective," Presentation to the American Correctional Association, August 9, 1998, BB 4952, SAA, p. 4.

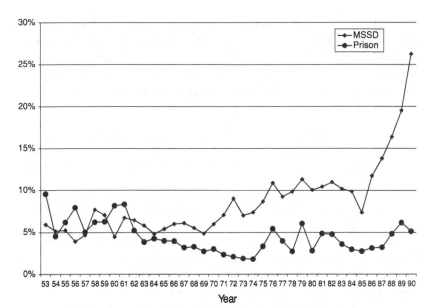

CHART 7.4. Seeker Rates: Corrections Services Versus MSSD, 1953–1990
Note: Prison conversion rates using the best formula (# seekers/# served) cannot be calculated for dates before 1953. Prison rates are somewhat inflated for recent dates because prisoners released to The Salvation Army are excluded from the denominator since earlier data did not reliably disaggregate those visited in prison from those supervised. A more accurate prison conversion rate in 1980, for instance, would be 2 percent. With more accurate numbers, the divergence depicted would be sharper.

services were relatively ineffective evangelical forums. Historian Lillian Taiz found that in the early twentieth century, the brevity of the contact most relief recipients had with the army made successful indoctrination unlikely.[10]

Before the reforms, the centers offered indigent men a temporary job, a clean place to sleep, and food in a wholesome Christian environment – but

[10] Taiz, *Hallelujah Lads and Lasses*, 160. One point of comparison might be the more evangelically successful Industrial Homes (where residence patterns were presumably longer) with the less-effective Working Men's Hotels (that offered primarily transient services). Figures from 1921 show that the Industrial Homes were ten times more likely to convert residents than were Working Men's Hotels. I arrived at this figure by determining the ratio of converts to beds offered by each institution. The Industrial Homes admitted 6,807 men during the year, of whom 9% were converted, and who were provided with 529,437 bed-nights. Hotels did not keep statistics on admittances, but reported only 205 converts for the 1,711,118 bed-nights provided. Barton, *Only One Thousand Dollars*, 76–7.

212   *American Protestantism in the Age of Psychology*

not much more. Besides Sunday services and the occasional birthday party or outing, the men were left on their own outside work hours. In 1959, a western territory MSSC officer reflected on how lonely beneficiaries were before the consolidation of Service-to-Man reforms when center staff did not have time to spend with the men under their care. He cited a "classic" joke that had made the MSSC rounds:

One of the men in the Center said to one of the other men: "What do you know, I have been here three weeks, and the Captain spoke to me today." The other man asked, "What did he say to you?" the reply was: "He said take that cigarette out of your mouth."[11]

The push toward rehabilitation changed all that. The army set out to create therapeutic institutions for homeless men. It was therefore necessary that beneficiaries stay for an extended period because personality change could not happen overnight. Forging relationships with staff – especially officers and counselors – was an essential part of the process. Men were forced to socialize with and learn to trust one another as well. They were forced to be part of a community and a fellowship. They had to "walk the Christian walk" and listen to Christian messages all around them – from those Salvationists in charge to those recovered men like themselves whom they emulated, from morning devotions to evening AA meetings. The therapeutic turn in the centers created a total environment in which Salvationists had the time and justification to probe thoroughly a beneficiary's mind, heart, and soul. They brought private and public influences to bear in persuading him of his deep spiritual need.

Although few testimonies from the millions of men treated in centers between 1940 and 1990 remain or are available to researchers, a recent statement gives a glimpse into how the centers' psychoreligious program worked. At a center in Flint, MI, Steven L., a 44-year-old man from an nonobservant Catholic family, explained his experience:

Then it happened.... Was working late night desk, took my work therapy assignment seriously, but always felt someone was behind me. Talked to Major Reed. He told me I had the devil mad, because I left him in the cold. So that night I went to the mercy seat [a special bench in chapel for penitents], asked Jesus to go to the Father for me, that I was ready to give my all to use me any way He chose. When I left the chapel, I then felt like what Paul talks about in 2 Cor. 5:17.[12]

---

[11] Johnson, "Fellowship Clubs," 33.
[12] Testimony of Steven L., "Contemporary Conversion Narratives," Central Territory ARC Command, Des Plaines, IL (2002), SAA.

New Creatures in Christ

Steven was referring to the scriptural verse, "if any man be in Christ, he is a new creature." For Steven and many others like him, therapy led him to the Word, which promised there was no cleavage between rehabilitation and salvation. Closeness to Jesus guaranteed rebirth in this world, and true recovery demanded submission to his will.

Conclusion

The therapeutic transformation of the MSSCs enabled them to redeem some of the nation's most marginalized citizens – in both the secular and sacred senses of the word. The personal connections, self-reflection, and pride that army rehabilitation was able to foster among some beneficiaries kindled or rekindled their faith. Historical and social scientific comparisons suggest that this psychotherapeutic approach was the most effective one to take with the highly isolated, troubled people who sought centers' assistance. The more purely religious tacks of the pre–World War II era were minimally successful evangelically. Over the postwar decades, the more centers implemented a fully psychoreligious program, the more they were able to reach residents spiritually. Other army ministries that lacked the opportunity to build extensive psychoreligious intersections, such as those devoted to prisoners, became relatively less and less successful compared to that of the centers.

A comparison of the Salvationist case with the previous two reveals an irony about the rise of the "therapeutic state."[13] Despite the fact that the army turned to rehabilitation services primarily as a way to deflect federal pressure, the maneuver worked brilliantly for its evangelical goals. In fact, a psychospiritual approach worked better for the centers than it did for the clinical pastoral education movement. This is despite the fact that the CPE movement endured no initial federal pressure. State pressure existed primarily in the form of clinical pastoral educators' need to justify themselves in secular terms to public and secular hospital administrators. But as CPE lost a good deal of its luster by the 1970s when clinical educators debated their complicity in nurturing secular narcissism, the army was just beginning to reap the full salvific fruit of its Service-to-Man reforms.

Although the initial governmental spur to pursue a psychospiritual approach did not predict the direction of the divergent outcomes, continued state pressure did. The centers benefited from their autonomy, which

[13] Nolan, *The Therapeutic State.*

they fiercely protected. The state did not shape their program or intervene in it once established. The norms and culture of the centers were shaped instead by an organic and entirely private accommodation between the diverse population of alienated beneficiaries and Salvationists. Center administrators were answerable first and last to the army. Their peers were other clergy. Their ministry's bottom line was the harvest of souls, the annual tally of converts.

Chaplains and their interns, meanwhile, answered ultimately to secular and even public institutions. The norms and culture of their interactions were shaped by the interaction between the diverse ranks of the institutionalized, the secular constraints of institutions, and the ministers. Their peers were doctors, nurses, social workers, and hospital administrators. Their ministry's bottom line was their ability to solace patients and help doctors cure them.

Of the groups examined in this study, the army was the only one that did not intend to use a psychotherapeutic approach as a democratic tool. Nevertheless, it was one. A psychotherapeutic approach enabled the army to adapt to the realities of a pluralistic democracy. It provided a rationale for reaching out to Catholic men whom they had limited hope of converting to Protestantism. It allowed centers to be more inclusive in practice without having to embrace ecumenism theologically. Additionally, it replaced more exclusive and coercive outreaches in which food was exchanged for a show of religious response or in which shelter was provided to those with the ability to help meet Industrial Homes' production goals. Furthermore, recasting evangelism as rehabilitation helped homeless people reintegrate into secular and even religious communities, thereby bolstering our coherence as a society. And it fostered a sense of mutual responsibility necessary for our liberal democratic republic.

8

Conclusion: American Psychology in an Age of Faiths

One aspect of the much-lamented "spread of a therapeutic ethos" was the extensive adoption of psychotherapeutic ideas and techniques by American religious groups after World War II. They pursued religious goals by forging convergences between spiritual and psychological systems. This was a difficult and contentious effort. Groups were always haunted by the possibility that they would sell a precious birthright of fellowship and holy wisdom for a potage of self-love and secular casuistry. And, in fact, believers overwhelmed by urgent earthly hungers occasionally made the trade off, as we saw among ministers who felt there was little nourishment left in traditional treatments of the Gospel. Yet they were a small minority compared with the larger groups of clergy and lay persons from across the American Protestant spectrum whose efforts were spiritually successful.

These men and women raided the cupboards of psychology for ways to strengthen and democratize their ministries, their evangelism, and their fellowships. Their efforts led to the opposite of the disenchantment and solipsistic individualism that has often been warned against. Instead, they fostered a sense of transcendence and even faith in God. They connected people socially. And they even inspired ethical striving. This was possible because believers recast psychotherapy in their own image. They relied in part on spiritually oriented paraprofessionals and lay persons to deliver therapy. And they expanded the definition of what constituted therapy to include religious traditions and spiritual activities. This expansion of psychology beyond its disciplinary borders into the larger culture – this "spread of a therapeutic ethos" – is precisely what enabled believers to use it for spiritual ends.

216 American Protestantism in the Age of Psychology

However, as I argued before, the results of these efforts varied. Although they were usually spiritually successful, they differed in the degrees to which they evangelized, united, and ennobled. Three sets of influences shaped the outcomes: the religious and personal backgrounds of those participating in psychospiritual programs; the religiosity and independence of the institutions in which those programs were conducted; and the vitality of faith and religious institutions in the larger society.

The histories recounted in this book demonstrate that a blended psychoreligious outreach was an effective form of ministry to people who were socially isolated or alienated. For example, The Salvation Army was less successful with homeless men before it began integrating psychological ideas and techniques into its traditional Bowery missions in the 1940s. Vagrants attended the worship services but cared mostly for the beans and coffee afterward. The men sometimes even drew straws to determine who had to fake a conversion so as to speed the service along toward the gastronomic portion of the program. The missionaries' coercion and the men's hypocrisy underscore the main point: Bowery denizens did not *really feel* it. Conversion required the sincerity of intense emotional response. Furthermore, real rejuvenation required forging sustained relationships. A psychologically astute outreach provided this.

A therapeutic approach was also spiritually effective with those who were indifferent or hostile to religion. Clergy and believers needed to persuade such people of the veracity and benefits of faith. A second language helped them to speak to those to whom an explicitly theological appeal was as likely to repulse as to attract. In Alcoholics Anonymous (AA), for instance, many doubters shunned "God talk." But they agreed to the desirability of becoming more "spiritual" when it was defined not by its core meaning (relatedness to the divine) but rather by its peripheral implications (social connectedness and obligation, serenity, and gratitude). This psychologically oriented interpretation did not preclude more theistic and traditional meanings. Meanwhile, it rendered disbelieving alcoholics more receptive to faith.

The distance from religious life that AA members, homeless men, and institutionalized people often felt had usually not been lifelong. Many had been taught to believe in God as children just as most of their fellow citizens had been. Some had had religious education, attended church, and known prayers and Scripture. This background made it more likely that they would experience and interpret psychospiritual programs in religious ways. This does not mean that atheists with no or very limited religious background were never converted through psychoreligious projects.

Certainly some were. But it did mean that, for example, atheists were more likely than others to avoid AA. Similarly, in clinical training, seminarians of deeper and more solid faith were far less likely than were their doubting peers to see perfect equivalences between theological experiences and psychological ones.

The backgrounds of Americans under the tutelage of the groups in this study were not the only thing that affected the outcomes of psychoreligious efforts. One of the factors that most determined a program's secularizing potential, not surprisingly, was proximity to traditional church and religious life. The closer the connection, the less likely it was that the spiritual faded amid the psychological. For example, pastors who counseled laity under ecclesiastical auspices were far more likely to integrate prayer and Scripture into the exchange than those who worked elsewhere. The army appears to have been more religiously effective in its care for men in its own para-church centers than were the chaplains who worked in secular institutions.

Proximity to traditional religious life was not the only factor, however, for AA was spiritually persuasive despite keeping its distance from all churches. Equally important was a group's detachment from secular institutions – that is, whether the group itself set the terms of its own psychoreligious efforts. Both AA and Men's Social Service Centers (MSSCs) were privately run and self-funded. They endured relatively little state interference in their activities. On the other hand, clinical pastoral education (CPE) by definition had to take place in spaces not controlled by chaplains. Their ministry had to be conducted in the interstices of alien institutions. They had only limited control over their interactions with patients. They were accountable to medical professionals, administrators, and civil servants. And they constantly had to prove themselves through a set of standards extrinsic to their vocation. All this constrained their religious efficacy.

Furthermore, secular institutions and ways of thinking became more culturally influential over the latter decades of the twentieth century. One might borrow from the Apostle Paul to say that psychospiritual programs served as a kind of "tutor" for a more full-fledged religious faith.[1] But to play this role, they depended on the vitality of a larger spectrum of religious communities, institutions, and cultural traditions. The contraction

---

[1] Paul's letters refer to things that are understood as having prepared mankind for Jesus as "tutors" (the New American Standard Bible). In Galatians 3:24, the Mosaic law of Jews is called a "tutor to lead us to Christ." In 1 Corinthians 4:15, Paul speaks of "countless tutors in Christ."

of this spectrum over the final third of the twentieth century made it somewhat less likely that Americans would perceive religious implications in psychospiritual programs. For example, the pressure on AA's committed atheists to "mature spiritually" lessened in the fellowship as atheism itself enjoyed greater respect in the broader culture.

Nevertheless, an opposing trend cut across this expansion of the public legitimacy of atheism, unchurched spirituality, heterodoxy, and irreligiosity. All of the groups described in this study either innovated a new program, or reoriented an older one, toward therapy and religion *simultaneously*. Clinical pastoral education enhanced institutional residents' access both to emotional and spiritual care. AA created a program that massively expanded the anti-alcoholism therapy and the spiritual outreach available to inebriates. The World War II–era Service-to-Man reforms simultaneously set MSSCs on the path to greater therapeutic *and* evangelical emphasis. This simultaneity is not as surprising if we recognize that historians have located both religious revivals and the "boom" in psychology in the aftermath of World War II. Many Americans in this period would have agreed with some variant of the idea that religion was God's psychiatry; at the same time, therapy provided by pastors, AA, and the army became a new form of spiritual revivalism.

Fundamentally, the vision of therapy articulated and promoted by believers in the decades after World War II did not run counter to the sociocultural needs of a pluralistic liberal democratic society as envisioned by Tocqueville and his intellectual heirs. Rather, it was shaped by these needs and intended to enhance them. All three groups adopted a therapeutic needs tack because it appeared to be a liberal democratic manner of interacting with the people they wanted to help. How? First, a psychotherapeutic approach facilitated outreach to diverse and isolated people. It helped civic organizations adapt to pluralism, whether or not they embraced ecumenism theologically. Psychotherapeutic ideas and techniques enabled programs to serve a wide variety of Americans, whose religious affiliations would otherwise have separated them. As we saw, the army, like many evangelicals and mid-century mainline Protestants, was wary of Roman Catholicism. But MSSCs granted all beneficiaries – regardless of religious background – the same opportunities for rehabilitation. Psychology should be recognized as one of the ways in which believers restructured not only American Protestantism but American Christianity as well.[2]

---

[2] Hunter, *Culture Wars*; Wuthnow, *The Restructuring of American Religion*.

Conclusion: American Psychology in an Age of Faiths   219

Second, the groups believed a psychotherapeutic approach was a way to embody Christian love while respecting individual difference and personal freedom. It emphasized the importance of allowing individuals to make their own choices while not withholding support that could help them heal. Thus, both army beneficiaries and AA members were helped to piece their lives back together irrespective of their spiritual decision making. CPE teachers attempted to be ecumenical as they nurtured their students emotionally and spiritually. As chaplain interns, these students tried to interact with patients in a similarly open-ended way. The universalism of the psychotherapeutic perspective thus helped these groups emphasize a form of Christian love that was egalitarian and "laity-centered."

Finally, all groups found in psychology a way to be more persuasive than coercive. Many ministers found in CPE a model of ministry that they felt enabled them to demonstrate the love of God rather than to goad parishioners into complying with religious forms out of fear or social conformity. Before AA, treatment for chronic inebriety depended largely on confinement or physical isolation. AA assumed a drinker would live and interact with the larger community. After the Service-to-Man reforms, the army ceased to dangle the lure of food over the heads of hungry men to get them to join in church services; a therapeutic approach offered the food and shelter first and relied on the entire program to encourage active spiritual participation.

That these programs had religious goals does not mean that they were religiously coercive. Independence allowed AA and the army to create flexible programs in which faith was paradigmatic but not hegemonic. They promoted religious structures but left the dogmas that had originally defined their shapes optional. This allowed a broad ecumenism to prevail. Even atheism was accommodated, although it was not preferred. A great example is the use of the language of the Higher Power in AA. Alcoholics Anonymous members insisted that such a power was the only thing that could keep an alcoholic sober, but they acknowledged that members could imagine it any way they chose. Members ranged in their affirmations from orthodox images of God, to a vaguely Platonic "go(o)d," to "G.O.D." ("group of drunks").

In fact, intrinsic forces constrained the coercive potential of autonomous groups. A heavy hand in the delicate work of convincing socially marginalized or addicted Americans to stick around, join the program, and participate willingly would have been counterproductive. Such a response could not be coerced, because the efficacy of these programs depended on the sincerity and enthusiasm with which people participated.

220   *American Protestantism in the Age of Psychology*

Furthermore, to incite such commitment from a highly diverse population, AA and the army had to make their programs capacious. Alcoholics Anonymous and army beneficiaries could leave at any time. The difficulty of forging new lives for themselves was reason enough to do so. The delights or debauch of the secular sphere in which they previously lived remained a constant alternative. Thus, groups could not insist members and beneficiaries believe their message. They had to persuade them. This restraint was reinforced by the fact that it did not impede their efficacy. As scholars have argued, Christian outreach historically has been *more* effective when it was *less* coercive.[3]

In fact, groups' willingness and interest in using psychology stemmed from its utility as a tool to democratize civil society. It was an aspect of what sociologist Peter Clecak has called a "democratization of personhood" in the latter half of the twentieth century. Clecak finds the origins of this movement in the 1950s and its flowering in the 1960s and 1970s. It comprised "the substantial extension of the many facilitating conditions for fulfillment of the self: enhanced cultural options, rising economic resources and rewards, strengthened legal guarantees, and augmented personal and political rights."[4] He argues that there was a redistribution of privileges, rights, and responsibilities.[5] Americans redistributed cultural authority to multiple competing centers in realms as diverse as the family, schools, work places, and other civil institutions.

This leveling between all kinds of people in all kinds of relationships applied not only to churches, but to spiritual communities both earthly and supernatural as well. As religious scholar Robert Orsi has recently argued, understanding religions as systems of meaning-making obscures the fact that believers understand their faith fundamentally as networks of relationships "between heaven and earth." Whether or not this applies trans-historically to all religions, it is an excellent way of making sense of the American Christian experience in the twentieth century. The networks that Orsi depicts were denser among Catholics than among Protestants, but the latter understood their faith as predicated on an intense relationship with Jesus, too.[6]

Psychotherapeutic approaches eroded the hierarchies between congregants, between clergy and laity, and between humans and the divine.

---

[3] Casanova, *Public Religions in the Modern World*; Hatch, *The Democratization of American Christianity*; Moore, *Selling God*.
[4] Clecak, *Ideal Self*.
[5] Ibid., 274.
[6] Orsi, *Between Heaven and Earth*; Prothero, *American Jesus*.

Conclusion: American Psychology in an Age of Faiths 221

This did not always entail total leveling. Clergy enrolled in CPE, for example, used their psychological expertise, in part, to regain the cultural prestige they saw themselves losing to the burgeoning professionals who laid claim to ever larger shares of their bailiwick. And yet the adaptation of psychology was an equalizer. It encouraged people in all groups studied to imagine God as an affable facilitator of the better person they wanted to become, rather than a stringent judge of the sinners they were. Fundamentally, the idea of a human–divine relationship characterized by emotional intimacy is itself one of familiarity and relative parity.

This increased equality did place greater emphasis on the human self in the relationship. Some critics suggest that *any* attention to the self is bad. But attention to the self in a liberal democratic republic is the inevitable result of its recognition of people as individuals rather than as members of corporate bodies. The question is what *kind* of attention to the self is paid; that is, what is demanded of it and how is it imagined? This psychoreligious project had at heart a vision of self appropriate for a liberal democratic society – it was one that balanced respect for pluralism and individuality with an emphasis on fulfillment through community and the search for transcendence.

Furthermore, it drew on an old Tocquevillian paradox about the function of religion in a liberal democratic republic: Americans were drawn into faith and its nobler concomitants of community, self-discipline, and cultural enhancement through the lure of individual well-being. Psychoreligious efforts were frequently effective in encouraging Americans to take on greater ethical responsibility while drawing them to faith and bringing them into fellowship with other citizens. The historical experience of the clinical pastoral education movement, AA, and MSSCs shows that psychology thus facilitated civil society and religious outreach in an individualistic, diverse liberal society.

Bibliography

Archival Sources

Pitts Theological Library, Emory University, Atlanta, Georgia
  Council for Clinical Training Collection
Southern Baptist Historical Library and Archives, Nashville, Tennessee
  Southern Baptist Association for Clinical Pastoral Education Collection
General Service Office Archives of Alcoholics Anonymous, New York, NY
Stepping Stones Foundation Archives, Bedford Hills, NY
The Salvation Army Archives, Alexandria, VA

Interviews

Bollwahn, Lt. Colonel Paul. National social services secretary, The Salvation Army. Interview by author, June 6, 2002, Alexandria, VA.

Cheydleur, John. Social services secretary, The Salvation Army, eastern territory. Interview by author, April 12, 2002 [telephone].

Gerkin, Charles. Interview by author, March 4, 2003, Atlanta, GA.

Hofman, Peter. Interviewed by Nicki Tanner, December 8, 1988. Acc. 89–26, transcript. The Salvation Army Archives, Alexandria, VA.

Hunter, Rodney. Interview by author, February 18, 2003, Altanta, GA.

Levine, Marsh. Associate editor, *The Grapevine*. Interview by author, April 15, 2003, New York, NY.

Marshall, Norman. Interviewed by Nicki Tanner, November 5, 1987. RG 20.90, transcript. The Salvation Army Archives, Alexandria, VA.

McPherson, Major Laurence. Assistant ARC commander, The Salvation Army, central territory. Interview by author, November 18, 2002 [telephone].

Norris, Richard. ARC commander, The Salvation Army, southern territory (retired). Interview by author, November 20, 2002 [telephone].

Robb, Anita. Interviewed by Nicki Tanner, September 17 and 22, 1986. Acc. 88–13, transcript. The Salvation Army Archives, Alexandria, VA.

Bibliography

White, Marilyn. National consultant for adult services, The Salvation Army. Interview by author, April 5, 2002, Alexandria, VA.

Articles, Books, and Papers

Twelve Steps and Twelve Traditions. 1995 pocket ed. New York: General Service Office of Alcoholics Anonymous, 1952.

Alcoholics Anonymous Comes of Age: A Brief History of AA. New York: Alcoholics Anonymous World Services, Inc., 1957.

Alcoholics Anonymous. Fourth ed. new and rev. at www.aa.org. New York: Alcoholics Anonymous World Services, Inc., 2001.

Alcoholics Anonymous: The Story of How More Than Fourteen Thousand Men and Women Have Recovered from Alcoholism. First ed. New York: Works Publishing Inc., 1945 (1939).

Came to Believe.... New York: Alcoholics Anonymous World Services, Inc., 1973.

Dr. Bob and the Good Oldtimers: A Biography, with Recollections of Early AA in the Midwest. New York: Alcoholics Anonymous World Services, Inc., 1980.

"Group I–Counselling." Paper presented at The Salvation Army Sessions, National Conference of Social Work, Cleveland, OH, 1963. SAA.

"Group II–Alcoholism." Paper presented at The Salvation Army Sessions, National Conference of Social Work, Cleveland, OH, 1963. SAA.

New York City Alcoholism Study: A Report. New York: National Council on Alcoholism, 1962.

Orders and Regulations for Officers of The Salvation Army. Rev. ed. St. Albans, UK: Campfield Press for The Salvation Army, International Headquarters, 1960. (Also: rev. ed. 1974.)

"Pass It On": Bill Wilson and How the AA Message Spread. New York: Alcoholics Anonymous World Services, Inc., 1984.

The Culture of Unbelief: Studies and Proceedings from the First International Symposium on Belief Held at Rome, March 22–27, 1969. Edited by Rocco Caporale and Antonio Grumelli. Berkeley: University of California Press, 1971.

The Little Red Book: An Orthodox Interpretation of the Twelve Steps of Alcoholics Anonymous. Center City, MN: Hazelden, 1957.

The Salvation Army Manual for Harbor Light Centers. New York: Salvation Army Commissioners' Conference, 1959. (Also: 2nd ed., 1966.)

The Salvation Army Men's Social Service Handbook of Standards, Principles and Policies. Edited by Commissioners' Conference. New York: The Salvation Army, 1960. (Also: rev. ed., 1987.)

The Salvation Army Social Service for Men: Standards and Practices. New York: National Research Bureau, Salvation Army, 1948.

"The 'Service-to-Man' Program of the Men's Social Service Department of The Salvation Army, Eastern Territory: A Report of the Institutes Held During 1944." New York: Salvation Army, Eastern Territory, 1944. SAA.

Twenty-Four Hours a Day. Rev. ed. Center City, MN: Hazelden, 1975.

Bibliography

Agnew, Ernest A. "The Casework Process in the Men's Social Service Center." Paper presented at the MSSD east, Officers' Councils, New York, NY, 1945. SAA.

Albanese, Catherine L. *America: Religions and Religion.* 2nd ed. Belmont, CA: Wadsworth Publishing Company, 1992.

Alexander, F., and M. Rollins. "Alcoholics Anonymous: The Unseen Cult." *California Sociologist* 7, no. 1 (1984): 33–48.

Alexander, Jack. "Alcoholics Anonymous: Freed Slaves of Drink, Now They Free Others." *Saturday Evening Post* (March 1, 1941).

Allen, John. "Teaching Mission." Paper presented at The Salvation Army, MSSD west, Officers' Councils, Pacific Grove, CA, 1959. SAA.

Baggs, Richard. "Answering the Challenge Through Men's Social Service." Paper presented at The Salvation Army Sessions, National Conference of Social Work, St. Louis, MO, 1943. SAA.

Bailey, Margaret, and Barry Leach. *Alcoholics Anonymous: Pathway to Recovery – A Study of 1,058 Members of the AA Fellowship in New York City.* New York: National Council on Alcoholism, 1965.

Baldwin, Albert. "Answering the Challenge Through Men's Social Service." Paper presented at The Salvation Army Sessions, National Conference of Social Work, St. Louis, MO, 1943. SAA.

Baldwin, Albert. "National Commission on Alcoholism Annual Report." Paper presented at The Salvation Army Sessions, National Conference of Social Work, Atlantic City, NJ, 1948. SAA.

Balogh, Brian. *Chain Reaction: Expert Debate and Public Participation in American Commercial Nuclear Power, 1945–1975.* Cambridge, UK: Cambridge University Press, 1991.

Barber, Roy. "Group Work in the Men's Social Service Center." Paper presented at The Salvation Army Sessions, National Conference of Social Work, Atlantic City, NJ, 1948.

Barber, Roy. "The Program at Work: The Group Approach." Paper presented at the Officers' Councils, Salvation Army, MSSD east, Atlantic City, NJ, 1954.

Barton, Bruce. *Only One Thousand Dollars: The Salvation Army Annual Report.* n.p.: The Salvation Army, 1922.

Battan, Jesse F. "The 'New Narcissism' in 20th-Century America: The Shadow and Substance of Social Change." *Journal of Social History* 17, no. 2 (1983): 199–220.

Bednarowski, Mary Farrell. *New Religions and the Theological Imagination in America.* Bloomington: Indiana University Press, 1989.

Beit-Hallahmi, Benjamin. "Psychology of Religion 1880–1930: The Rise and Fall of a Psychological Movement." *Journal of the History of the Behavioral Sciences* 10, no. 1 (1974): 84–90.

Bellah, Robert N. "The Protestant Structure of American Culture: Multiculture or Monoculture?" *The Hedgehog Review* 4, no. 1 (2002): 7–28.

Bellah, Robert N., Richard Madsen, William M. Sullivan, Ann Swidler, and Steven M. Tipton. *Habits of the Heart: Individualism and Commitment in American Life.* Berkeley: University of California Press, 1985.

Bibliography

Bjork, Daniel W. *The Compromised Scientist: William James in the Development of American Psychology*. New York: Columbia University Press, 1983.

Bodine, Paul E. "The 1959 Yale Summer School on Alcohol: Impressions and Reactions." Paper presented at The Salvation Army, MSSD west, Officers' Councils, Pacific Grove, CA, 1959. SAA.

Booth, William. *In Darkest England and the Way Out*. New York: Funk & Wagnalls, 1890.

Boyer, Paul. *By the Bomb's Early Light: American Thought and Culture at the Dawn of the Atomic Age*. Chapel Hill: University of North Carolina Press, 1985.

Bromet, Evelyn, Rudolf H. Moos, and Fredric Bliss. "The Social Climate of Alcoholism Treatment Programs." *Archives of General Psychiatry* 33 (1976): 910–16.

Bruder, Ernest E., and Marian L. Barb. "A Survey of Ten Years of Clinical Pastoral Training at Saint Elizabeth's Hospital." Washington, DC: Department of Health, Education, and Welfare, Saint Elizabeth's Hospital, Chaplain Services Branch, 1956: 69–71. SAA.

Buber, Martin. *I and Thou*. Translated by Walter Kaufmann. New York: Charles Scribner's Sons, 1970.

Bufe, Charles. *Alcoholics Anonymous: Cult or Cure?* San Francisco: See Sharp Press, 1991.

Cahalan, Margaret Werner. *Historical Corrections Statistics in the United States, 1850–1984*. Rockville, MD: Westat, Inc., for Bureau of Justice Statistics, U.S. Department of Justice, 1986.

Cain, Arthur. "Alcoholics Anonymous: Cult or Cure?" *Harpers* 226 (February 1963): 48–52.

Cain, Arthur. "Alcoholics Can be Cured – Despite AA." *Saturday Evening Post* (September 19, 1965): 6–8.

Caplan, Eric. *Mind Games: American Culture and the Birth of Psychotherapy*. Berkeley: University of California Press, 1998.

Cary, Phillip. *Augustine's Invention of the Inner Self: The Legacy of a Christian Platonist*. New ed. New York: Oxford University Press, 2003.

Casanova, Jose. *Public Religions in the Modern World*. Chicago: University of Chicago Press, 1994.

Cheever, Susan. *My Name Is Bill*. New York: Simon & Schuster, 2004.

Chesham, Sallie. *Born to Battle: The Salvation Army in America*. Chicago: Rand McNally & Co., 1965.

Chesler, Phyllis. *Women and Madness*. Garden City, NY: Doubleday, 1972.

Clebsch, William A. *American Religious Thought: A History*. Edited by Martin E. Marty for *Chicago History of American Religion* series. Chicago: University of Chicago Press, 1973.

Clebsch, William A., and Charles R. Jaekle. *Pastoral Care in Historical Perspective: An Essay with Exhibits*. 1967 paperback ed. New York: Harper Torchbooks, Harper & Row, Publishers, 1964.

Clecak, Peter. *America's Quest for the Ideal Self: Dissent and Fulfillment in the 60s and 70s*. New York: Oxford University Press, 1983.

Bibliography

Clinebell Jr., Howard J. *Understanding and Counseling the Alcoholic Through Religion and Psychology.* New York: Abingdon Press, 1956.

Coben, Stanley. *Rebellion Against Victorianism: The Impetus for Cultural Change in 1920s America.* New York: Oxford University Press, 1991.

Cohen, Lizabeth. *Making a New Deal: Industrial Workers in Chicago, 1919–1939.* Cambridge, UK: Cambridge University Press, 1990.

Cohen, Lizabeth. *A Consumer's Republic: The Politics of Mass Consumption in Postwar America.* New York: Knopf, 2003.

Cotkin, George. *Existential America.* Baltimore: Johns Hopkins University Press, 2003.

Coutts, Frederick. *The History of The Salvation Army: The Weapons of Goodwill, 1946–1977.* Vol. VII. London: Hodder and Stoughton, 1947.

Coutts, John. *The Salvationists.* London: The Salvation Army, 1977.

Croce, Paul Jerome. *Science and Religion in the Era of William James.* Vol. 1, Eclipse of Certainty, 1820–1880. Chapel Hill: University of North Carolina Press, 1995.

Crowley, Michael. "L. Ron Hubbard: Scientology's Esteemed Founder." *Slate* (July 15, 2005) at www.slate.com.

Cushman, Philip. *Constructing the Self, Constructing America: A Cultural History of Psychotherapy.* Boston: Addison-Wesley, 1995.

Danzinger, Kurt. *Constructing the Subject: Historical Origins of Psychological Research.* Cambridge, UK: Cambridge University Press, 1990.

Davis, Joseph. *Accounts of Innocence: Sexual Abuse, Trauma, and the Self.* Chicago: University of Chicago Press, 2005.

Demos, John. "Oedipus and America: Historical Perspectives on the Reception of Psychoanalysis in the United States." In *Inventing the Psychological: Toward a Cultural History of Emotional Life in America*, edited by Joel Pfister and Nancy Schnog, 63–78. New Haven, CT: Yale University Press, 1997.

Douglas, Ann. *Terrible Honesty: Mongrel Manhattan in the 1920s.* New York: Farrar, Straus, and Giroux, 1995.

Duplain, George W. "The Use of Professional Workers on the Staff." Paper presented at The Salvation Army, MSSD west, Officers' Councils, Pacific Grove, CA, 1959. SAA.

Eberly, Don E., ed. *The Essential Civil Society Reader: The Classic Essays.* Lanham, MD: Rowman and Littlefield Publishers, Inc., 2000.

Ellenberger, Henri F. *The Discovery of the Unconscious: The History and Evolution of Dynamic Psychiatry.* New York: Basic Books, Inc., 1970.

Ellwood, Robert S. *Alternative Altars: Unconventional and Eastern Spirituality in America.* Edited by Martin E. Marty for *Chicago History of American Religion* series. Chicago: University of Chicago Press, 1979.

Ellwood, Robert S. *The Sixties Spiritual Awakening: American Religion Moving from Modern to Postmodern.* New Brunswick, NJ: Rutgers University Press, 1994.

Ellwood, Robert S. *The Fifties Spiritual Marketplace: American Religion in a Decade of Conflict.* New Brunswick, NJ: Rutgers University Press, 1997.

Bibliography

Emrick, Chad D., J. S. Tonigan, H. Montgomery, and L. Little. "Alcoholics Anonymous: What Is Currently Known?" In *Research on Alcoholics Anonymous: Opportunities and Alternatives*, edited by Barbara S. McCrady and William R. Miller, 41–76. New Brunswick, NJ: Publications Division, Rutgers Center of Alcohol Studies, 1993.

Fiedler, Leslie A. "The Birth of God & the Death of Man." *Salmagundi*, no. 21 (1973): 3–26.

Findlay, James. *Church People in the Struggle: The National Council of Churches and the Black Freedom Movement, 1950–1970*. New York: Oxford University Press, 1993.

Finke, Roger, and Rodney Stark. *The Churching of America, 1776–1990: Winners and Losers in Our Religious Economy*. New Brunswick, NJ: Rutgers University Press, 1992.

Fitzgerald, Timothy. *The Ideology of Religious Studies*. New York: Oxford University Press, 2000.

Foote, Loren. "Theory and Practice – Applying the Yale Material to Our Programs." Paper presented at The Salvation Army, MSSD west, Officers' Councils, Pacific Grove, CA, 1959. SAA.

Ford, David F., ed. *The Modern Theologians: An Introduction to Christian Theology in the Twentieth Century*. Cambridge, UK: Blackwell Publishers, 1997.

Ford, David F. "Introduction to Modern Christian Theology." In *The Modern Theologians: An Introduction to Christian Theology in the Twentieth Century*, edited by David F. Ford, 1–16. Cambridge, UK: Blackwell Publishers, 1997.

Foucault, Michel. *The Birth of the Clinic: An Archaeology of Medical Perception*. Translated by A. M. Sheridan Smith. New York: Pantheon, 1973.

Foucault, Michel. *Madness and Civilization: A History of Insanity in the Age of Reason*. Translated by Richard Howard. New York: Pantheon, 1965.

Fox, Richard Wightman. *Jesus in America: Personal Savior, Cultural Hero, National Obsession*. San Francisco: HarperCollins Publishers, 2004.

Freud, Sigmund. *Civilization and Its Discontents*. Translated and edited by James Strachey. New York: W.W. Norton & Company, 1961.

Freud, Sigmund. *The Future of an Illusion*. Translated and edited by James Strachey. New York: W.W. Norton & Company, 1961.

Fuller, Robert C. *Mesmerism and the American Cure of Souls*. Philadelphia: University of Pennsylvania Press, 1982.

Fuller, Robert C. *Americans and the Unconscious*. New York: Oxford University Press, 1986.

Fuller, Robert C. *Stairways to Heaven: Drugs in American Religious History*. Boulder, CO: Westview Press, 2000.

Fuller, Robert C. *Spiritual, but Not Religious: Understanding Unchurched America*. New York: Oxford University Press, 2001.

Furedi, Frank. "The Silent Ascendancy of Therapeutic Culture in Britain." *Society* 39, no. 3 (2002): 16–24.

Furedi, Frank. *Therapy Culture: Cultivating Vulnerability in an Uncertain Age*. New York: Routledge, 2003.

Bibliography

Gifford, Sanford. *The Emmanuel Movement: The Origins of Group Treatment and the Assault on Lay Therapy*. Boston: Harvard University Press for the Francis Countway Library of Medicine, 1997.

Gilbert, James. *Redeeming Culture: American Religion in an Age of Science*. Chicago: University of Chicago Press, 1997.

Gilbert, William. "The Salvation Army Men's Service Center: Group Therapy, Final Report." Syracuse, NY, 1963. Acc. 78–24, SAA.

Gillespie, C. Kevin. *Psychology and American Catholicism: From Confession to Therapy?* New York: The Crossroad Publishing Company, 2001.

Gilkey, Langdon. *Naming the Whirlwind: The Renewal of God-Language*. Indianapolis, IN: Bobbs-Merrill, 1969.

Green, Roger J. "William Booth's Theology of Redemption." *Christian History* 9, no. 2, Issue 26 (1990) at http://www.ctlibrary.com.

Gross, Martin L. *The Psychological Society: The Impact – and the Failure – of Psychiatry, Psychotherapy, Psychoanalysis and the Psychological Revolution*. New York: Random House, 1978.

Guldenschuh, Frank. "Aiding Alcoholics." Paper presented at the MSSD east, Officers' Councils, New York, NY, 1945. SAA.

Gutmann, David. "Psychology as Theology." *Social Research* 45, no. 3 (1978), 452–66.

Hale, Nathan G. *The Rise and Crisis of Psychoanalysis in the United States: Freud and the Americans, 1917–1985*. Vol. II, *Freud in America*. New York: Oxford University Press, 1995.

Hall, Charles E. *Head and Heart: The Story of the Clinical Pastoral Education Movement*. Atlanta, GA: Journal of Pastoral Care Publications, Inc., 1992.

Hall, David. *Worlds of Wonder, Days of Judgment: Popular Religious Belief in Early New England*. Cambridge, MA: Harvard University Press, 1989.

Hall, David, ed. *Lived Religion in America: Toward a History of Practice*. Princeton, NJ: Princeton University Press, 1997.

Hamblett, Mark. "AA at State-Funded Facility May Be Permissible." *The Legal Intelligencer*, April 26, 2001, at http://web.lexis-nexis.com.

Hamilton, Malcolm B. *The Sociology of Religion: Theoretical and Comparative Perspectives*. London: Routledge, 1995.

Hatch, Nathan O. *The Democratization of American Christianity*. New Haven, CT: Yale University Press, 1989.

Heinze, Andrew R. "Peace of Mind (1946): Judaism and the Therapeutic Polemics of Postwar America." *Religion and American Culture* 12, no. 1 (2002): 31–58.

Heinze, Andrew R. *Jews and the American Soul: Human Nature in the Twentieth Century*. Princeton, NJ: Princeton University Press, 2004.

Herman, Ellen. "Being and Doing: Humanistic Psychology and the Spirit of the 1960s." In *Sights on the Sixties*, edited by Barbara Tischler, 87–102. New Brunswick, NJ: Rutgers University Press, 1992.

Herman, Ellen. *The Romance of American Psychology: Political Culture in the Age of Experts*. Berkeley: University of California Press, 1995.

Heron, Alasdair I. C. *A Century of Protestant Theology*. London: Lutterworth Press, 1980.

230   *Bibliography*

Heschel, Abraham Joshua. *Man Is Not Alone: A Philosophy of Religion*. New York: Farrar Straus & Young, 1951.

Hiltner, Seward. *Pastoral Counseling*. New York: Abingdon-Cokesbury Press, 1949.

Hiltner, Seward. *Preface to Pastoral Theology*. Nashville, TN: Abingdon Press, 1958.

Hofman, Peter. "Answering the Challenge Through Men's Social Service." Paper presented at The Salvation Army Sessions, National Conference of Social Work, St. Louis, MO, 1943. SAA.

Hofman, Peter. "Relating The Salvation Army Program on Alcoholism to the Community." Paper presented at The Salvation Army Sessions, National Conference of Social Work, Chicago, IL, 1945. SAA.

Hofman, Peter. "Serving the Client and the Community through the Men's Social Service Center." Paper presented at the National Conference of Social Work, 1947. SAA.

Hofman, Peter. "Keynotes." Paper presented at The Salvation Army, MSSD west, Officers' Councils, Pacific Grove, CA, 1959. SAA.

Holifield, E. Brooks. "The Hero and the Minister in American Culture." *Theology Today* 33, no. 4 (1977): 370–9.

Holifield, E. Brooks. *A History of Pastoral Care in America: From Salvation to Self-Realization*. Nashville, TN: Abingdon Press, 1983.

Holifield, E. Brooks. "Ministry in America: Past and Present." *Virginia Seminary Journal* (2004): 9–23.

Holifield, E. Brooks. *God's Ambassadors: A History of the Christian Clergy in America*. Grand Rapids, MI: William B. Eerdmans Publishing Company, 2007.

Hollinger, David A. *Science, Jews, and Secular Culture*. Princeton, NJ: Princeton University Press, 1996.

Hudnut-Beumler, James. *Looking for God in the Suburbs: The Religion of the American Dream and Its Critics, 1945–1965*. New Brunswick, NJ: Rutgers University Press, 1994.

Hunter, James Davidson. *Culture Wars: The Struggle to Define America*. New York: Basic Books, 1991.

Hunter, James Davidson. *The Death of Character: Moral Education in an Age Without Good or Evil*. New York: Basic Books, 2000.

Hunter, James Davidson. "When Psychotherapy Replaces Religion." *The Public Interest*, no. 139 (2000): 5–21.

Hunter, Rodney J., ed. *Dictionary of Pastoral Care and Counseling*. Nashville, TN: Abingdon Press, 1990.

Hutchison, William. *The Modernist Impulse in American Protestantism*. Cambridge, MA: Harvard University Press, 1976.

Hutchison, William. *Between the Times: The Travail of the Protestant Establishment in America, 1900–1960*. New York: Cambridge University Press, 1989.

Imber, Jonathan B., ed. *Therapeutic Culture: Triumph and Defeat*. New Brunswick, NJ: Transaction Publishers, 2004.

International Marketing Group Inc. "The Second Hundred Years: A Strategy Plan for The Salvation Army, U.S.A." McLean, VA: n.p., 1980. SAA.

Bibliography

James, William. *The Varieties of Religious Experience*. Edited with an introduction by Martin Marty. New York: Penguin Books, 1982.

Jenson, Robert W. "Karl Barth." In *The Modern Theologians: An Introduction to Christian Theology in the Twentieth Century*, edited by David F. Ford, 21–36. Cambridge, UK: Blackwell Publishers, 1997.

Johnson, Warren C. "Fellowship Clubs." Paper presented at The Salvation Army, MSSD west, Officers' Councils, Pacific Grove, CA, 1959. SAA.

Johnstone, Arthur. "Alcoholics Anonymous Groups." In *Report on Men's Social Service Councils*. Pacific Grove, CA: Salvation Army, 1960. SAA.

Joint Commission on Mental Illness and Health. *Action for Mental Health*. New York: Basic Books, 1961.

Judge, John J. "Alcoholism Treatment at The Salvation Army; A New Men's Social Service Center Program." *Quarterly Journal of Studies on Alcohol* 32 (1971), 462–7.

Kaminer, Wendy. *I'm Dysfunctional, You're Dysfunctional: The Recovery Movement and Other Self-Help Fashions*. New York: Vintage Books, 1993.

Katz, Lawrence. "The Salvation Army Men's Social Service Center, I. Program." *Quarterly Journal of Studies on Alcohol* 25, no. 2 (1964): 324–32.

Katz, Lawrence. "Alcoholic Rehabilitation Project: Men's Social Service Center, San Francisco, CA." n.p.: 1966. SAA.

Katz, Lawrence. "The Salvation Army Men's Social Service Center, II. Results." *Quarterly Journal of Studies on Alcohol* 27, no. 4 (1966): 636–47.

Kaufmann, Walter, ed. *Existentialism from Dostoevsky to Sartre*. New York: Meridian Books, 1956.

Kimball, Marion. "Experiences in Lessening Racial Tensions." Paper presented at The Salvation Army Sessions, National Conference of Social Work, Chicago, IL, 1945. SAA.

Kovel, Joel. "The American Mental Health Industry." In *Critical Psychiatry: The Politics of Mental Health*, edited by David Ingleby, 72–101. New York: Pantheon Books, 1980.

Kugelmann, Robert. "Neoscholastic Psychology Revisited." *History of Psychology* 8, no. 2 (2005): 131–75.

Kugelmann, Robert. *Psychology and Catholicism: Contested Boundaries*. Cambridge, UK: Cambridge University Press, forthcoming.

Kurtz, Ernest. *Not-God: A History of Alcoholics Anonymous*. Center City, MN: Hazelden Educational Services, 1979.

LaPiere, Richard Tracy. *The Freudian Ethic*. New York: Duell, Sloan and Pearce, 1959.

Larson, Edward J. *Summer for the Gods: The Scopes Trial and America's Continuing Debate over Science and Religion*. New York: Basic Books, 1997.

Lasch, Christopher. *The Culture of Narcissism: American Life in an Age of Diminished Expectations*. New York: W. W. Norton & Company, Inc., 1978.

Laune, Ferris Finley. "A Survey of The Men's Social Service Center." Honolulu, HI, 1961. SAA.

Leahey, Thomas Hardy. *A History of Modern Psychology*. 2nd ed. Englewood Cliffs, NJ: Prentice Hall, 1994.

Bibliography

Lears, T. J. Jackson. *No Place of Grace: Antimodernism and the Transformation of American Culture, 1880–1920.* New York: Pantheon, 1981.

Lears, T. J. Jackson. "From Salvation to Self-Realization: Advertising and the Therapeutic Roots of the Consumer Culture, 1880–1930." In *The Culture of Consumption: Critical Essays in American History 1880–1980,* edited by T. J. Jackson Lears and Richard Wightman Fox, 1–38. New York: Pantheon Books, 1983.

Levine, George, ed. *Constructions of the Self.* New Brunswick, NJ: Rutgers University Press, 1992.

Lunbeck, Elizabeth. *The Psychiatric Persuasion: Knowledge, Gender, and Power in Modern America.* Princeton, NJ: Princeton University Press, 1995.

Macquarrie, John. *God-Talk: An Examination of the Language and Logic of Theology.* New York: Harper & Row, Publishers, 1967.

Madsen, William. *The American Alcoholic: The Nature-Nurture Controversy in Alcoholic Research and Therapy.* Springfield, IL: Charles C. Thomas Publisher, 1974.

Makela, Klaus, Ikka Arminen, Kim Bloomfield, et al. *Alcoholics Anonymous as a Mutual-Help Movement: A Study in Eight Societies.* Madison: University of Wisconsin Press, 1996.

Malpass, Leslie. "Techniques of Counseling and Their Application: The Theoretical Bases of Personal Counseling." Paper presented at The Salvation Army Sessions, National Conference of Social Work, Cleveland, OH, 1953. SAA.

Marty, Martin E. *Modern American Religion.* Vol. 1, The Irony of It All, 1893–1919. Chicago: University of Chicago Press, 1986.

Marty, Martin E. *Modern American Religion.* Vol. 2, The Noise of Conflict, 1919–1941. Chicago: University of Chicago Press, 1991.

Marty, Martin E. *Modern American Religion.* Vol. 3, Under God, Indivisible, 1941–1960. Chicago: University of Chicago Press, 1996.

Maslow, Abraham. "Eupsychia – The Good Society." *Journal of Humanistic Psychology* 1(2): 11.

Matthews, F. H. "The Americanization of Sigmund Freud: Adaptations of Psychoanalysis before 1917." *Journal of American Studies* 1, no. 1 (1967): 39–62.

Maxwell, Milton A. "Alcoholics Anonymous: An Interpretation." In *Society, Culture, and Drinking Patterns,* edited by David J. Pittman and Charles R. Snyder, 577–85. New York: John Wiley and Sons, 1962.

McCarthy, Katherine. "Early Alcoholism Treatment: The Emmanuel Movement and Richard Peabody." *Journal of Studies on Alcohol* 45, no. 1 (1984): 59–74.

McClay, Wilfred. *The Masterless: Self and Society in Modern America.* Chapel Hill: University of North Carolina Press, 1994.

McKinley, Edward H. *Marching to Glory: The History of The Salvation Army in the United States of America, 1880–1980.* 1st ed. San Francisco: Harper & Row, 1980. (Also: 2nd ed. Grand Rapids, MI: William B. Eerdmans Publishing Co., 1995.)

McKinley, Edward H. *Somebody's Brother: A History of The Salvation Army Men's Social Service Department, 1891–1985.* Lewiston/Queenston, NY: The Edwin Mellon Press, 1986.

Bibliography

McKinley, Edward H. "'A Lodging Place for Men-and More!' The Salvation Army Residential Rehabilitation Program for Men in Historical Perspective." Paper presented at the Protestant Health and Welfare Association Conference, Salvation Army Sessions, New Orleans, LA, 1987. SAA.

Meador, Keith G. "'My Own Salvation': *The Christian Century* and Psychology's Secularizing of American Protestantism." In *The Secular Revolution*, edited by Christian Smith, 269–309. Berkeley: University of California Press, 2003.

Meyer, Donald. *The Positive Thinkers: A Study of the American Quest for Health, Wealth and Personal Power from Mary Baker Eddy to Norman Vincent Peale.* Garden City, NY: Doubleday & Company, Inc., 1965.

Mills, C. Wright. *White Collar: The American Middle Classes.* New York: Oxford University Press, 1951.

Mills, C. Wright. *The Power Elite.* New York: Oxford University Press, 1956.

Moore, R. Laurence. *In Search of White Crows: Spiritualism, Parapsychology, and American Culture.* New York: Oxford University Press, 1977.

Moore, R. Laurence. *Selling God: American Religion in the Marketplace of Culture.* Oxford, UK: Oxford University Press, 1994.

Moos, Rudolf, John W. Finney, and Ruth C. Cronkite. *Alcoholism Treatment: Context, Process, and Outcome.* New York: Oxford University Press, 1990.

Moos, Rudolf, Barbara Mehren, and Bernice Moos. "Evaluation of a Salvation Army Alcoholism Treatment Program." *Journal of Studies on Alcohol* 39, no. 7 (1978): 1267–75.

Morris, Andrew J. F. *The Limits of Voluntarism: Charity and Welfare from the New Deal Through the Great Society.* New York: Cambridge University Press, 2009.

Moskowitz, Eva S. *In Therapy We Trust: America's Obsession with Self Fulfillment.* Baltimore: Johns Hopkins University Press, 2001.

Murdoch, Norman H. *Origins of The Salvation Army.* Knoxville: University of Tennessee Press, 1994.

Niebuhr, H. Richard. *Christ and Culture.* San Francisco: Harper San Francisco, 2001.

Nolan, James L. *The Therapeutic State: Justifying Government at Century's End.* New York: New York University, 1998.

Noll, Richard. *The Jung Cult: Origins of a Charismatic Movement.* Princeton, NJ: Princeton University Press, 1994.

Noll, Richard. *The Aryan Christ: The Secret Life of Carl Jung.* 1st ed. New York: Random House, 1997.

Oates, Wayne E., ed. *An Introduction to Pastoral Counseling.* Nashville, TN: Broadman Press, 1959.

Ogborne, Alan, and Frederick B. Glaser. "Characteristics of Affiliates of Alcoholics Anonymous." *Journal of Studies on Alcohol* 42 (July 1981): 661–75.

Orsi, Robert. "Everyday Miracles: The Study of Lived Religion." In *Lived Religion in America: Toward a History of Practice*, edited by David Hall, 1–21. Princeton, NJ: Princeton University Press, 1997.

Orsi, Robert. *Between Heaven and Earth: The Religious Worlds People Make and the Scholars Who Study Them.* Princeton, NJ: Princeton University Press, 2005.

Bibliography

Petigny, Alan. *The Permissive Society: America 1941–1965.* New York: Oxford University Press, 2009.

Pfister, Joel. "Glamorizing the Psychological: The Politics of the Performances of Modern Psychological Identities." In *Inventing the Psychological: Toward a Cultural History of Emotional Life in America,* edited by Joel Pfister and Nancy Schnog, 167–213. New Haven, CT: Yale University Press, 1997.

Pfister, Joel, and Nancy Schnog, ed. *Inventing the Psychological: Toward a Cultural History of Emotional Life in America.* New Haven, CT: Yale University Press, 1997.

Pines, Deborah. "Judge Again Backs Atheist in AA Dispute." *New York Law Journal,* July 15, 1997, at http://web.lexis-nexis.com.

Pisani, Vincent. "Milieu Therapy and the Multi-Treatment Approach." In *Alcoholism: The Total Treatment Approach.* Edited by Ronald Catanzaro, 255–67. Springfield, IL: Charles C. Thomas Publisher, 1968.

Prothero, Stephen. *American Jesus: How the Son of God Became a National Icon.* New York: Farrar, Straus and Giroux, 2003.

Putnam, Robert D. *Bowling Alone: The Collapse and Revival of American Community.* New York: Simon and Schuster, 2000.

Rice, John Steadman. *A Disease of One's Own: Psychotherapy, Addiction, and the Emergence of Co-Dependency.* New Brunswick, NJ: Transaction Publishers, 1996.

Rieff, Philip. *The Triumph of the Therapeutic: Uses of Faith after Freud.* New York: Harper Torchbooks, Harper & Row, 1966.

Rieff, Philip. *Freud: The Mind of the Moralist.* 3rd ed. Chicago: University of Chicago Press, 1979.

Rieff, Philip. *My Life among the Deathworks: Illustrations of the Aesthetics of Authority.* Edited by Kenneth S. Piver. Vol. I, Sacred Order/Social Order. Charlottesville: University of Virginia, 2006.

Riesman, David, Nathan Glazer, and Reuel Denney. *The Lonely Crowd: A Study of the Changing American Character.* New Haven, CT: Yale University Press, 1969.

Robb, Anita. "The Yale Summer School of Alcohol Studies." Paper presented at The Salvation Army Sessions, National Conference of Social Work, San Francisco, 1947. SAA.

Roberts, David E. *Psychotherapy and a Christian View of Man.* New York: Charles Scribner's Sons, 1950.

Rogers, Carl R. *On Becoming a Person.* Boston: Houghton Mifflin Company, 1961.

Roof, Wade Clark. *A Generation of Seekers: The Spiritual Journeys of the Baby Boom Generation.* San Francisco: Harper San Francisco, HarperCollins Publishers, 1993.

Room, Robin. "Alcoholism and Alcoholics Anonymous in U.S. Films, 1945–1962: The Party Ends for the 'Wet Generation.'" *Journal of Studies on Alcohol* 50, no. 4 (1989): 368–83.

Room, Robin. "'Healing Ourselves and Our Planet': The Emergence and Nature of a Generalized Twelve-Step Consciousness." *Contemporary Drug Problems* 19, no. 4 (Winter 1992): 717–40. At InfoTrac OneFile, http://web6.infotrac/galegroup.com.

Bibliography

Room, Robin, and Thomas Greenfield. "Alcoholics Anonymous, Other 12-Step Movements and Psychotherapy in the US Population, 1990." *Addiction* 88 (1993): 555–62.

Rose, Nikolas. *Inventing Our Selves: Psychology, Power, and Personhood*. Cambridge, UK: Cambridge University Press, 1996.

Rose, Nikolas. *Governing the Soul: The Shaping of the Private Self*. 2nd ed. London: Free Association Books, 1999.

Rossinow, Doug. *The Politics of Authenticity: Liberalism, Christianity, and the New Left in America*. New York: Columbia University Press, 1998.

Rudy, David, and Arthur Greil. "Is Alcoholics Anonymous a Religious Organization? Meditations on Marginality." *Sociological Analysis* 50, no. 1 (1988): 41–51.

Russell, Mina. "Building a Healthy Personality Through Religious Service." Paper presented at The Salvation Army Sessions, National Conference of Social Work, St. Louis, MO, 1956. SAA.

Sandall, Robert. *The History of The Salvation Army*. Vol. III: Social Reform and Welfare Work, 1883–1953. London: Thomas Nelson and Sons Ltd., 1947.

Scott, Daryl. *Contempt and Pity: Social Policy and the Image of the Damaged Black Psyche, 1880–1996*. Chapel Hill: University of North Carolina Press, 1997.

Seligman, Adam. *The Idea of Civil Society*. New York: The Free Press, 1992.

Selke, Raymond. "Group Therapy Approaches to The Salvation Army Beneficiary." Rochester, NY, 1959. Acc. 78–24, SAA.

Shinn, Roger Lincoln. *Man: The New Humanism*. Edited by William Hordern. Vol. 6, New Directions in Theology Today. Philadelphia: The Westminster Press, 1968.

Silkworth, W. D. "A New Approach to Psychotherapy in Chronic Alcoholism." *Journal-Lancet* (July 1939). Reprinted in *Alcoholics Anonymous Comes of Age: A Brief History of AA*. New York: Alcoholics Anonymous World Services, Inc., 1957: 302–8.

Smith, Christian, ed. *The Secular Revolution*. Berkeley: University of California Press, 2003.

Sommers, Christina Hoff, and Sally Satel. *One Nation Under Therapy: How the Helping Culture Is Eroding Self-Reliance*. New York: St. Martin's Press, 2005.

Spence, Clark C. *The Salvation Army Farm Colonies*. Tucson: The University of Arizona Press, 1985.

Spencer, Gary. "Religious Freedom Not an Issue in 12-Step Sobriety Program." *New York Law Journal*, May 19, 1995, at http://web.lexis-nexis.com.

Spencer, Gary. "Prison Condition a Religious Violation; Required Attendance at Alcohol Program Ruled an Unconstitutional Infringement." *New York Law Journal*, June 12, 1996, at http://web.lexis-nexis.com.

Stearns, Peter N. *American Cool: Constructing a Twentieth-Century Emotional Style*. New York: New York University Press, 1994.

Steinberg, Stephen. *The Academic Melting Pot: Catholics and Jews in American Higher Education*. New York: Carnegie Foundation, McGraw-Hill Book Company, 1974.

Bibliography

Stevens, Leonard F., and Doyle D. Henrie. "A History of Psychiatric Nursing." *Bulletin of the Menninger Clinic* 30, no. 1 (1966): 32–8.

Stokes, Allison. *Ministry after Freud*. New York: The Pilgrim Press, 1985.

Straus, Robert. "Alcohol and the Homeless Man." *Quarterly Journal of Studies on Alcohol* 7, no. 3 (1946): 360–404.

Summers, Thomas. *Hunkering Down*. Columbia, SC: Edisto Press, 2000.

Susman, Warren. "'Personality' and the Making of Twentieth-Century Culture." In *Culture as History: The Transformation of American Society in the Twentieth Century*, 271–86. New York: Pantheon Books, 1984.

Szasz, Thomas S. *The Myth of Mental Illness: Foundations of a Theory of Personal Conduct*. New York: Hoeber-Harper, 1961.

Taiz, Lillian. *Hallelujah Lads and Lasses: Remaking The Salvation Army in America, 1880–1930*. Chapel Hill: University of North Carolina Press, 2001.

Taves, Ann. *Fits, Trances, and Visions: Experiencing Religion and Explaining Experience from Wesley to James*. Princeton, NJ: Princeton University Press, 1999.

Taylor, Charles. *The Ethics of Authenticity*. Cambridge, MA: Harvard University Press, 1991.

Taylor, Charles. *Varieties of Religion Today: William James Revisited*. Cambridge, MA: Harvard University Press, 2002.

Taylor, Charles. *A Secular Age*. Boston: Belknap Press/Harvard University Press, 2007.

Telfer, A. P. "Pasadena Alcoholics Anonymous." Paper presented at The Salvation Army, MSSD west, Officers' Councils, Pacific Grove, CA, 1959. SAA.

Thornton, Edward E. *Professional Education for Ministry: A History of Clinical Pastoral Education*. Nashville, TN: Abingdon Press, 1970.

Tiebout, Harry M. "Therapeutic Mechanism of Alcoholics Anonymous." *American Journal of Psychiatry* (January 1944). Reprinted in *Alcoholics Anonymous Comes of Age: A Brief History of AA*. New York: Alcoholics Anonymous World Services, Inc., 1957: 309–19.

Tillich, Paul. *Systematic Theology*. 3 vols. Chicago: University of Chicago Press, 1951–1956.

Tillich, Paul. *The Courage to Be*. New Haven, CT: Yale University Press, 1952.

Tillich, Paul. *The Meaning of Health: Essays in Existentialism, Psychoanalysis, and Religion*. Edited by Perry LeFevre. Chicago: Exploration Press, 1984.

Tillich, Paul. *The Essential Tillich*. Edited by F. Forrester Church. Chicago: University of Chicago Press, 1987.

Tobin, E. K. "Group Therapy and Clinics." Paper presented at The Salvation Army, MSSD west, Officers' Councils, Pacific Grove, CA, 1959. SAA.

Tocqueville, Alexis de. *Democracy in America*. Edited by Phillips Bradley, translated by Henry Reeve and Francis Bowen. New York: Vintage Books Edition, 1990.

Tonigan, J. Scott, W. R. Miller, and Carol Schermer. "Atheists, Agnostics, and Alcoholics Anonymous." *Journal of Studies on Alcohol* 63, no. 5 (2002): 534–41.

Bibliography

Trice, Harrison M., and Paul M. Roman. "Sociopsychological Predictors of Affiliation with Alcoholics Anonymous." *Social Psychiatry* 5, no. 1 (January 1970): 51–9.

Turner, James. *Without God, Without Creed: The Origins of Unbelief in America*. Baltimore: Johns Hopkins University Press, 1985.

Vaillant, George E. *The Natural History of Alcoholism*. Cambridge, MA: Harvard University Press, 1983.

Vitz, Paul C. *Psychology as Religion: The Cult of Self-Worship*. 2nd ed. Grand Rapids, MI; Carlisle, UK: W. B. Eerdmans Pub. Co.; Paternoster Press, 1994.

Vitz, Paul. "Psychology in Recovery." *First Things* (March 2005): 17–21.

Waldron, John D., ed. *Creed and Deed: Toward a Christian Theology of Social Services in The Salvation Army*. Oakville, Ontario: The Salvation Army of Canada and Bermuda, 1986.

Walker, Pamela J. *Pulling the Devil's Kingdom Down: The Salvation Army in Victorian Britain*. Berkeley: University of California Press, 2001.

Warren, Heather A. "The Shift from Character to Personality in Mainline Protestant Thought, 1935–1945." *Church History* 67, no. 3 (1998): 537–55.

Warren, Heather A. "Will It Preach? Turning Inward in Mainline Protestantism, 1954–1964." Paper presented to the Twentieth Century History Workshop, University of Virginia, Charlottesville, 2001.

Webster, Richard. *Why Freud Was Wrong: Sin, Science, and Psychoanalysis*. New York: BasicBooks, HarperCollins Publishers Inc., 1995.

White, Andrew Dickson. *A History of the Warfare of Science with Theology in Christendom*. 1896. Reprint, New York: George Braziller, 1955.

White, William L. *Slaying the Dragon: The History of Addiction Treatment and Recovery in America*. Bloomington, IL: Chestnut Health Systems/Lighthouse Institute, 1998.

Whitley, Oliver. "Life with Alcoholics Anonymous: The Methodist Class Meeting as a Paradigm." *Journal of Studies on Alcohol* 38, no. 5 (1977): 831–48.

Whyte, William H. *The Organization Man*. New York: Simon and Schuster, 1956.

Wilcox, Danny M. *Alcoholic Thinking: Language, Culture, and Belief in Alcoholics Anonymous*. Westport, CT: Praeger, 1998.

Winston, Diane H. *Red-Hot and Righteous: The Urban Religion of The Salvation Army*. Cambridge, MA: Harvard University Press, 1999.

Wisbey, Herbert A. *Soldiers Without Swords: A History of The Salvation Army in the United States*. New York: The MacMillan Company, 1955.

Wolfe, Alan. *The Transformation of American Religion: How We Actually Live Our Faith*. New York: Free Press, 2003.

Wolfe, Tom. "The Me Decade and the Third Great Awakening." In *Mauve Gloves and Madmen, Clutter and Vine*, 126–67. New York: Farrar, Straus, and Giroux.

Wood, Gordon. *The Radicalism of the American Revolution*. New York: A. A. Knopf, 1992.

Woods, Lester. "Group Therapy." In Report on Men's Social Service Councils, 22–7. Pacific Grove, CA: The Salvation Army, 1960.

Bibliography

Worth, L. M., V. K. Westphal, and J. Scott Tonigan. "Longitudinal Perspective of Changes in Religiosity and Spirituality Among Three AA Exposed Groups in Project MATCH [poster paper]." Clinical Research Branch, Center on Alcoholism, Substance Abuse, and Addictions, University of New Mexico at http://casaa.unm.edu.

Wrieden, Jane E. *The Pattern of Social Work in The Salvation Army*. New York: National Research Bureau, Salvation Army, 1948.

Wuthnow, Robert. *The Restructuring of American Religion: Society and Faith since World War II*. Princeton, NJ: Princeton University Press, 1988.

Wuthnow, Robert. *Sharing the Journey: Support Groups and America's New Quest for Community*. New York: The Free Press, 1994.

Wuthnow, Robert. *After Heaven: Spirituality in America since the 1950s*. Berkeley: University of California Press, 1998.

Dissertations and Theses

Bloomfield, Kim Audrey. "Community in Recovery: A Study of Social Support, Spirituality, and Voluntarism among Gay and Lesbian Members of Alcoholics Anonymous." PhD diss., University of California at Berkeley, 1990.

Dexter, Robert William. "Aspiration Level in Relation to the Homeless Man." MSW thesis, Sacramento State College, 1968.

Johnson, Hazel Cameron. "Alcoholics Anonymous in the 1980s: Variations on a Theme." PhD diss., University of California at Los Angeles, 1987.

Leparte, Michael Gene. "Rehabilitation of the Homeless Man: The Effects of an Informal Social System on a Resident Rehabilitation Program." MA thesis, University of Rhode Island, 1967.

Lukens, Graham S., and William R. Scott. "Some Characteristics of Two Hundred Transient Men Who Received Aid from The Salvation Army, Shawnee, Oklahoma, from January 1, 1958 to December, 31, 1958." MSW thesis, University of Oklahoma, 1960.

Morris, Andrew J. F. "Charity, Therapy, and Poverty: Private Social Service in the Era of Public Welfare." PhD diss., University of Virginia, 2002.

Petigny, Alan Cecil. "The Permissive Turn and the Challenge to Bourgeois Values: Psychology, Secularization, and Sex in the United States, 1940–1965." PhD diss., Brown University, 2003.

Posey, Charles Robert. "A Study of the Correlation between the God-Image of the Alcoholics and the Degree of Difficulty in Accepting the AA Third Step." Doctor of Ministry thesis, Garrett-Evangelical Theological Seminary, 1988.

Sheehy, Peter. "The Triumph of Group Therapeutics: Therapy, the Social Self and Liberalism in America 1910–1960." PhD diss., University of Virginia, 2002.

Smith, Brian Dean. "The Moral Treatment of Psychological Disorder: A Historical and Conceptual Study of Selected Twentieth Century Pastoral Psychologists." PhD diss., University of Washington, 1989.

Wagner, Charles A. Van. "The AAPC: The Formative Years: A History of the American Association of Pastoral Counselors." Doctor of Sacred Theology thesis, Emory University, 1986.

Index

Abbott, Lyman, 7
Adult Rehabilitation Centers. *See* Men's
Social Service Centers
Alcoholics Anonymous, 2, 3–4, 9
12-step program, 85–86
atheism in, 136–140
Bible reading in, 124–126
Christian interpretation of, 146–149
as civil society, 86–87, 88–89, 90–91,
113, 156
criticism of, 108–109
democratic nature of, 81, 82, 86, 87, 89,
110
General Service Office, 90, 99
Higher Power, 88, 114, 136–149, 219
history, 83–85, 89–91
meetings, 86–89
in Men's Social Service Centers, 181,
189–193
prayer in, 88, 118–124
relationship to professional
psychotherapy, 98–110
spiritual education in, 112, 115
spiritual experience and growth in,
106–107, 131–136, 149–155
as therapy, 91–98
Alcoholics Anonymous (book), 84, 85, 86,
90, 92, 118, 124–126
Alcoholics Victorious, 128, 193
alienation, 18–20, 157, 180, 213, 216
American Association of Pastoral
Counselors, 43

American Council for Pastoral Education,
30. *See also* Council for Clinical
Training
antipsychiatry movement, 18
atheism, 10, 108–109, 129, 216–217.
See also secularism
in Alcoholics Anonymous, 136–140
among Salvation Army beneficiaries,
171–172
authenticity, 22. *See also* therapeutic
outlook

Calix, 128–129
case study rationale, 23–24
Catholicism and psychology, 2, 8, 10, 14
Catholics in psychospiritual programs,
218. *See also* Calix
in Alcoholics Anonymous, 93, 114, 119,
127, 152
in clinical pastoral education, 45
in Men's Social Service Centers,
169–171, 196
chaplain interns, 3, 31–32, 54–55
chaplain supervisors, 40, 41, 42, 43,
55
Christian Century, 8
civil society, 2, 4, 75, 81, 86–87, 107,
213–214, 217–219
in Alcoholics Anonymous, 113, 156
in Men's Social Service Centers,
173–174, 180–181
in The Salvation Army, 169

239

Index

Clecak, Peter, 220
clinical pastoral education, 2–3, 9
  CPE organizations, 30
  curriculum, 31–32, 46
  develops self-awareness, 31–36,
    62–66
  develops social savvy, 36–39, 62–66
  institutional setting, 31, 54–56
  promotes pastoral counseling, 39–44
  resistance to, 3, 33, 52
  resolves vocational doubts, 66–71
  as secularizing force, 52–58
  strengthens ministers, 60, 61, 77
  and theology, 30, 47–52
  as therapy, 40–42
  understanding of ministry in, 29–30,
    39–40, 43–44, 52, 67, 77–78
community. *See* fellowship
conversion, 173, 175, 205–213. *See also*
    evangelism
Council for Clinical Training, 26, 29, 30,
    60
Council for the Clinical Training of
    Theology Students (CCTTS), 26, 28,
    29. *See also* Council for Clinical
    Training
counseling, 3, 4, 12, 14. *See also* pastoral
    counseling
  in Men's Social Service Centers,
    182–189
The Culture of Narcissism. See Lasch,
    Christopher
democratic culture, 2, 15–16, 217, 220,
    221. *See also* Alcoholics Anonymous
  promoted by psychology, 14–15, 17,
    22–23, 217, 218–219, 220
  undermined by psychology, 20

Dunbar, Helen Flanders, 25

Emmanuel Movement, 9, 25
ethical development. *See* moral
    development
evangelism, 138, 172, 173, 174, 195–196.
    See also conversion

Fair Labor Standards Act of 1938, 163
fellowship, 3, 78, 79, 92, 97–98, 110, 136,
    173–174, 180, 198, 212
Freud, Sigmund, 10, 11, 12, 53, 200.
    See also psychoanalysis

The Grapevine (AA magazine), 85, 90, 92,
    138–139
group therapy, 3, 4
  in Alcoholics Anonymous, 96–98
  in clinical pastoral education, 41, 47
  in Men's Social Service Centers,
    196–198, 201–202

Hiltner, Seward, 51
Hofman, Peter, 190, 194, 201, 202
humanistic psychology, 16–17
Hunter, James D., 20

individualism, 16, 17. *See also* alienation
Industrial Homes. *See* The Salvation Army

James, William, 8, 9, 115, 131
Jews and psychology, 13, 20

Kant, Immanuel, 5

Lasch, Christopher, 19, 20, 175
Liebman, Joshua Loth, 13
Lindsay-Stewart, Rev. William, 200

Maslow, Abraham, 16, 17
Men's Social Service Centers, 159, 162,
    168. *See also* The Salvation Army
  anti-addiction therapy, 189–196
  case work, 182–189
  Catholic beneficiaries, 169–171
  conversion, 205–213
  counseling, 182–189
  finances of, 175–176
  history of, 162–164
  Men's Social Service Departments
    (MSSD), 163, 166–167
  milieu therapy, 178–182
  profile of beneficiaries, 169, 171–172,
    177, 179–180, 207–209
  Service-To-Man Program, 163, 164,
    173, 213, 218
  spiritual rehabilitation, 168–175
  use of psychotherapy, 196–203
  work therapy, 175–178
ministry, 216, 219. *See also* clinical
    pastoral education
moral development, 4, 14, 77, 85, 140, 149
MSSC. *See* Men's Social Service Centers
MSSD (Men's Social Service Department).
    See Men's Social Service Centers

Index

Orsi, Robert, 220
Oxford Group, 84, 93, 102, 113

pastoral counseling, 3, 4, 9, 29, 39–44,
    186. *See also* counseling
  in clinical pastoral education, 29
  in Men's Social Service Centers, 187,
    200–201
  shepherding perspective, 30
Pastoral Psychology (journal), 14
Peale, Norman Vincent, 13
pluralism, 170, 218–219
  in Alcoholics Anonymous, 119,
    127–128, 152, 196. *See also* Catholics
    in psychospiritual programs
  in Men's Social Service Centers,
    170–171, 214
  in The Salvation Army, 169–171, 196
Protestantism, 5, 23
  and psychology, 8, 25, 53–54, 56–57
  and science, 7
  theology, 5–6, 7, 131, 145
psyche, 6, 7, 10, 11
  as understood by clinical pastoral
    educators, 39–40
psychoanalysis, 10, 12–13, 94. *See also*
    Freud, Sigmund
psychologists, 10, 12, 13. *See also* James,
    William
psychology and psychiatry, 10–11,
    215–216
  acceptance of Alcoholics Anonymous by,
    94, 98–107
  democratization of, 14–15
  discipline of, 8, 9–10, 12, 53
  in Men's Social Service Centers,
    196–203
  promoted in Alcoholics Anonymous,
    102–104
psychology of religion movement, 8,
    10
psychoreligious. *See* psychospiritual
    programs
psychospiritual programs, 2, 24, 79, 84,
    111, 115, 128, 156, 162, 203, 218
psychotherapists. *See* therapists

Quimby, Phineas Parkhurst, 7, 8

Rational Recovery, 109
recovery movement, 109–110

religious experience. *See* spirituality
Rieff, Philip, 1, 18, 19, 20
Robb, Anita, 191
Rogers, Carl, 16, 78

The Salvation Army, 2, 3–4. *See also* Men's
    Social Service Centers
  corps, 165, 168
  history of, 161
  Industrial Homes, 159, 162, 175,
    182
  relationship to Catholicism, 169–171
  Schools for Officer Training, 165–166
  theology of, 165, 170
Schleiermacher, Friedrich, 5
science and religion, 15–16
secularism, 54–56, 108–109, 151–153,
    175–176, 217. *See also* clinical
    pastoral education
Secular Organizations for Sobriety,
    109
self, 6, 22–23, 220, 221. *See also*
    individualism
Shoemaker, Sam, 113
Silkworth, W. D., 95
Smith, Robert, 84, 99
soul, 6, 10, 11, 91
  as understood by clinical pastoral
    educators, 39–40, 49–50
spiritual experience, 5, 7, 10–12.
    See also Alcoholics Anonymous
spirituality, 2, 150–153, 216,
    217–218
Spock, Benjamin, 13
Szasz, Thomas, 18

Taylor, Charles, 20, 22–23
Temple, Frederick, 5
therapeutic ethos. *See* therapeutic outlook
therapeutic outlook, 2, 4, 12–14, 15,
    215–217
  in Alcoholics Anonymous, 102–104,
    107–110, 113, 155
  in clinical pastoral education, 37–38,
    42–43, 44–47
  criticism of, 2, 18–22. *See also*
    antipsychiatry movement
  in Men's Social Service Centers,
    202
therapists, 12, 13, 183, 199–200
Thornton, Edward, 29

Tiebout, Harry, 95, 105
Tillich, Paul, 52
Tocqueville, Alexis de, 22, 113, 151, 156, 218, 221
The Triumph of the Therapeutic. See Rieff, Philip

U.S. Department of Labor, 163, 177

Varieties of Religious Experience. *See* James, William

Wilson, Bill, 83, 95, 99, 102
Witmer, Lightner, 8
Women for Sobriety, 109

Yale School for Alcohol Studies, 167, 190